The Return of Great Power Rivalry

MATTHEW KROENIG

The Return of Great Power Rivalry

Democracy versus Autocracy

from the Ancient World to the

U.S. and China

OXFORD
UNIVERSITY PRESS

Oxford University Press is a department of the University of Oxford. It furthers
the University's objective of excellence in research, scholarship, and education
by publishing worldwide. Oxford is a registered trade mark of Oxford University
Press in the UK and certain other countries.

Published in the United States of America by Oxford University Press
198 Madison Avenue, New York, NY 10016, United States of America.

CIP data is on file at the Library of Congress
ISBN 978–0–19–008024–2

9 8 7 6 5 4 3 2 1

Printed by Sheridan Books, Inc., United States of America

To Eleanora

CONTENTS

ALSO BY MATTHEW KROENIG

Author or Coauthor

The Logic of American Nuclear Strategy: Why Strategic Superiority Matters
A Time to Attack: The Looming Iranian Nuclear Threat
Exporting the Bomb: Technology Transfer and the Spread of Nuclear Weapons
The Handbook of National Legislatures: A Global Survey

Coeditor

Nonproliferation Policy and Nuclear Posture: Causes and Consequences for the Spread of Nuclear Weapons
Causes and Consequences of Nuclear Weapons Proliferation

PREFACE

I N AUGUST 2008, I began my job as an assistant professor at Georgetown
University. A few weeks later, Lehman Brothers Bank collapsed and the
world found itself in the worst financial crisis since the Great Depression. The
American economic model was badly tarnished and the Chinese, state-led
capitalism approach looked better in comparison. Many began to ask whether
China possessed the superior economic and political system. Moreover, some
wondered whether the days of U.S. global leadership were coming to an end
and China might soon become the world's leading global economic and geopolitical power. I became fascinated by this possibility and its implications
for global geopolitics.

A few semesters later, I taught a PhD seminar in advanced international
relations theory. The syllabus covered cutting-edge research published in the
field's best journals. Over the past few decades, social scientists have been
obsessed with studying whether democracies are different from autocracies
with regard to specific types of international political behavior, and my
course focused intensely on these debates. Many of the studies found that
democracies are better at a number of discrete functions: economic growth,
international finance, alliance building, and warfare. I made a connection
between these sets of issues. If it is the case that democracies perform better
in all of these discrete issue areas, then should they not also perform better
overall? If so, then it stood to reason that the United States was actually
much better positioned for the coming competition with China than many
experts and pundits seemed to believe. I wanted to further investigate this
intriguing and potentially important insight. This book is the result.

I have aimed to write a book that will advance scholarly debates about great power competition while also appealing to a broader readership. Accomplishing either of these tasks on its own would be challenging, and attempting to do both is ambitious. Still, I have done my best to speak to both audiences. I hope political scientists will excuse me for not clogging the narrative with extensive digressions into scholarly literature and research methodology. My apologies to non–political scientists for the occasional discussions of "variables" and the presentation of some simple statistics.

My name is on the cover of this book, but many other institutions and individuals helped to make it possible. Many thanks to my home academic institution, Georgetown University. We often appear at or near the top of rankings for the world's best programs in international relations and foreign affairs. If the ranking is deserved, the credit should go to our ambitious and talented students, who frequently amaze me with the impressive feats they accomplish after leaving campus. From our classrooms, students have gone on to become members of Congress, ambassadors, military officers, professors, White House officials, and much more. I am relieved that my influence has not yet been too great an obstacle to their progress.

I am also grateful to the Atlantic Council, where I am currently the Deputy Director of the Scowcroft Center for Strategy and Security. Sitting in on discussions with current and former high-level policymakers is a type of daily field work into the people, ideas, and developments shaping contemporary international relations. These interactions have also helped to inspire and inform my writing and have forced me to ground my arguments in reality, while also drawing out concrete implications for contemporary policy debates.

For constructive feedback on parts of this book, I thank participants at seminars at the American Political Science Association Annual Meeting, the Atlantic Council, Georgetown University, and Princeton University. The concepts for this book were initially sketched in an essay in *The National Interest*, and I am grateful to the editors for the right to expand on those themes in this longer opus.[1] Marc Shaffer, a Junior Fellow at the Atlantic Council, was the best research assistant I could have hoped for and made significant contributions at every stage of this book project. Thanks also to the Smith Richardson Foundation and the Hertog Foundation for providing me with the resources necessary to transform my previous work on this subject into a book manuscript for broader public consumption. Other research assistance was provided by Anastasia Kazteridis, Jake Galant, Ilari Papa, Luan Tian, Christian Trotti, Mark Massa, and Lorenzo Lau.

This book would not have been possible without the loving support of my family. Olivia, you have sacrificed much in order to be a superb wife to me and mother to Eleanora. For that, there is no way I can fully repay you, but I am trying my best.

Finally, I would like to celebrate my daughter, Eleanora. You can achieve anything you set your mind to. And, if the argument of this book is correct, you can do it right here in the United States of America. This book is dedicated to you.

Introduction

THE UNITED STATES of America has been the most powerful country in the world for the past seventy-five years, but will Washington's reign as the world's leading superpower continue? At the end of World War II, the United States and its victorious allies built the world we know today. American military supremacy deterred great power war and undergirded international peace and security. The U.S. economy was a consistent source of technological innovation, an engine for global growth, and a model for how other countries structure their domestic markets and politics. Democratic forms of governments, inspired by the United States, spread around the world, and by the late 2000s, more people were living under freedom than at any time in world history.[1] U.S. diplomats led the way in erecting the international institutions that govern contemporary global politics, including the United Nations, the North Atlantic Treaty Organization, and the World Trade Organization. And U.S. culture permeated the globe from blue jeans, Hollywood, and Coca-Cola during the Cold War, to hip-hop, the National Basketball Association, and Instagram today. These cultural contributions provided the United States with a significant reservoir of "soft power" and made planet Earth a richer and more vibrant home.[2]

To be sure, Washington's leadership was not uncontested. During the Cold War, from 1945 to 1989, it faced an intense geopolitical competitor in the form of the Soviet Union, but the Berlin Wall came crashing down, leaving the United States as the globe's sole and undisputed hegemon. It would not be an exaggeration to say that from 1989 to 2014, the United

States may have been the world's most dominant state at any time since ancient Rome.

But all of this may be coming to an end. After twenty-five years of virtually uncontested U.S. global leadership, Russia and China have emerged as great power competitors. In recent years, Russia has invaded its neighbors, Ukraine and Georgia, and intervened forcefully in Syria, establishing itself as a Middle Eastern power broker for the first time since the 1970s. Fueled by petrodollars, Russian President Vladimir Putin has made modernization of the Russian military a top priority. He has built a formidable force, and a U.S. think tank recently estimated that if Putin decided to invade, he could take the capitals of two NATO allies, Estonia and Latvia, within sixty hours.[3] Putin is interfering in Western politics, including the 2016 U.S. presidential election, with the objective of discrediting democracy and weakening the NATO alliance. He has declared the collapse of the Soviet Union "the greatest geopolitical catastrophe of the 20th century" and his promises to resurrect a greater Russia could very well force a major clash with the United States and its allies.[4]

The challenge from China is even more daunting. Since putting in place sound economic reforms in the 1970s, China's economy has expanded at eye-popping rates. It is now the world's second-largest economy, and many economists predict that China could surpass the United States within the decade.[5] China's state-led capitalism model of economic growth is proving more appealing to many around the world than the U.S. template of free markets and open politics. In addition, military prowess often follows economic might, and China is ploughing its economic gains into military hardware. The balance of power in East Asia has greatly shifted in recent years, and some U.S. military planners doubt whether the United States still has the ability to defend long-standing allies and partners in the region, such as Taiwan. China is projecting its power further afield, conducting military exercises with Russia in Europe and establishing military outposts in Africa and Latin America.[6] Beijing is making major infrastructure investments around the world, expanding its economic and political clout in every major world region, including Europe. It is also asserting itself politically on the world stage, with President Xi Jinping disingenuously presenting China as a champion of free trade, clean energy, and respect for global norms. China is not shy about its ambitions. Indeed, its leaders promise that by 2049, the 100th anniversary of the Chinese Communist Party (CCP), China will be a global superpower.[7]

Many believe that things look grim for the United States. CNN host Fareed Zakaria may represent the conventional wisdom when he announced several years ago that we are entering a "post-American world."[8] Some predict that after America, the world will return to a "multipolar" balance of power system among multiple competing great powers, each lording it over its own respective sphere of influence.[9] Others forecast a rising China usurping global mastery from the United States.[10] Or, perhaps most frighteningly, a power transition between a rising China and declining America could result in World War III. Harvard scholar Graham Allison is one of many who believes these two giants may be "destined for war."[11]

Washington is belatedly awakening to these challenges to its global leadership. After two decades of squandering strategic attention and resources, fighting in the desert in Iraq and Afghanistan, Washington announced in the 2017 National Security Strategy of the United States of America that "great power competition with Russia and China" is now the number one threat to U.S. security and economic well-being.[12]

How will this competition play out? Is China bound to lead, as many now seem to believe? Are we returning to a multipolar balance of power system, in which Russia, China, and the United States will establish spheres of influence within their own respective regions? Or will Washington manage to fend off these formidable competitors and refresh its position as the world's leading superpower?

To answer these questions, we lack a crystal ball. But history and political theory can serve as a guide, and they suggest a clear answer: democracies enjoy a built-in advantage in long-run geopolitical competitions.

The idea that democracies are better able to accumulate and maintain power in the international system has a distinguished pedigree. Herodotus, Machiavelli, and Montesquieu are among the classical political thinkers who argued that republican forms of government are best able to harness available domestic resources toward national greatness. And recent social science research concurs. For the past two decades, cutting-edge research in economics and political science has been obsessed with the issue of whether democracies are different, and the consistent finding is that they perform a number of key functions better than their autocratic counterparts. They have higher long-run rates of economic growth.[13] They are better able to raise money in international capital markets and become international financial centers.[14] They build stronger and more reliable alliances.[15] They are more likely to make and keep international agreements.[16] They are less likely to fight wars (at least against other democracies).[17] And they are more likely to win the wars that they fight.[18]

This book takes this line of thinking a step further by aggregating these narrower findings into a broader argument about the relative fitness of democracy and autocracy in great power political competitions. The central claim of this book is that democracies do better in major power rivalries. After all, it is not much of a logical leap to assume that states that outperform on important economic, diplomatic, and military tasks will do better in long-run geopolitical competitions than those that do not. According to this view, the very constraints on government power and a strict rule-of-law system that some may see as signs of democratic weakness are, in fact, democracy's greatest strengths.

In other words, this book makes the hard-power case for democracy. The argument is not that democracy is a superior system because it protects human rights and civil liberties, although it does that too. Rather, this book argues that democratic countries are better able to amass power, wealth, and influence on the world stage than their autocratic competitors. Democracy is a force multiplier that helps states punch above their weight in international geopolitics.

This hunch is supported by the empirical record. As this book will show, autocrats often put up a good fight, but they fail to ultimately seize lasting global leadership. Xerxes, Napoleon, Nazi Germany, and the Soviet Union are among the examples of authoritarians that launched campaigns for world domination, but came up short. On the other hand, states with relatively more open forms of government have often been able to establish themselves as the international system's leading state, from Athens and the Roman Republic in the ancient world to the British Empire and the United States in more recent times. According to some scholars, the world's leading state since the 1600s has also been among its most democratic.[19] It is hard to argue with an undefeated record of four centuries and counting.

Indeed, a leitmotif of this book is that the history of Western civilization can be thought of as the passing of the torch of liberal hegemony from Athens to Rome, to Venice, Amsterdam, and London, and on to its current resting place in Washington, DC.

America's greatest strength in its coming competition with Russia and China, therefore, is not its military might or economic heft, but its institutions. For all of its faults, America's fundamentals are still better than Russia's and China's. There is good reason to believe, therefore, that the American era will endure and the autocratic challenges posed by China and Russia will run out of steam.

The idea that democracies dominate may seem counterintuitive. After all, throughout history, and in contemporary policy debates, many have argued that dictators have a foreign policy advantage.[20] Autocrats can be ruthless when necessary, but democracies are constrained by public opinion and ethical and legal concerns. Autocrats take decisive action, but democracies dither in endless debate. Autocrats strategically plan for the long term while democracies cannot see beyond a two- or four-year election cycle. Many today laud Russia and China's autocratic systems for precisely these reasons.[21] Russians play chess and Chinese play go, but Americans play checkers, as the aphorism has it.

It is true that autocracies are better at taking swift and bold action, but impulsive decisions uninformed by vigorous public debate often result in spectacular failure. Hitler, for example, was able to harness new technology to create blitzkrieg warfare and conquer much of Western Europe in the early stages of World War II, but he also foolishly invaded Russia and declared war on the United States. Unfortunately for autocracies, this story is all too common. As Machiavelli wrote in his *Discourses on Livy* in the 16th century: "Fewer errors will be seen in the people than in the prince—and those lesser and having greater remedies."[22] "Hence it arises that a republic has greater life and has good fortune longer than a principality."[23]

There is good reason to hope that this argument is true, because continued American leadership would be beneficial to the United States and the rest of the free world. The decline of American power would certainly be unwelcome for the United States. Americans have grown accustomed to the benefits that accrue to the world's leading power. But billions of others also have a stake in America's success. For all of its faults, the United States has been a fairly benevolent hegemon. While far from perfect, it has gone to extraordinary lengths to provide security, promote economic development, and nurture democracy and human rights. The world is certainly safer, richer, and freer today than it was before the dawn of the American era.

Indeed, China itself has been among the greatest beneficiaries of a U.S.-led international order. American military and economic power have provided the peace and macroeconomic stability that allowed China to grow into the major power that it is today.

There is little reason to believe that Russia and China will be as kind. These autocratic powers long to establish spheres of influence in their near abroad, and they have shown little concern for the sovereignty or personal freedoms of their own citizens or subjected populations. To get a vision of a world led by Russia or China, just look at how they treat the people that fall under their influence today. Russian dictator Vladimir Putin invades neighboring countries and murders critical journalists. And China takes contested territory from its neighbors through brute force and locks up one million Muslim minorities in "re-education" camps. And this is but a small taste of the brutality of these governments. If readers doubt these claims, they can simply ask citizens of American allies in Eastern Europe or East Asia whether they desire continued American leadership, or whether they would prefer to live under the thumb of Moscow or Beijing, respectively.

Moreover, just as consequentially for the globe, the decline of the United States could very well result in war. As noted earlier, international relations theory maintains that the decline of one dominant power and the rise of another often results in great power conflict.[24] According to this telling, World War I and World War II were primarily the result of the decline of the British Empire and the rise of Imperial and then Nazi Germany. Falling powers fight preventive wars in a bid to remain on top, and rising powers launch conflicts to dislodge the reigning power and claim their "place in the sun."[25] Many fear that a power transition between Beijing and Washington would produce a similar catastrophic result.[26] Continued American leadership, therefore, could forestall this transition and may be necessary for continued peace and stability among the major powers.

There are many other works on related subjects, but this book is distinctive. Since the time of Aristotle, scholars have debated the virtues and vices of democratic versus autocratic constitutions, and some, including Machiavelli in his masterpiece *Discourses on Livy*, argued that republican forms of government were better suited for international ascendance.[27] But these arguments have not been updated with the latest advances in social science research nor applied to contemporary cases, like the United States, Russia, and China.

Other scholars have written more about whether the American era is coming to an end or enduring, but they do not provide a generalizable argument for why great powers rise and fall or inform their understanding of the current situation with a systematic study of historical cases.[28] Fareed Zakaria's *The Post-American World* and Joseph Nye's *Is the American Century Over?*, despite coming to opposite conclusions, serve as dueling prime examples of this kind of work.[29]

Others have written about the rise of China and its implications for the future of international politics, but, similarly, they do not embed this analysis in a broader story about what determines the outcomes of long-run geopolitical competitions historically and theoretically.[30] Henry Kissinger's *On China* fits this description.[31]

There are many good books on contemporary Russia, including Michael McFaul's *From Hot War to Cold Peace*, but none make their central focus the question of how Russia's domestic political institutions affect its ability to project power and influence on the international stage or compete with the United States and China.[32]

International relations "power transition" theory, including Graham Allison's *Destined for War*, deals with the conditions under which power transitions cause great power war, but they largely take the rise of one power and decline of another as a given and do not conduct a systematic investigation into the prior question of why these power transitions happen in the first place.[33]

Paul Kennedy's magisterial work *The Rise and Fall of the Great Powers* describes a long cycle of great power competition, but, like other works in this genre, his historical approach does not provide a clear social scientific explanation of the root causes of power in international affairs and, since the book was published decades ago, he does not focus on the contemporary great power competition among the United States, Russia, and China.[34]

Finally, there has been much social science research on a possible democratic advantage in discrete areas, such as economic growth and war outcomes, but none has aggregated these mid-range findings into a broader theory about democratic advantages in long-run, great power competitions.[35] Daron Acemoglu and James Robinson's *Why Nations Fail*, for example, focuses on how open institutions affect economic growth, and *Democracies at War* by Allan Stam and Dan Reiter explains the democratic wartime advantage, but these works do not tell the larger story of democratic fitness for great power competition across a wide range of economic, political, and military dimensions.[36]

In sum, this book is distinctive in at least four ways. First, it provides an innovative argument about how domestic political institutions are the key to a state's ability to amass power and influence in the international system. Second, it studies the causes of power transitions. Or, in other words, it seeks to explain why great powers sometimes ascend to and maintain their position atop the international system and are at other times surpassed by rivals. Third, it tests this argument with a sweeping historical analysis of democratic and autocratic competitors from ancient Greece through the Cold War. Fourth, and finally, it employs this framework to understand and analyze the state of today's competition between the democratic United States and its autocratic competitors, Russia and China.

The findings of this book have implications, not just for those in the ivory tower but also for those working in the corridors of power. It suggests that despite all the talk of American decline, the United States is well positioned to remain the world's leading nation for the foreseeable future. History also shows, however, that while democracies tend to win in the end, the path from here to there can get messy. Washington must, therefore, prepare to defend itself and its allies from the serious Russian and Chinese threats in the meantime. And this book lays out a strategy for doing just that.

Furthermore, this book recommends that U.S. leaders take seriously growing concerns about a possible erosion in the quality of American democracy. Washington must be careful to nurture its greatest source of strength: its democratic institutions.

The book will continue in four parts. Part I lays out the central argument. It draws on ideas from the political philosophy canon and the latest social science research to advance the idea that democracies do better in long-run geopolitical competitions. It also considers and critiques the competing arguments about a possible autocratic advantage.

The second part of the book examines the empirical basis for this idea through simple quantitative analysis and a historical study of democratic and autocratic competitors from the ancient world to the present. Specifically, the book will examine the following seven cases: Athens, Sparta, and Persia; the Roman Republic, Carthage, and Macedon; the Venetian Republic, the Byzantine Empire, and the Duchy of Milan; the Dutch Republic and the Spanish Empire; Britain and France in the 18th and 19th centuries; the United Kingdom and Germany in the late 19th and early 20th centuries; and the United States and the Soviet Union during the Cold War. This section of the book does not show that democracies always achieve everlasting hegemony, but it does demonstrate that they tend to excel in great power rivalry and for the precise reasons identified by the theoretical framework.

Part III is the real payoff of the book. What does all of this mean for contemporary international politics? This section examines the United States, Russia, and China. It studies how their domestic political systems prepare them for the coming competition and finds that U.S. institutions are a continuing source of strength, while Russian and Chinese institutions are dragging down their attempts to amass international wealth and power.

Part IV takes stock of what we have learned and draws out the implications for U.S. foreign policy and also looks ahead to the future. How can the United States best shore up its sources of strength? How can, or should, it seek to exploit its opponents' weaknesses? And, given the previous arguments, will the American era endure?

PART I | Democracy versus Autocracy

CHAPTER I │ The Democratic Advantage in Theory

NICCOLÒ MACHIAVELLI WAS the political genius of the Italian Renaissance. When people recall this remarkable period of artistic productivity and intellectual flourishing, they often emphasize the scientists, painters, architects, and sculptors: Leonardo, Raphael, Brunelleschi, and Michelangelo. But Machiavelli was the Michelangelo of politics. Like his contemporaries in the arts, Machiavelli ushered his field out of the dark ages and into the modern world. He is often considered the first modern political scientist and among the first "realist" international relations scholars.

Machiavelli was born into a middle-class family in the Santo Spirito neighborhood of Florence, Italy, in 1469.[1] At the tender age of twenty-nine, he had risen to become the secretary of the Ten of Liberty and Peace. Essentially what we would today call the national security adviser of Florence, Machiavelli was responsible for all matters of foreign and defense policy. This was the time of the Great Italian Wars, and Florence was a medium-sized city-state, surrounded by competitors, including Venice, Milan, and the Papal States, all of which were constantly threatened by the great powers, France and the Holy Roman Empire, lurking just over the Alps. Machiavelli racked up many achievements while in office. He served as a diplomat, established Florence's first standing militia, and commanded a successful military operation to retake Florence's longtime rival Pisa. But, after a fourteen-year run in office, his career in politics came to a sudden halt when the powerful Medici family, with the military backing of the pope, returned to retake Florence by force of arms. The new Medici rulers did not look kindly on the holdovers from the previous government, and they had Machiavelli removed from office, tortured, and exiled to his family estate in Sant'Andrea in Percussina, eleven miles south of Florence.

Machiavelli went to his grave believing that this had been his life's greatest tragedy, and he constantly longed to return to power in the city that, on a clear day, he could see from his country home. Fortunately, for the world and his own legacy, however, his time in exile allowed him to become the Machiavelli we know today. With little else to do other than drink wine and play cards in the local tavern (which we know from his personal correspondence he did quite a bit), he had time to write some of the greatest masterpieces in Western political philosophy.

Machiavelli is best known for his short work of advice to the new Medici ruler, *The Prince*.[2] The book was something of a job application, as Machiavelli hoped it would demonstrate his usefulness to the Medici and cause them to recall him back into public service. The book advised the new prince on how to consolidate power and recommends the use of any means necessary, no matter how diabolical, to protect the city-state in a turbulent and violent era. Unfortunately for Machiavelli, the book did not cause the Medici to reinstate him to his former government post. Subsequent generations, however, took note. Indeed, due to the widespread fame (or infamy) of *The Prince*, the adjective "Machiavellian" has become synonymous with cunning, double-dealing, and immorality.

In actuality, however, Machiavelli was a republican with a small "r." (Ancient political theorists drew a distinction between democratic and republican forms of government, with "democracy" meaning direct majority rule of the people and "republicanism" connoting a system with a division of power among various branches of government, rule by elected representatives, and strong protections for minority rights.) Before the Medici returned and established themselves as princely rulers, Florence had been a republic with an elected leader and representation from the major families in Florence. Machiavelli believed this was the superior form of government.

He makes this case for the democratic advantage most clearly in what many consider to be his greatest masterpiece, *The Discourses on Livy*.[3] While less well-known than *The Prince, The Discourses* is nothing short of a full-throated defense of republican government. In fact, in this work, Machiavelli goes so far as to advise a wise prince to use his fleeting time in office not to rule with an iron fist, but, rather, to establish a republic. This he argues, is what will do most to contribute to the well-being of his people and to the prince's own legacy. As he writes, "he to whom the heavens have given such an opportunity should consider that there are two paths: one that will make him secure during his lifetime and glorious after his death, and the other that will make him live in constant anguish and after his death leave behind a legacy of everlasting infamy."[4]

The Discourses is so named because it contains Machiavelli's reflections on the monumental *History of Rome*, written by Roman historian Titus Livius (often translated as "Livy" in English). Machiavelli was fascinated by how Rome, at first a small city-state surrounded by other hostile powers (much like his beloved Florence), had risen to become the most dominant political entity the world had ever known.

Machiavelli's conclusion is straightforward: Rome's republican institutions were the secret to its success. As he writes, "For it is seen through experience that cities have never expanded either in dominion or in riches if they have not been in freedom."[5] Foreshadowing contemporary arguments about open political institutions and economic growth, Machiavelli argued that polities governed by republican constitutions are better able to harness the talents and ambitions of a broad segment of society and apply them toward state expansion. "The reason is easy to understand, for it is not the particular good but the common good that makes cities great. And without doubt this common good is not observed if not in republics."[6] According to Machiavelli, "The contrary happens when there is a prince, in which case what suits him usually offends the city and what suits the city offends him." For this reason, "as soon as a tyranny arises . . . the least evil that results for those cities is not . . . to grow more in power or riches, but usually—or rather always—it happens that they go backward."

Note that Machiavelli was somewhat "Machiavellian" in his defense of democracy. He does not extol republican systems of government because they protect the freedoms and human rights of their citizens, but rather for a more instrumental reason: they help the state to become more powerful.

Machiavelli was far from the only thinker in the political theory canon to argue that democracies dominate. In fact, in arguing that ancient Rome owed its success to an open political system, Machiavelli was following in the footsteps of Polybius. Polybius was a Hellenic Greek historian who wrote a contemporary history of Rome in the 2nd century BC. Polybius's work had an important influence on later thinkers, including the framers of the U.S. Constitution. To this day, scholars debate whether Machiavelli had access to and read Polybius's work, but, either way, both scholars' analysis of Rome's rise to power is remarkably similar.[7]

In *The Histories*, Polybius provides a history of ancient Rome, but his primary purpose is to explain the sources of Rome's success. As he writes, "the most admirable and educational part of my project was that it would let my readers know and understand how, and thanks to what kind of political system, an unprecedented event occurred—the conquest of almost all the known world in somewhat under fifty-three years, and its submission to just one ruler, Rome."[8] Polybius's explanation should by now be familiar: "The chief cause of either success or the opposite is, I would claim, the nature of a state's system of government."[9] It was the strength of Rome's domestic political institutions, according to Polybius, that allowed it to best its competitors and conquer the known world. "If one thinks the finer and nobler thing is to be a world-class leader, with an extensive dominion and empire, the center and focal point of everyone's world—then one must admit that the Spartan constitution is deficient, and that the Roman constitution is superior and more dynamic. The facts themselves demonstrate the truth of this."[10]

The French philosopher Montesquieu would pick up these themes in his *Greatness of the Romans and Their Decline*, published in 1734. Montesquieu also credited Rome's international standing to its domestic political institutions. On the basis of republican institutions, for its international standing Rome rose to prominence, but the demise of the republic under Caesar and the tyranny of subsequent emperors sowed the seeds of decay. "By means of their maxims they conquered all peoples, but when they had succeeded in doing so, their republic could not endure. It was necessary to change the government, and contrary maxims employed by the new government made their greatness collapse."[11]

Before Rome, Athens was a leading state in the ancient world. Like the commentators on Rome mentioned earlier, ancient Greeks also attributed Athens's success in international affairs to its open political institutions at home. Ancient Greece gave birth to many firsts in Western Civilization, including its first historian: Herodotus.

Herodotus's best-known work, *The Histories*, focuses on the origins of the Greco-Persian Wars. The book examines how Athens, just a small city-state, was able to stand up to, and then defeat, the mighty Persian Empire. Herodotus concludes that Athens's greatest asset was its democratic form of government:

> The Athenians had increased in strength, which demonstrates that an equal voice in government has a beneficial impact not merely in one way, but in every way: the Athenians, while ruled by tyrants, were no better in war than the peoples living around them, but once they were rid of tyrants, they became by far the best of all. Thus it is clear that they were deliberately slack while repressed, since they were working for a master, but that after they were freed, they became ardently

devoted to working hard so as to win achievements for themselves as individuals.[12]

This judgment was also shared by ancient Greece's, and arguably the world's, first physician, Hippocrates. In his *Airs, Waters, and Places*, he considers how one's environment affects one's health and well-being. It is a sweeping work that also considers how governmental institutions shape human attitudes and, in turn, the vitality of the state. Hippocrates maintained that freedom domestically contributes to expansion internationally. He writes:

> where there are kings, there must be the greatest cowards. For men's souls are enslaved, and refuse to run risks readily and recklessly to increase the power of somebody else. But independent people, taking risks on their own behalf and not on behalf of others, are willing and eager to go into danger, for they themselves enjoy the prize of victory.[13]

In sum, for centuries, some of the world's greatest minds argued that Athens and Rome rose to power on the basis of their open institutions. Perhaps, unsurprisingly, better understanding the determinants of world domination has fallen out of favor in the modern academy, but the democratic advantage thesis has nevertheless re-emerged in subtler forms.

Toward a Modern Theory of Democratic Advantage

For the past several decades, social scientists have been obsessed with the question of whether democracies are different. And the answer they have found, in a wide range of discrete issue areas, from economic growth to military effectiveness, is that democracies do better.

Before we review this research, however, let us take a step back and consider what it takes for a country to become a leading power in the international system.

First, to become a great power, a state must have a strong economy. With amassed wealth, a state can influence other states. It can promise economic aid and access to its markets to friends. Contrarily, it can threaten to revoke economic access or impose economic penalties on enemies or those who defy its commands.

Perhaps most importantly, a state can translate economic weight into military power. According to Cicero, "money are the sinews of war."[14] Wealthy states can fund major military buildups, underwrite international commitments, and sustain the high costs of international warfare. As Yale diplomatic historian Paul Kennedy argued, "the history of the rise and later fall of the leading countries in the great power system . . . shows a very significant correlation over the longer term between productive and revenue-raising capacities on one hand and military strength on the other."[15]

To be a global leader, a state can also benefit from deep and liquid capital markets. Being a financial powerhouse relates to the previous point as functioning markets allocate capital efficiently and help to maintain high levels of economic growth. Granting or denying access to capital to other nations is also an important tool of diplomatic statecraft. Perhaps most importantly, however, the ability to borrow allows states to finance arms buildups and large wars in excess of normal revenue.[16] In addition, easy access to credit allows states to engage in "tax smoothing," financing extraordinary expenditures through debt rather than through large tax increases, which reduces economic and societal disruptions. As political scientists Karen Rasler and William Thompson write, "winners in the struggle for world leadership owed a significant portion of their success to their ability to obtain access to credit inexpensively, to sustain relatively large debts, and in general to leverage the initially limited base of their wealth in order to meet their staggering military expenses."[17]

Second, to become an enduring global leader, a state must also be effective diplomatically. It is hard to become a leading global power without strong and reliable alliances and partnerships to help achieve one's international objectives. Allies can help a state in international diplomacy, carrying the water for the powerful state in international fora. This can provide greater international legitimacy to the hegemon's efforts and shield it from criticism. Allies can also contribute resources and manpower to share in the burdens of diplomatic efforts, defense buildups, and combat. They can also provide bases or allow the free passage of military forces that can help the powerful state project power beyond its own borders.

Enduring global leaders must also be effective not only at building their own alliances, but at preventing rivals from forming counterbalancing coalitions. Even the most powerful state can be brought down, if the rest of the world gangs up against it. See the fates of Napoleon and Hitler for evidence on this point.

Some might counter that alliances are more of a burden than a boon. They could claim that a sprawling alliance network increases a state's commitments and provides little in return. This can sometimes be true. Not all allies are created equal, and more allies are not always better. Indeed, weak or unreliable allies are likely worse than none at all. The value of an alliance, therefore, depends on its quality and reliability. Most things are easier with capable and reliable friends, and geopolitics is no different.

The final ingredient for global mastery is military power. Military power may be the most important resource in an anarchic international system. There is no world government and so there is no international 911 a state can call if it gets into trouble.[18] This makes international politics a "self-help" system. Militarily powerful states are able to defend themselves in a dangerous world. States with effective militaries can use military power to their advantage in other ways as well. They can promise to protect friends. And they can threaten to hurt enemies.

An effective military force can help states achieve objectives short of war by deterring rivals. As the ancient Romans used to say, if you want peace, prepare for war.

War is, however, a recurring feature of international politics, and military power helps states to win wars. States that win wars are better able to accumulate and maintain power than those that lose them. Nations victorious on the battlefield can eliminate threats to their security and gain political influence and access to resources that help them improve their position. Losing a war disastrously, on the other hand, may be the most direct way in which a state can squander power. In 1941, for example, Nazi Germany possessed 20 percent of world power, but by 1945, following its catastrophic defeat in World War II, Germany's share of global power resources plummeted to a mere 8 percent.[19] Over the same time period, however, one of the victors of World War II, the United States of America, saw its share of global power increase from 24 percent to 38 percent. As Kennedy writes, "The triumph of any one Great Power in this period [the years 1500 to 2000] or the collapse of another, has usually been the consequence of lengthy fighting by its armed forces."[20]

In sum, to achieve global mastery, a state must have a strong economy, strong diplomacy, and a strong military.

Recent social science research suggests that democracies may do all of these things better than their autocratic rivals. To be clear, recent research has not theorized the sources of world domination directly. But social scientists have examined whether democracies are better at discrete tasks: economic growth, finance, alliance building, and military effectiveness. And the repeated finding is that democracies appear to have an advantage.

DEFINING DEMOCRACY

As noted earlier, ancient political theorists drew a distinction between democratic and republican forms of government (with a small "d" and a small "r").

They praised republican or "mixed" systems, but denigrated direct democracy for its tendency to devolve into mob rule and tyranny of the majority. They were correct about the dangers of direct democracy, as we will see later in our examination of ancient Athens.

But this distinction has become less important over time. It is simply not practical to have every citizen debate and vote on every issue in the modern world. In practice, what we today call democracy is what the ancients would have called a "republican" form of government. This book is really about the advantages of "republican" forms of government, and it concurs with past philosophers who saw downsides to direct democracy. Still, in this book we will follow standard usage and refer to these modern republics as democracies.

Contemporary political scientists define democracies as political systems in which political officeholders are selected through competitive, popular elections.[21] Thicker definitions add a broad set of political and civil liberties, such as freedom of speech and assembly, that are necessary to make an electoral political system work.

Autocracies lack these characteristics. Autocracies come in many forms and can include dictatorships, like Kim Jong Un in North Korea; single-party states, such as the Chinese Communist Party (CCP) in China; monarchies, like Saudi Arabia; military juntas, as in Thailand; and other forms as well. What unites autocratic forms of government, however, is that their leaders are either unelected or have been selected through sham elections in which the outcome was rigged by authorities. Their citizens also lack the broad sets of political and civil freedoms enjoyed in more open societies. There are often restrictions on free speech and assembly, for example, because autocratic leaders fear that allowing people to openly criticize the government, or hold massive public protests, could threaten their hold on power.

Political regime type is generally conceptualized as a continuous variable, ranging from most democratic at one end to most autocratic at the other, with various shades of gray in between. More democratic states have greater constraints on executive authority, and their citizens enjoy more political and civil liberties. More autocratic states place fewer constraints on the executive, and their citizens possess fewer rights.

The widely used Polity scores measure the level of democracy of every country in the world from 1800 to the present on a twenty-point scale, ranging from –10 (most autocratic) to +10 (most democratic).[22] According to these rankings, Mexico, for example, is considered more democratic than North Korea, but less so than the United States. In this way, countries can be compared to each other as more or less democratic. Social scientists have tended to find, however, that the greatest benefits of open government tend to kick in for those states grouped toward the highest end of this scale, measured at roughly + 6 or above. What are some of these identified democratic advantages?

DEMOCRACY AND ECONOMIC STRENGTH

In their book *Why Nations Fail*, Daron Acemoglu and James Robinson tell the story of the contrasting fates of North and South Korea. These countries straddle the 38th parallel and are separated by a demilitarized zone, but they still have much in common. They share a nearly identical climate and natural resource endowment. The ethnic and cultural makeup of their populations are roughly the same. Yet, despite all these commonalities, there is a stark difference in levels of economic development. The South Korean side of the border is richer. The infrastructure is better. And life expectancy is higher. Why?

The question of why some countries achieve higher levels of economic development than others is among the most important subjects in the field of economics. Theories on the deep causes of economic growth point to factors such as culture, climate, or natural resources.[23] But all of these cultural, geographic, and resource conditions are basically the same on both sides of the border on the Korean Peninsula.

Acemoglu and Robinson argue that the only variable that can explain these countries' very different fortunes is institutions. Institutions are "the rules of the game in a society or, more formally . . . the humanly devised constraints that shape human interaction."[24] Countries with good economic institutions, like those found in South Korea, have higher long-run rates of economic growth, whereas countries with poorer economic institutions, such as in North Korea, suffer from lower rates of growth.

Good economic institutions are those that incentivize people to work hard, engage in productive economic activity, and make themselves and their nations richer. They include protections for private property rights, allowing individuals and firms to develop businesses, properties, and products without fear that their assets will be seized by other individuals or the state itself. They contain courts that reliably enforce contracts, so economic actors can transact with confidence that business agreements will be upheld. The rules need to be nondiscriminatory so as to encourage wide swathes of the population to participate in growth-enhancing economic activity. In addition, good economic institutions incentivize innovation by encouraging entrepreneurship, thinking outside the box, and risk-taking.

On the other hand, countries that lack good economic institutions generally suffer from economic underdevelopment. There is little reason to devote time and resources to improving one's property or experimenting with innovative new products or services if it is unclear whether you will ultimately benefit from your efforts. Business is discouraged in countries where there is a reasonable chance that if you are cheated, the courts will be too corrupt or inept to rectify the situation. If a country systematically discriminates against large segments of its population, it is wasting human resources that could be contributing to economic development. And radical innovation does not tend to happen in societies that enforce conformity and discourage new ways of thinking or doing things.

A country's economic institutions are, in turn, heavily shaped by its political institutions. In autocratic countries where power is concentrated, the narrow elite have incentives to put in place economic institutions that disproportionately benefit themselves but fail to protect the economic interests of broad swathes of society. Autocrats set up instructions to extract wealth from society to redistribute to themselves and their cronies. This makes the rulers richer, but undermines conditions for stable, long-run growth.

Contrariwise, countries with inclusive political institutions that distribute political power to a broad segment of society, i.e., democracies, are more likely to produce good economic institutions. In democratic countries in which political power has a broader base, the power holders themselves have economic incentives to develop economic institutions that protect the economic interests of a broad segment of society. In addition, constraints on executive power allow rulers to credibly commit to protecting individual property rights, encouraging citizens to engage in long-term planning, investment, and economic activity.

Democracies also facilitate innovation. The great economist Joseph Schumpeter wrote about the need for "creative destruction" in healthy economies.[25] Entrepreneurs with new ideas tear down old ways of doing business and create new ones, providing innovative products or services. Democracies are comfortable with the rough and tumble of creative destruction. Individuals are educated and encouraged to be independent and think for themselves. Future entrepreneurs are incentivized to take risks and try new approaches, motivated by the knowledge that they and their families can profit from their innovations. (Democracies may be more innovative in other areas as well. They tend to push the technological frontier and develop new operational concepts in military affairs. And, important for the development of "soft power" in international diplomacy, they often set the style for new cultural movements and artistic expression.)

In contrast, autocratic governments are less comfortable with the tumult and disruption necessary for radical innovation. Thinking outside the box and challenging standard practices is generally discouraged. It is a good way to land oneself in trouble with the authorities. Radical breakthroughs mean innovation and disruption, but autocratic leaders hate innovation and disruption because it might threaten their ability to control society. They like stability.

Acemoglu and Robinson argue that autocrats could fix this economics problem in theory, by putting in place inclusive economic institutions despite their closed politics, but they argue that this is difficult, if not impossible, in practice because it would undermine the autocrats' own base of power. Inclusive institutions would enrich and therefore empower individuals and businesses outside of the government. And autocrats do not like independent centers of power that could challenge their rule.

So, dictators face a dilemma. They can put in place policies that encourage economic growth only by threatening their own power. Or they can opt for suboptimal economic performance and the protection of their privileged position. Since humans are not angels, it should come as no surprise that they often choose the latter.

In short, economic theory suggests that democracies should enjoy higher long-run rates of economic growth. North and South Korea have such divergent economic outcomes primarily because the rules that incentivize economic activity in the two cities are so different. Social scientists call this a "natural experiment." Although the research was not performed in a lab, all of the important variables were held constant except the "treatment." One of the countries was treated with good institutions. The other was not. And it made all the difference.

Indeed, a quick glance around the world today shows that the states with the highest standards of living are also among the most democratic: Canada and the United States in North America; Germany and the United Kingdom in Europe; and Australia and Japan in Asia. In contrast, the poorest nations on Earth, such as Congo, North Korea, and Haiti, suffer from poor political and economic institutions.

At this point, some readers may object and ask about the prominent exceptions. What about China? It has maintained remarkable rates of economic growth since the early 1970s despite being ruled by the authoritarian Chinese Communist Party (CCP). Acemoglu and Robinson grant that some autocratic states like the Maya Empire, the Soviet Union during the Cold War, and China in recent decades, can temporarily generate high growth rates by using centralized planning to allocate resources from less to more productive sectors, but these models of growth have limits. In China's case, moving mass numbers of unproductive workers from farms in the country-side to more productive manufacturing jobs in cities was an easy fix. Once the gains are achieved from this more efficient allocation of resources, however, the model does not provide continued growth. The state must find another area where resources are underutilized and force re-allocation. But centrally planned economies do not have a great record at making these bets. Perhaps China will be the sole exception, but every other state-planned economy in history has hit a wall at some point.

Democracies also benefit economically due to their greater openness to international flows of goods, people, and money. Ever since Adam Smith and David Ricardo wrote about comparative advantage we have understood that trade is an important engine of economic development. By specializing in the goods and services they can produce most efficiently and engaging in inter-national trade for the rest, nations are richer than when they close themselves off from the international economic system.[26]

And democracies are more likely to be open to international trade by al-most any measure.[27] A higher percentage of their GDP comes from imports and exports. They have lower tariffs. They sign more free trade agreements. The logic is the same for trade as for economic institutions. The biggest ben-eficiary of free trade is the average consumer, who can buy a wide range of products from around the world at lower prices. Democratic leaders care more about the average consumer (who is also the average voter) than do autocrats. On the other hand, autocrats can benefit from protectionism. By placing tariffs on incoming goods, for example, autocrats hurt their own people, who must pay higher prices for these imported goods. But they can reward themselves and elite supporters by shielding selected domestic industries from foreign competition. They can also use the taxes they collect at the border to invest in the apparatus of the state, shoring up their power relative to society. Indeed, autocrats are often threatened by free trade because they fear that the free flow of goods, people, and ideas across their borders could contaminate a system that is working well for them. For example, the Kim dynasty in North Korea has intentionally selected economic isolation and deprivation for decades over international economic engagement in part for this reason.

Democracies also benefit economically from the freer flow of people. Democracies tend to be more open to immigration because they are more tolerant of outsiders and less afraid of the disruptions they might bring.[28] Openness to immigration allows states to attract high-skilled laborers, causing a brain drain in their favor that is pro-growth and pro-innovation.

It is estimated that without migration, U.S. growth, for example, would be much lower.[29] Autocracies tend to be more closed to immigration, because leaders like to maintain strict control and the free flow of people and the ideas that they bring are seen as a threat.

Democracies are also more open to international monetary flows and, therefore, enjoy a financial advantage.[30] Would you rather invest your retirement savings in a democracy or an autocracy? Why? Capital markets do not flourish in autocratic states. This is largely because investors feel that their money is more secure in democratic societies. It is no coincidence that the leading financial centers in the world today, New York and London, also reside in two of the world's oldest continuous democracies. Before Wall Street and The City rose to prominence, the center of global finance could also be found in what at the time were the world's most open societies. Many consider the Venetian Republic to be the first international financial center from the 9th through the 14th centuries. And freewheeling Amsterdam of the 17th and 18th centuries was the center of global finance before London assumed the title in the 19th century.[31]

One area in which this democratic financial advantage manifests itself most clearly today is in sovereign debt. Nation-states borrow to cover their expenses by issuing government debt. U.S. Treasury bonds are the most prominent and well-known example. Stanford University political economists Douglas North, Barry Weingast, and Kenneth Schultz have argued that democracies enjoy a sovereign debt advantage because they are able to "credibly commit" to repaying their loans.[32]

Democracies have this credibility advantage because their executives are constrained. If a dictator decides to default on his nation's debt repayments, he could do so with little resistance. But a democratic leader cannot unilaterally default because there are checks and balances in the system. Other branches of government, public opinion, and forces within the executive branch itself would make it difficult for a democratic leader to make a decision of this magnitude. Just imagine the uproar if a U.S. president announced they planned to stop payments on U.S. Treasury bonds. And if the leader went ahead with the decision anyway, they and their party could be punished later in public opinion polling, party donations, or at the ballot box. Moreover, since many of the nation's bondholders are also its citizens and its elected representatives, they themselves have a stake in ensuring regular debt repayments. The openness of democratic systems means that even international bond holders are not completely shut out, as they too can access veto points in the system and lobby for repayment.[33]

In other words, democracies can make "credible commitments" to repay their debt because it would be difficult for them to default even if they wanted to. On the other hand, autocratic governments cannot make similar commitments because their decisions to default would face little resistance. Investors understand this dynamic, and it is why they prefer to invest in democracies. Indeed, when investors talk about a "flight to safety" in uncertain economic times, they often mean buying U.S. Treasury bonds, which are seen as the most reliable investment on the planet. They certainly do not mean stashing their cash in Russia or China.

Since investors are eager to hold the sovereign debt of democracies, democracies have easier access to credit at lower interest rates. On the other hand, bond holders fear that autocratic governments will be more likely to default on their loan payments and, therefore, demand a higher interest rate in order to cover this risk premium.[34]

The democratic advantage in finance extends beyond sovereign debt, however, to stock markets. Capital controls are tools governments use to regulate the money flowing in and out of their countries. And scholars have found that autocratic states rely more heavily on capital controls than democracies.[35] Since capital controls are often implemented through taxes on cross-border capital flows, autocratic governments can capture these rents and, consistent with the model of exclusionary economics discussed earlier, re-allocate them to themselves and their supporters. Capital controls also allow autocratic states greater influence over the money flowing in and through their economies.

One of the problems with capital controls, however, is that they prevent the development of functioning stock and bond markets. Capital markets rely on the free flow of capital, and economists have shown that stock and bond markets tend to become deeper and more liquid following capital control liberalization.[36]

This is important because stock markets are a driver of economic growth. A functioning stock and bond market improves the allocation of capital and enhances prospects for long-term economic growth. But capitalism does not work without capital markets. [37]

In sum, national economies work primarily according to a political logic, not an economic one, and the political logic in democracies facilitates the type of economic institutions, practices, and policies that tend to promote economic growth. In autocracies, the countervailing political logic encourages institutions that constrain economic development. It should come as no surprise, therefore, that the world's economic, financial, and trading powerhouses tend also to be the most democratic.

DEMOCRACY AND DIPLOMATIC STRENGTH

On August 23, 1939, the Soviet Union and Nazi Germany signed the infamous Molotov-Ribbentrop Pact, named after the countries' foreign ministers, Vyacheslav Molotov and Joachim von Ribbentrop, respectively. Under the terms of this secret alliance, the powers agreed to divide Eastern Europe between themselves, with the Soviet Union taking the eastern half of Poland, parts of Romania, Finland, and the Baltic states, and Nazi Germany annexing western Poland. Additionally, the powers also committed to a nonaggression pact. They agreed not to invade each other and not to assist any third parties at war with either side. The states immediately followed through in implementing the "sphere of influence" component of the agreement. Germany invaded Poland on September 1, 1939, and the Soviet Union followed, taking its portion of Eastern Europe sixteen days later. But the alliance did not last long. Once Hitler had consolidated his gains in western Poland, his appetite for territorial conquest increased. He now set his sights back on Moscow's holdings. In direct violation of the nonaggression pact, Hitler attacked Soviet positions along the eastern front in Operation Barbarossa on June 22, 1941.

Compare the Soviet-Nazi alliance to the North Atlantic Treaty Organization (NATO), founded less than a decade later, in 1949. The organization began as a club of mostly democracies in Western Europe and North America, united by fears of Soviet aggression. While NATO faced tough times during the Cold War, it stuck together. When the Cold War ended in 1989, some predicted that NATO had lost its raison d'être and would, therefore, dissolve. Instead, it went in the other direction and expanded to incorporate much of the former Soviet bloc. Today, the Alliance includes twenty-nine democratic nations stretching from the United States to Estonia. Its newest member, Montenegro, joined in 2017. The Alliance has been successful in deterring major conflict against its members. When it came under threat in the 9/11 terror attacks against the United States, Alliance members invoked the Article 5 mutual defense clause of the Atlantic Charter and joined the United States in its war in Afghanistan.

Far from anomalous, political science research suggests that these cases are representative: democracies build larger, more durable, and reliable alliances. In his landmark study *Origins of Alliances*, Stephen Walt argued that the "balance of threat" was the primary driver of alliance formation; the enemy of your enemy is your friend.[38] Walt is in the Realist school of international relations and is skeptical that domestic politics matter much in an anarchic international system. But even he acknowledges that common ideology is an important impetus for alliance formation, and democratic states are especially likely to collaborate. He argued this was because, unlike in other systems, the domestic political ideologies of democratic states do not threaten, but rather reinforce, the legitimacy of other like-minded states.

More recent research suggests that democracies do flock together, but this is because of the checks and balances in their domestic political systems. Constraints on the executive branch and domestic political "audience costs" in democracies make it difficult for leaders to quickly shift policies or renege on international commitments.[39] Audience costs are the domestic political costs that a leader pays when he or she makes a public commitment and then backs away. Domestic political audiences, including opposition political parties, other branches of government, or the general public, seek to criticize or punish a leader for failing to live up to the country's international commitments. (Just think of the heat President Trump took, for example, for raising questions about the value and continued relevance of NATO). Since democratic leaders are constrained by their domestic political circumstances, they are hesitant to take on international commitments they do not intend to keep. As a corollary, they are more likely to actually abide by the commitments they do take on. For this reason, (and as we saw previously in the discussion of sovereign debt), it is thought that democracies are better able to make "credible commitments" in international politics.[40] Other nations tend to believe the promises (and threats) of democracies.

When a U.S. president announces that America's alliances are "ironclad," U.S. partners can generally rest assured that Washington has their back. When a dictator makes the same promise, on the other hand, allies better watch their back.

Statistical analysis has found that democracies make more reliable partners. They are more likely to uphold their alliance commitments even in times of war and they might make more effective partners during wartime.[41] Alliances between democracies are larger and last longer than those between other states.[42] Unlike in autocracies, democratic alliances endure even as leaders come and go.[43]

Just think of the major democracies fighting victoriously together on the same side in World War I and World War II. Compare NATO's seventy-year lifespan and more than two dozen members to the short-lived Molotov-Ribbentrop Pact. There is no autocratic equivalent to NATO. The Soviet-led Warsaw Pact was held together only by coercion. Indeed, the primary fighting experienced by the Warsaw Pact was invading its own members, including attacks against Hungary in 1956 and Czechoslovakia in 1968. The Pact crumbled quickly at the end of the Cold War, and Moscow's erstwhile allies eagerly switched sides as soon as they had the chance.

Much like modern marriage in which the most desirable partners seek each other out for long-term relationships, democracies prefer to align with other democracies. They eschew formal defense commitments with unreliable autocrats. Indeed, this preference is explicit in the NATO alliance; democratic governance has become a requirement for membership. Scholars have also found in statistical analysis that democracies are more likely to align with other democracies.[44]

Beyond alliance commitments, democracies appear to be more likely to make and comply with diplomatic commitments of all kinds. We have very few laws in political science, but this may be one of them. Take the Treaty on the Nonproliferation of Nuclear Weapons (NPT) as an example. Many consider this to be the most successful treaty in history, and it enjoys near-universal adherence and compliance. In recent years, however, the international community has wrestled with countries, like Iran and North Korea, that have signed the NPT but failed to live up to their treaty obligations. Indeed, these countries seem to be preying on the treaty, using their membership as a cover under which to develop covert bomb programs. What may be less well known, however, is that a democracy has never attempted this path.[45] There are democracies that sign the NPT and comply, like Belgium and Canada. There are other democracies that decide that they would like to build nuclear weapons and, therefore, refuse to join the institution, like Israel and India. But never has a democracy signed the NPT and then attempted to build nuclear weapons anyway. In contrast, the list of autocracies that signed the NPT and then secretly pursued the bomb despite their public commitment is long and includes Iran, Iraq, Libya, North Korea, and Syria. It also includes Romania, Taiwan, and South Korea in the past when they were ruled by autocratic governments.

In addition to the NPT, democracies are more likely to sign and/or comply with international agreements in a wide range of other areas including human rights, the environment, trade, international monetary affairs, and arms control.[46]

There are several reasons why democracies may be willing and able to make "credible commitments" internationally. As discussed earlier, democratic leaders may fear "audience costs" for making international agreements and then failing to comply. In addition, democracies will often change their domestic political laws to accord with their international legal agreements, which locks in the international commitment and makes noncompliance illegal domestically. Signing an international treaty may also empower domestic political interest groups by providing them with resources, legitimacy, and information. These groups are then better positioned politically to press their governments to keep their international commitments.

The democratic advantage in international diplomacy goes beyond formal commitments, however. Democracies also enjoy more "soft power."[47] Political scientist Joseph Nye defines hard power as the ability to influence others through economic or military threats or promises. He contrasts that with soft power—a term he coined—to mean achieving one's goals by getting others to want what you want. Nye argued that the United States, due to its attractive political system, culture, and foreign policies, built up large reservoirs of soft power during the Cold War. It was often able to achieve its goals without resorting to bribes or punishments because other nations generally liked the United States and believed in what it stood for. (The American model may have been somewhat tarnished in recent years; this is a subject to which we will return later in the book.) In contrast, the Soviet Union, with its authoritarian politics at home and abroad, lacked soft power and was forced, therefore, to rely more heavily on brute force. These are not isolated examples. Democracies tend to display the types of values, policies, and vibrant cultures that appeal to others. Indeed, according to a recent ranking of soft power, the top twenty nations with the most soft power around the world are all democracies.[48] Since democracies also tend to be perceived as less threatening to other states, they are better able to amass power internationally without generating significant resistance or counterbalancing coalitions.[49]

Finally, democracies may also be better at foreign policy decision-making in general. As we will see later, scholars have argued that democracies may enjoy a wartime advantage due to two factors.[50] First, democratic leaders may make better decisions about war and peace due to the free flow of information and open debate in their societies. And second, democracies may produce more capable military officers who are empowered to take initiative on the battlefield. While recent scholarship has focused on how these factors affect war, in theory, these same dynamics should apply to diplomacy as well. The same mechanisms that allow leaders to make better decisions about war initiation may also lead them to more astutely navigate a wide range of diplomatic issues that fall short of war and peace. If democratic warriors are better able to take initiative on the battlefield, then democratic diplomats may also be more effective at the negotiating table. In addition, scholars have argued that when democracies make foreign policy mistakes, they are better able to self-correct.[51]

In sum, democracies stand out as more reliable, attractive, and judicious (and less threatening) diplomatic partners in an often dodgy, ugly, rash, and dangerous world.

DEMOCRACY AND MILITARY STRENGTH

On December 7, 1941, Japan attacked the U.S. naval base at Pearl Harbor. Tokyo intentionally picked a fight with the world's largest economic power on the assumption that the United States did not have the stomach for a major war in the Pacific. A few years later, on September 2, 1945, Japan formally surrendered on the decks of the USS Missouri in Tokyo Bay.

On October 25, 1983, the United States invaded the tiny Caribbean island nation of Grenada. A military junta had just executed the country's leader, and the United States intervened to overthrow the upstart military government. The fighting was over within a week, and the United States helped install a democratic system that governs the country to the present day.

The democratic peace theory—the idea that democracies do not fight other democracies—is well known. What is less well known is that democracies win the wars they fight.[52] Indeed, since 1815, democracies have won over 76 percent of their wars. Compare this to the much lower success rate of autocracies, which have been victorious in only 47 percent of cases. Statistical tests reveal that regime type is an important determinant of victory in war even after controlling for other factors that might matter, such as military power, terrain, strategy, allies, and distance.

There are several reasons why democratic states may enjoy an advantage in international conflict. First, as the examples above indicate, democracies are more likely to choose wars they can win, or at least ones in which losses will not be devastating. Democracies go to war with Serbia, while autocracies invade Russia in winter. Democratic leaders may be pickier about the wars they fight because they conduct foreign policy with an eye to the ballot box. Losing a war is a good way to lose popular support and re-election. Winning a war, on the other hand, rallies the country around the flag and boosts one's support and prospects for remaining in office.

In addition, democratic states facilitate free flows of information, which allow leaders to make more accurate assessments about their prospects for victory. Before a democratic leader makes a decision to go to war, he or she has been informed by vigorous debates within his or her own government and in the broader public. These debates weigh the available options and the associated costs and benefits.

Autocratic leaders, on the other hand, do not benefit from hearing all sides of an argument. They tend to be surrounded by "yes men" who tell the dictator what he wants to hear. When Saddam Hussein received unwelcome news, for example, it was not uncommon for him to literally shoot the messenger.

Moreover, broader public debate over a state's policy are not welcomed in a closed society. Foreign policy wonks in the United States can burnish their credentials and advance their career prospects by consistently pointing out the flaws in U.S. foreign policy in op-eds, journal articles, and books. The same behavior in China would land one in jail. Leaders in autocratic states, therefore, may make less sound judgments on issues of war and peace because they need not worry about losing power at the ballot box and because they are less likely to have access to the best information about their chances of prevailing in armed conflict.

In addition, democratic states produce better soldiers. To fight effectively, officers must be prepared to take initiative on the battlefield. No plan survives contact with the enemy, and a good military officer must be able to make real-time decisions consistent with political guidance as conditions on the ground change. Higher levels of education and the individualistic culture fostered in democratic states produce soldiers who make good leaders and take initiative on the battlefield. Improvising in an autocratic army, on the other hand, can be risky. Individual initiative may be seen as insubordination. It is much safer to wait for orders from above. Moreover, autocrats do not tend to empower lower-level officers because they like to maintain strict control from the top. Additionally, democratic soldiers are often more motivated because they believe they are fighting for their own nation's freedom, not because they are forced into battle.

Furthermore, democracies are known to comply with the laws of war and treat prisoners humanely. This makes surrender an easier proposition for enemy soldiers. Just think of Saddam Hussein's army surrendering in droves without much of a fight in the 1991 and 2003 Gulf Wars. Contrariwise, autocracies have less compunction about killing or mistreating enemy POWs. Why not fight to the finish if the alternative may be execution or years of grueling torture in the Hanoi Hilton?

Democracies also enjoy a military advantage due to their innovation edge.[53] Wars are often won by the state with the superior military technology or the more innovative military operational concepts.[54] Military competition is not static; it is a constant cat-and-mouse game, with both sides seeking advantage. The offense creates more powerful artillery; the defense builds better walls. The defense deploys trenches, barbed wire, and machine guns; the offense develops tanks and aircraft. The offense builds aircraft carriers; the defense fields anti-ship missiles. States that push the technological frontier of military technology and, importantly, that can develop the new operational concepts to employ the technology on the battlefield, have an advantage over those that do not.[55] It is widely believed that democracies hold a technology and innovation edge in the civilian economy for the reasons discussed previously, and I argue here that democracies also tend to be better innovators in military/technological competitions. They are more likely to develop innovative military technologies and to devise ingenious operational concepts for their employment.

Perhaps democracy's greatest advantage over autocracy in international warfare, however, is that democrats have the luxury of focusing their militaries on international warfare. Autocratic leaders, on the other hand, fear their own people more than foreign powers. They must devote considerable attention to domestic threats to their rule. Autocratic systems often lack legitimacy and clear mechanisms for leadership succession. Because of this, autocracies are more likely than democracies to experience irregular leadership turnover in assassinations, coups, and revolutions. To deal with this problem, autocrats must balance against both external and internal threats.[56] They, therefore, focus their security apparatus inordinately on domestic challenges.

Sometimes autocratic leaders are even forced to make concessions to external powers, so that they can concentrate on more pressing problems at home. Taylor Fravel has written about how China, for example, becomes more aggressive abroad in periods of domestic tranquility.[57] But when it is facing domestic political turmoil, it looks to settle disputes with international rivals.

Autocratic leaders sometimes even intentionally hobble their own militaries in a strategy known as "coup proofing." If the dictator's army is weak and poorly trained, it will not be capable of overthrowing the dictator.[58] The strategy can work, but it also renders one's military less effective against external adversaries. Saddam Hussein, for example, denied his military training in urban combat because he did not want it capable of orchestrating a coup. It may have had its intended effect, but it allowed the U.S. military to march into Baghdad virtually uncontested in the spring of 2003.

In sum, democracies enjoy a military advantage because they make better decisions on matters of war and peace, their soldiers take initiative on the battlefield, they are more innovative in military-technological competitions, and they have the luxury of focusing on external enemies.

The Democratic Advantage in Great Power Competition

We have just seen that there is substantial theory and evidence to suggest that democracies have a meaningful advantage over autocracies in a number of separate economic, diplomatic, and military arenas.

Of course, social science is not physics. The strongest relationships we have are general tendencies, not hard and fast rules. And most of these findings have been challenged by other scholars and are the subject of on-going debate.[59] Yet, there is more than enough theory and evidence to suggest that there is something different about democracies.

Moreover, the advantages possessed by democracies are not trivial, but are central to gaining and maintaining global mastery. To become a leading global power, a state must possess economic, diplomatic, and military strength. Democracies, on average, possess stronger economies, diplomacy, and militaries than their autocratic competitors. We can, therefore, aggregate these mid-level findings about a democratic advantage in discrete areas into a bigger theory about domestic political institutions and international power and influence. Democracies should enjoy a systematic advantage in international geopolitics.

Some see the constraints on government power in democracies as a weakness, but, in fact, they are democracy's greatest strength. These constraints facilitate economic growth by giving individuals and businesses confidence that they will be able to reap the rewards of their labors, investments, and innovations. They help democracies attract capital and develop as financial centers, because investors know their money will be safe and will likely generate positive rates of return over the long run. They make for stronger alliances and international diplomacy, because democratic commitments tend to be more reliable and because others have less to fear from powerful democracies. They lead to superior military performance; since people do not fear their governments, their governments need not fear them, and governments can focus on external enemies. They innovate in military technology and operational concepts. In addition, protections for free speech lead to open debate that informs democratic leaders in foreign policy, including on matters of war and peace.

Combined, this is an impressive array of positive attributes and should lead us to conclude that democracies, on average, will be better able to amass international power and influence than their autocratic rivals.

To put the argument in the language of social science, the central independent variable of this study is domestic political institutions. It is a continuous variable that ranges from most democratic to most autocratic. The further one goes back in time, the fewer states that meet contemporary standards of democracy, but some states were more open than others even in the ancient world, and this book contends that those differences matter.

The intervening variables are economic, diplomatic, and military strength. Economic strength means having a large and growing economy and deep and liquid financial markets. A state possesses diplomatic strength when it has a large network of effective and reliable allies and partners and when it does not face a formidable counterbalancing coalition. Military strength exists when a state possesses a quantitative and/or qualitative military advantage over its rivals.

The dependent variable is international power and influence. Robert Dahl famously defined power as the ability to get others to do something that they otherwise would not do.[60] Sometimes the exercise of power can be witnessed directly, but usually it cannot. To get around this problem, political scientists often study power resources that can be measured. Hard-power resources include economic and military strength; soft power resources include policies, values, and culture that are attractive to others. If this argument is correct, then we should expect that democracies tend to possess more hard and soft power resources than do autocracies. In a sense, therefore, these are both intervening and dependent variables according to this theoretical framework.

Further, if democracies are better at amassing power resources, then other implications should follow as well. For political scientists, here comes another list of dependent variables. We should expect that democracies will, on average, hold greater shares of global power. We should expect that democracies will feature disproportionately among the great powers. We should expect that democracies are more likely to become the leading state in the international system and that these liberal leviathans will enjoy more enduring periods of ascendancy.[61] We should expect that democracies are more likely to emerge victorious in long-run geopolitical rivalries. We might also expect that, while autocracies may launch serious challenges for world domination, they will tend to fail in their bids. Finally, we should expect that power transitions, situations in which a rising challenger overtakes a declining hegemon, will be less likely when there is a reigning democratic hegemon and a rising autocratic challenger.

To convey this information graphically, the central argument of the book is outlined in Figure 1.1.

According to this argument, domestic political institutions are not the only thing that matters, but they are a central, and perhaps the most important, fundamental driver of international power. The other factors that we often believe leads to power and influence on the world stage, like economic wealth, alliances, and military power, are themselves the products of domestic political institutions. In sum, we should expect that democracies tend to excel in international affairs.

An important clarification is, however, in order. Many of the democratic advantages reviewed above attend to any open society, whether democracy

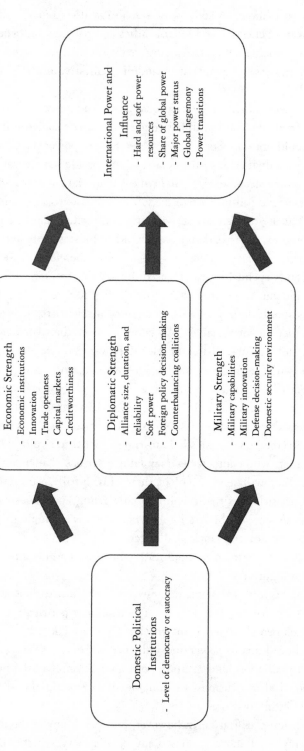

FIGURE 1.1 A Schematic of the Argument

or republic. But some of the benefits, especially those that rely on checks and balances within the system, do not apply to direct democracies in which simple majority opinion can result in decision making that is every bit as rash as in autocracies. Direct democracies should tend to do better than autocracies, therefore, but not as well as republics. It is republics, or what we today call democracies, that should benefit from the full range of democratic advantages.

The idea that democracies have an edge in the rough and tumble of international politics may come as a shock to many. Indeed, for centuries, a countervailing autocratic advantage hypothesis has also existed. According to this perspective, succeeding in international politics requires the ability to make big, bold decisions, to develop a long-term strategy and stick to it, and to act with cutthroat ruthlessness when necessary. These are all traits, some claim, that come more naturally to dictators than to democrats.

Does the argument of this book have it exactly wrong? Is it actually the case that autocrats have the advantage in international politics? It is to this question that we will turn in the next chapter.

CHAPTER 2 | The Autocratic Advantage?

I N 1831 ALEXANDER DE TOCQUEVILLE visited the United States. Tocqueville was an aristocrat and diplomat in his native France sent to this fledgling democracy across the Atlantic to study its prison system and prepare a report for the French government. Tocqueville succeeded in this task over the course of his nine-month visit and also found spare time to write up the notes from his travels. The result of his scribbles, *Democracy in America*, has become a landmark in the political philosophy canon.[1] Harvey Mansfield, a professor of government at Harvard University, has said it is "at once the best book ever written on democracy and the best book ever written on America."[2]

Tocqueville marveled at the novel experiment taking place in the new world. He examined why republican institutions had flourished in the United States while failing elsewhere. And he extolled the virtues of American political and socioeconomic equality as superior to the entrenched inequality found in his native France. In sum, he saw many upsides to the untrammeled freedom and independence permitted in the United States.

But he saw downsides as well. He was prescient in predicting that slavery would eventually tear America apart. He worried about materialism, isolation, and the tyranny of the majority. And he judged that American arts and science left something to be desired. (He did not live to be proven wrong by the discoveries of James Watson, the paintings of Jackson Pollack, or the writing of Ernest Hemingway).

Most importantly for our purposes, he also seemed to have missed the mark when it came to assessing U.S. foreign policy. Tocqueville believed that the American system was simply unable to stack up against the monarchies of Europe in this domain. He wrote that "as for myself I have no hesitation in avowing my conviction, that it is most especially in the conduct of foreign relations that democratic governments appear to me to be decidedly inferior to governments carried on upon different principles."

He argued that a successful foreign policy requires a state to develop and adhere to a clear grand strategy. It also demanded the ability to act covertly when necessary to achieve one's objectives. But Tocqueville assessed that "a democracy is unable to regulate the details of an important undertaking, to persevere in a design, and to work out its execution in the presence of serious obstacles. It cannot combine its measures with secrecy, and it will not await their consequences with patience." He concluded that "these are qualities which more especially belong to . . . an aristocracy; and they are precisely the means by which (a state) attains to a predominant position."

As a thoughtful and balanced observer, Tocqueville recognized the "natural defects of aristocracy" as well, but he thought their negative "influence is comparatively innoxious in the direction of the external affairs of a state." He observed that "the capital fault of which aristocratic bodies may be accused is that they are more apt to contrive their own advantage than that of the mass of the people," but that when it comes to "foreign politics it is rare for the interest of the aristocracy to be in any way distinct from that of the people." Note that this is nearly the exact opposite claim made by Machiavelli just over three centuries before, when he explained that what suits the prince generally offends the city and vice versa. In contrast to Machiavelli, Tocqueville concluded that "Foreign politics demand scarcely any of those qualities which a democracy possesses; and they require, on the contrary, the perfect use of almost all those faculties in which it is deficient."

Tocqueville was not the first, nor would he be the last, thinker to disparage democracies' foreign policy acumen. In the ancient world, Plato argued that a philosopher king possesses superior judgment to the excesses of democratic mob rule.[3] Thomas Hobbes, writing in the early modern period, argued that a strong monarch was necessary to protect populations from the "war of all against all" that is the state of nature in international affairs.[4] And in the 20th century, fascist and communist dictators, including Adolf Hitler, chastised democracy, claiming that it made people soft, operated too slowly, and pitted factions within society against each other.[5] Similarly, Vladimir Lenin assessed that "democratic-republican" systems were "rotting alive."[6] Even some democratic statespersons feared that they were at the helm of a creaky ship of state as their adversaries captained more seaworthy vessels. Henry Kissinger, for example, sometimes feared that the Soviet Union's autocratic system would give Moscow a leg up in its Cold War rivalry with America's democracy.[7]

By the end of the 20th century, however, fascism and communism had been consigned to the ash heap of history and the idea that autocracy might provide the superior model for organizing domestic politics and economics was mostly buried along with them.[8] Social science research tends to follow real-world events, and in the post–Cold War period open-market democracies flourished, as did new thinking about democratic advantages in the social sciences.

As Russia and China have re-emerged as serious autocratic competitors in recent years, however, the autocratic advantage thesis has also been resurrected from the dead.

Contemporary Autocratic Advantage Theory

While not as rigorously developed, or entrenched in the scholarly research, there is a folk wisdom developing among some that America's dysfunctional political system will never be able to compete with our ruthless and efficient autocratic competitors in Russia and China. We will call this developing folk wisdom "contemporary autocratic advantage theory."

Contemporary autocratic advantage theory begins from the conviction that autocracies can set out long-term strategies and stick to them, while policy directions in a democracy change with every election. In autocracies, the same party, or maybe even the same leader, will be in power for decades, so autocrats can chart a consistent strategic course. Autocrats need to worry less about internal bureaucratic bickering or public opinion because the strongman can overrule dissent and keep the nation on a steady course.

The Chinese Communist Party (CCP), for example, has committed to controlling the commanding heights of the 21st-century economy by becoming a leader in the most important high-tech industries of the future through its plan, formerly referred to as "Made in China 2025." Beijing's Belt and Road Initiative (BRI) is a grand proposal to expand China's control throughout the developed and developing world through massive investments in infrastructure, such as roads, ports, and bridges. And, most ambitiously, China's leaders have broadcast a goal for the country to become a global superpower by 2049.[9] The CCP, and maybe even President Xi himself, will be in power for decades and can ensure the country remains committed to these outlined paths.

Democracies, on the other hand, are fickle and unstable. Leaders focus on the next election. U.S. Presidents choose policies designed to maximize performance for only four or eight years, at which point any problems are kicked down the road to their successor. New governments are elected with a desire to distinguish themselves from their predecessor, zigzagging the country in entirely new directions every few years.

In the United States, for example, we are glued to the next presidential election. With every new administration, we move off in a new direction. Commentators joked that the George W. Bush administration's policy would be ABC, Anything but Clinton. Obama vowed to show more humility on the world stage, following what he perceived as the hubris of the George W. Bush years. Trump appears intent to rip up Obama's foreign policy legacy, from the Iran nuclear deal to the Paris climate accord. And Democratic candidates line up to portray themselves as the anti-Trump.

Beyond inconsistency, the next pillar of the autocratic advantage thesis holds that, when it comes to implementing national strategy, autocracies can take big, bold actions, whereas democracies dither in endless debate. When autocratic leaders make an important decision, they can impose their will on the system. They pull a lever and things get done. They can mass resources behind important national objectives. Political opposition or the potential losers from needed change are bulldozed over in the name of national progress.

In democracies, on the other hand, a politician's proposal is often just the opening bid in a drawn-out negotiation. Debates drag on for months or years and most promising policy ideas end up in a desk drawer. The potential losers from necessary policy change mobilize to resist, adding to the gridlock. The government cannot impose decisions. Resources are scattered as diverse private actors move off in different directions. Nothing gets accomplished as momentum is slowed through endless debate. The policies that do actually make it through are no longer recognizable as they get watered down in political compromise and horse trading.

Take China's massive infrastructure spending or investments in new technology as an example. When the CCP wants to build a road, a bridge, or a dam, or invest in clean energy, it completes the work quickly. *New York Times* columnist Thomas Friedman, for example, has fantasized what it would be like if the United States could be "China for a day." He said, "What if we had a government here that could actually make decisions? Okay? That could actually come together, Democrats and Republicans, and make a long-term plan and pursue it?"[10]

The third supposed autocratic advantage is that autocracies can be ruthless when necessary, but democracies are constrained by morality, domestic politics, and international law. International politics is a free-for-all, and, to succeed, a state must be willing to do whatever it takes to secure one's interests, including actions that many find morally repugnant, such as spying, dissembling, assassination, and decimating enemies in international warfare. Autocracies are willing and able to take such actions. They do not care about international or domestic public opinion. Secrets are kept due to strict controls on free speech and the fear of punishment. And they are perfectly comfortable brutalizing their own people, so doing the same to foreigners when necessary is not a hard call.

Democracies, on the other hand, are constrained by ethical and legal constraints. Domestic public opinion, international law, and normative commitments to human rights prevent democracies from really taking the gloves off. Democracies cannot keep secrets because private government deliberations in open societies are immediately leaked to the press or penetrated by foreign intelligence organizations. According to an old joke in Washington, DC, the difference between Top Secret and the front page of the *Washington Post* is two weeks. With the arrival of *BuzzFeed* and *Politico*, that may have changed to two hours. Moreover, the foreign policy of democracies is decided principally by voters who wish to avoid footing large tax bills or sending their sons and daughters off to die in war. They are, therefore, overly cautious and lack the stomach for international conflict.

Some military analysts, for example, claim that the United States was handcuffed in its fight against ISIS in Iraq and Syria by restrictive rules of engagement.[11] Meanwhile, we saw Russian President Vladimir Putin and Syrian leader Bashar al-Assad bomb hospitals and gas innocent civilians with chemical weapons. The behavior may have been evil, but what was the end result? Today it is Putin and Assad, not the United States and its allies, calling the shots in Syria.

Or take China's commitment to pursuing next-generation technologies, such as artificial intelligence (AI). Developing effective AI algorithms requires access to large amounts of data. The CCP has no qualms about collecting all manner of private information on its citizens. And they are using this information to develop world-class facial recognition technology that can identify and track the daily activities of the Chinese people. In contrast, the United States and other democracies do not have access to such wide-ranging personal data (because, you know, the Bill of Rights) and some tech experts bemoan this data shortage as a democratic handicap in the new tech arms race.

The final autocratic advantage is that politics in democracies are simply too messy, whereas autocratic politics are clean and efficient. In autocracies, there is less infighting because the lines of authority are clear. Any politicking that does occur is done in backrooms, and the image portrayed to the nation and to the outside world is one of serene stability. Instead of choosing factions, the people have little choice but to stay silent or unite behind a single national government.

Politics in democracies, on the other hand, are characterized by constant gridlock, vituperation, political infighting, and scandal. Politicians denigrate each other on the campaign trail and in office. Society is divided by party, and political opponents are vilified. Almost daily there seems to be some new scandal with a disgraced politician in hot water. The foolishness of government policy is attacked by opponents both inside and outside the governing administration. In sum, politics in democracies are fractious and demoralizing.

Today this point is sometimes made by contrasting the constant chaos surrounding the Trump administration in the United States to President Xi's rise to power. Indeed, after the 2016 election, some colleagues in Washington bemoaned the U.S. electoral system and pined for a system like China's, in which a small circle of elites choose a leader from among their own ranks. "If only we had a system like China's," they argued, "we could have had a dignified and normal leader, like Joe Biden, Hillary Clinton, or even Jeb Bush. Instead, democracy brought us Donald Trump."

In another recent example, the president of a prominent Washington, DC, think tank wrote that the 2019 U.S. government shutdown would undermine national security. The message to the world would be that "fractious, paralyzed democracies simply can't muster the will to deliver the goods their people want." Autocracies would use the event to argue that the rest of the world should embrace "an effective, tech-fueled autocracy that can move nimbly to pursue national interests and spread prosperity."[12]

This line of argument has been taken a step further in recent years given the autocratic meddling in the domestic politics of democracies, like Russia's interference in the 2016 U.S. presidential election. The openness of democratic systems makes them more vulnerable to foreign manipulation. Russia and China have preyed on the divisions within democratic societies in an attempt to turn us against each other, weaken us, and strengthen their own relative position. In contrast, we are unable or unwilling to fight fire with fire.

In sum, according to the autocratic advantage argument, democracies are at a disadvantage because they are astrategic, indecisive, pusillanimous, and fractious.

It is a damning condemnation. But is it true?

Questioning the Autocratic Advantage

It is the case that autocracies may have certain advantages in foreign affairs, but these are often overstated. And, indeed, many of these alleged advantages are nothing of the sort. Almost all of the above arguments were encountered and then countered by the maestro, Machiavelli, himself. Let us consider each in turn.

First, there is good reason to doubt that constancy in policy is actually an advantage of autocrats. After all, autocrats have proven themselves to be quite fickle over the millennia. Autocratic leaders are unconstrained, so they have an easier time ripping their countries in new and radically different directions. Then, if the dictator happens to change his mind, he can do it again. Mao's autocratic China ricocheted from one failed policy to another, from the Great Leap Forward to the Cultural Revolution. Mao aligned with the Soviet Union in 1950. Then he nearly fought a nuclear war with Moscow two decades later. Since Deng Xiaoping, China pursued a fairly constant strategy of "hiding its capabilities and biding its time," but President Xi discarded that doctrine and launched the country on a new and more confrontational path. Since Xi is the most powerful Chinese leader since Mao, this might mean that his whims, like Mao's, will once again jerk China in several different new directions and back again. Indeed, the strategies that commentators currently see as evidence of China's long-range planning, like "Made in China 2025" and BRI, are each only several years old and, therefore, hardly evidence of enduring dedication toward a strategic vision.

Moreover, autocracies are less constant in another more fundamental way; their regimes are less stable. While institutionalized political successions in democracies often lead to changes of policy, political successions in autocracies often result in regime collapse, civil and international war, and the formation of brand new political regimes that take the country on a new path. Tsar Nicholas II, for example, was supportive of Russia's involvement in World War I until he was imprisoned and executed. Russia's new government withdrew from the conflict. In contrast, Revolutionary France beheaded a king and started a war. Iran went from being a close strategic partner of the United States to its bitter enemy in just a few months following the Iranian Revolution in

1979. The Soviet Union had a fairly constant foreign policy direction until the system collapsed. Autocratic foreign policy changes much like Hemingway went bankrupt: "gradually, then suddenly." If Putinism or the CCP were to come to an end tomorrow, which is at least plausible, it is likely that Russian and Chinese grand strategy would also undergo a seismic shift.

On the other hand, democracies are slower to react, but once they lock-in on a grand strategy that works, it is harder to upend the domestic political consensus. After all, Washington was committed to its successful bipartisan grand strategy of deterrence and containment of the Soviet Union for a half century. Since then, "realist" critics of U.S. foreign policy have bemoaned what they see as America's unshakeable bipartisan commitment to liberal internationalism in the post–Cold War era.[13]

Indeed, Washington has arguably followed the same basic grand strategy since 1945: building, expanding, and maintaining a rules-based, liberal international order. It is a simple three-step strategy. First, set up an open system with international institutions, free trade, and support for democracy and human rights. Second, invite other countries to join the order. Third, defend the order against challengers.[14]

Some have argued that Washington is currently abandoning this strategy at its peril. That is a subject that is up for debate and to which we will return in the conclusion. Still, a seventy-five-year commitment to a single grand strategy is impressive evidence of unwavering commitment to a long-term goal.

To be sure, where the stakes are lower, democracies can afford to have intense political disagreements—and often do—but on the big issues, they often show remarkable unity of purpose.

Moreover, unlike in autocracies, democratic political regimes themselves are stable. In consolidated democracies, regime change is rare. While new politicians seek to improve on their predecessor's policies, democracies do not see the drastic change in strategic orientation that comes with the collapse of one governing system and the rise of another.

When critics claim that autocracies are better at strategy, they often seem to be saying that autocracies are better at developing plans for mid-level issues. Autocracies are better able to micromanage their societies. Many strategists in the United States envy that level of control as they call on the United States to develop a "whole-of-government strategy" for pet issue X. (I must admit that I myself have been guilty of this.)

But a whole-of-government approach dictated by the government is not desirable for most issues. The "China for a day" thesis assumes that it is big, government actions that really get things done. But the most important decisions for the future wealth and power of nations often do not come from the top down, but from the bottom up. The best ideas do not reside in the politburo but in talented individuals in the boardroom, or the battlefield, closest to the action. A government that gets out of the way and lets societal actors fill the void have often proven more successful. Indeed, too much government control can stifle creativity and crowd out the energies of society where the real innovations take place. China has a coordinated government strategy for developing new energy technologies, and yet the shale gas revolution happened in the United States.

So, in sum, democracies have demonstrated themselves to be pretty good at long-term planning where it is most crucial and avoiding it for smaller matters where it is unhelpful. In contrast, autocracies attempt to impose plans on a wide range of mid-level issues, but their systems allow greater capacity for overnight and radical change in strategic orientation. I, for one, would award the prize for constancy in strategic purpose to the U.S.-led international order over "Made in China 2025" any day.

Indeed, as Machiavelli argued:

> I, therefore, disagree with the common opinion that a populace in power is unstable [and] changeable. . . . The prince . . . unchecked by laws, will be more . . . unstable, and imprudent than a populace.

Having dispensed with one argument, what about the supposed autocratic ability to make big, bold decisions, and mass resources behind a national objective? First, it bears noting that this is not necessarily a desirable trait. Just because a decision is quick and efficient does not mean it is the right one. Impulsive decisions in our personal lives often turn into regrets, and international politics is no different. Big, bold decisions can become big, bold mistakes. Hitler's decision to invade Russia was bold and efficient, but it also turned out to be his undoing. Since the 2008 financial crisis, China has executed vast infrastructure investment plans, but this included many wasted capital expenditures on white elephant projects in the middle of nowhere. At present, the CCP is throwing a ton of money into developing new technology, like AI, but there is no guarantee they are making the right bets. Perhaps they are investing in the AI equivalent of Betamax as the rest of the world coordinates around VHS.

Endless debate in democracies can certainly result in gridlock, but it also means that national-level decision-makers are more informed about the costs and benefits of ambitious undertakings. Democracies are less likely to make big mistakes. Moreover, in times of emergency, when a national consensus is forged, democracies can get their act together quite quickly. Witness the United States launching the Manhattan Project, inventing nuclear weapons, and employing them to win the War in the Pacific in just over three years. So, when there is national unity behind a decision (which often means it is a good idea) democracies can be just as efficient as autocracies. When there is intense political disagreement, democracies cannot act boldly, but these are precisely the instances in which it would more likely be a mistake to act decisively.

So, yes, democratic governments are slow and plodding in normal political times, but this also means that they get out of the way and let the blooming, buzzing confusion within their societies advance a multitude of options with a greater chance that at least one of them leads to major breakthroughs. It also means that they are more cautious and, therefore, less likely to make major blunders.

As Machiavelli claimed, "one will see fewer mistakes in the populace than in the prince, and these will be less serious and easier to resolve."[15]

Let us now turn to the argument that democracies are not ruthless or deceptive enough for international politics. This argument has it backward. The democratic commitment to international agreements and transparency is an advantage, and the autocratic habit of quotidian ruthlessness and deception a weakness. In the last chapter we saw that the ability to make "credible commitments" is an important asset in economic, diplomatic, and military realms. A state can be more effective if its promises and threats are generally believed. But other nations do not take autocracies at their word. The autocratic advantage in deception must be balanced by the inability to make credible commitments.

Russia, for example, has repeatedly demonstrated that it is comfortable saying one thing and doing another. It meddles in America's elections, tests and deploys missiles in violation of arms control treaties, and sends Russian "little green men" into Ukraine, all while denying it is doing any such thing. But this comes at a cost: the international community does not trust Moscow in other domains where credibility matters. They do not trust that Russia will not appropriate foreign direct investments, they do not trust that Russia will abide ceasefires in Ukraine or Syria, and the list goes on. As we will discuss later in the book, this behavior has led to a growing counterbalancing coalition against Russian actions.

Moreover, a reputation for ruthlessness has other downsides in a modern and globalized international system. At the time of writing, Chinese tech giant Huawei was struggling to deploy its 5G technology in Europe because democratic governments do not believe the CCP when it says that it would not use the data flowing over its infrastructure for espionage. As a result, many democratic governments including Australia, Japan, and the United

States have banned Huawei's technology and others are considered doing the same. It is hard to become a tech leader if no one trusts your technology.

So, generic ruthlessness is not necessarily an advantage.

Indeed, when it comes to the Law of Armed Conflict, there is certainly a noticeable difference between democracies and autocracies. Democracies are more constrained by the Law of Armed Conflict and often go to great lengths to distinguish between civilian and military targets in warfare and to treat prisoners of war humanely. But complying with international law does not reduce democratic effectiveness. There is not much evidence that brutal tactics, such as intentional victimization of civilian populations provide much of an advantage.[16] Moreover, a reputation for complying with international law does provide a concrete advantages on the battlefield; enemy soldiers are more likely to surrender because they believe they will be treated humanely in captivity.

Moreover, democracies are capable of rising to the occasion when the going gets tough. Desperate times call for desperate measures, and democracies have proven themselves quite willing to punch a bully in the face.[17] As we will see in the chapters to come, democracies have been sufficiently ruthless when necessary to defeat autocratic rivals. Indeed, while democracies are more peaceful in general, they often respond with a vengeance when attacked.

Let us now turn to the argument about the inherent messiness of democracy. It is true that democracies are messy; and that is what makes them great. Debates provide information that result in improved decision-making. Gridlock is a guardrail against major strategic blunders. Frequent elections and changes of government provide opportunities for the infusion of fresh ideas and needed course corrections, without bringing down the entire system. Political infighting seems more frequent only because it plays out in public view, rather than in backroom torture chambers.

Democracies are more open to foreign interference, but they are also more resilient. Open systems are already awash in information, and foreign entries into the debate rarely make a noticeable difference. Importantly, unlike autocracies, democracies do not need to worry very much that foreign information operations will lead to the very collapse of their political system.

Autocracies, on the other hand, must inoculate themselves against foreign interference because they know it could be fatal to their brittle systems of government. Times of leadership succession are especially fraught. In 2020, Trump will either be re-elected or a successor will be chosen. But what happens when Putin and Xi die? Will one of their henchmen step in, or will their personalized systems crumble altogether? Democratic elections may be messy, but not as messy as a Chinese civil war.

In the *Discourses*, Machiavelli countered those who found fault in the ancient Roman Republic for its constant political fights. Rather, he argued that open political disagreement helped Rome flourish. He stated that "those who censure the discord between the nobles and the plebians . . . consider only the tumult and shouts generated by such disorder, rather than the good results they generate."[18] He argued that "all the laws that are passed in favor of liberty arise from . . . discord." Moreover, he advised that if leaders want a country to "expand in dominion and power as did Rome [then] . . . it is necessary to give place to tumults and general dissensions as best he can."[19]

Domestic Political System Does Not Matter

There is of course a third possibility. It might be that domestic political institutions are completely irrelevant. Perhaps neither democracy nor autocracy has the advantage in great power rivalries.

Realist international relations scholars have long argued that domestic political institutions are immaterial to international politics because the demands of the international system force all states to respond in similar ways.[20] In a dangerous world, states will do what they must to survive, regardless of their domestic political situations. If they cannot, they reason, they will be eliminated in a Darwinian struggle for survival.

In recent years, other scholars have pushed back on the democratic advantage argument by claiming that democratic and autocratic institutions are actually not that different when it comes to foreign policy decision-making.[21] To be sure, there is a clear difference between a personalist dictatorship, like Kim Jong Un's North Korea, and the United States, they argue. But in a single-party state, like the CCP in China, the leader is at least somewhat accountable to the other members of the Politburo Standing Committee and to the Party more broadly.[22] These systems with broader political audiences operate more like democracies, these scholars claim.

Others have argued a similar point, but from the opposite direction. They maintain that decision-making in democracies is actually pretty autocratic. At the end of the day, they argue the most important decisions about foreign policy take place among a handful of elites, not the broader public.[23]

These are important injections to the discussion, but it seems implausible that there is absolutely no difference between how foreign policy decisions are made in democratic and autocratic political systems. Perhaps the differences can sometimes be exaggerated, but there are differences. Furthermore, these recent debates have focused on the relatively narrow question of how foreign policy decisions are made, not on the broader issue of international ascendancy tackled in this book. Even granting for the sake of argument that autocracies and democracies make foreign policy decisions in similar ways, there are likely still differences in how these institutions affect long-run rates of economic growth, innovation, finance, alliances, soft power, military effectiveness, and much more.

Another set of objections might hold that democracy does not matter for global ascendancy because other causes are more important. Perhaps international political success is all about geography, sea power, economic growth, technological-military revolutions, or some other factor.[24]

It is certainly the case that other factors likely matter. This book does not argue that domestic institutions are the only cause of success in international politics, but rather that they are an important (and perhaps the most important) one. All else being equal, states with democratic institutions will tend to do better than their autocratic rivals.

Furthermore, many of the causes of international ascendancy others have pointed to, such as geography, sea power, economic growth, or technological-military revolutions, are only proximate causes of international success. They themselves are in part the results of a state's domestic political institutions. Open states are more likely to acquire territory, pursue commercial relations and sea power, grow their economies, revolutionize warfare, and so on.

Alfred Thayer Mahan, for example, famously wrote about the importance of sea power in history and his writings influenced many subsequent military strategists.[25] But Mahan viewed sea power, not as fixed, but as a capability states could choose whether to pursue. Pre-World War I Germany is one example of a country that built naval capabilities in response to Mahan's ideas. Indeed, there is no strict geographical reason, for example, why the United States was destined to become a sea power or China a land power. Both have plenty of coastline and land borders with neighbors. As we will see in this book, however, open states, like the United States, are more likely to pursue overseas commercial relations and, therefore, to require naval capabilities to defend trading routes. Indeed, Mahan even referenced Great Britain's domestic system of government and commercial interests as a reason why it developed into a naval power. Open states become sea powers and sea powers often become global powers. But it is domestic political institutions that is causing both. Naval power is the mere intervening variable.

So those pointing to these other factors are not incorrect, but they are overlooking the root cause of international power and influence.

A final objection might be that domestic political institutions are not the cause of power and wealth, but their effect. Perhaps wealthier states are more likely to become democratic. Indeed, recent social science research on democratization finds that transitions to democracy are more likely as states modernize their economies, become wealthier, and build a middle class.[26] What comes first, the chicken or the egg? To deal with this problem, however, we need only to look at the sequencing in the historical case studies to follow. As we will see, every democratic great power studied in this book became a democracy before it became a great power, not the other way around.

At this point, therefore, it is necessary to bring evidence to bear. After all, these are debates that cannot be settled through pure deduction. We will begin our empirical analysis, therefore, in the next chapter by taking a look at the numbers.

PART II | The Democratic
Advantage in History

CHAPTER 3

The Democratic Advantage
by the Numbers

Are democratic states more likely to accumulate power, become great powers, and achieve global hegemony? We will begin to answer these questions by looking at some simple statistics.

It is notable how often democracies appear at or near the top of global power rankings. And this is even more remarkable when one considers how historically rare this form of government has been. Athens was the world's first democracy, and it became leader of the Greeks. Rome was a lonely republic in the ancient world, yet it rose to become the most dominant polity of antiquity. The leading power of Renaissance Italy was the Venetian Republic, the only major Italian city-state to retain its status as an independent republic throughout this time period. The Dutch Republic was the first republic of early modern Europe, and it overthrew the Spanish yoke and established its own global empire. The sun never set on the British Empire at a time when Britain was the world's most liberal state. And, even by 1945, the year marking America's ascendancy, there were only about a dozen other democratic countries in the world.

Democracies are rare. Yet, they keep coming out on top.

In his long-cycle theory of international politics, political scientist William Thompson claims that in every era, there is a leading country that establishes an international system that suits its interests.[1] But no nation can remain on top forever, he argues, and the world's leading country is inevitably replaced by a rising challenger. This new hegemon then reshapes international politics more to its liking. Eventually, this state also declines and the cycle repeats. According to Thompson, the leading states in the international system for the past four hundred years (the timeframe of his study) have been: the Dutch Republic (1609–1713), Great Britain (1714–1945), and the United States (1945–present). These states were also among the most democratic of their time. According to this reckoning, therefore, liberal leviathans have led the world for the past four centuries and counting.

Now, to be sure, democracies of earlier eras would not qualify as full democracies according to contemporary definitions. After all, the Utrecht Sodomy Trials in the Dutch Republic do not quite square with modern conceptions of civil liberty. But, nevertheless, these were more open than their contemporaries.

To go beyond this subjective accounting, let us now look at the hard data. Political scientists have collected information on democracy and power (and many other variables) for all countries in the international system from 1816 to 2007. These data cover a large swathe of modern history from the end of the Napoleonic Wars through the last decade.

Some readers may be skeptical about using numbers to measure something as messy and imprecise as great power politics, but political scientists have come to understand that quantitative analysis, in addition to other tools, can greatly aid our understanding of international affairs. After all, we commonly employ statistics in other domains of life that are equally messy and imprecise, such as economics and medicine.

Political scientists measure a state's power in the international system, using the Correlates of War Composite Index of National Capabilities, or CINC score.[2] The CINC score measures a state's share of total material power in the international system. So, for example, if a great power possessed 10 percent of all the power in the international system, its CINC score would be 0.10. If a smaller country possessed only one half of one percent of the total power in the world, its score would be 0.005. The total of the CINC scores for all countries in the world, in any given year, therefore, sums to one. To construct this index, the CINC score aggregates information on six components of national power: total population, urban population, energy consumption, iron and steel production, military manpower, and military expenditures.

To be clear, the CINC score is a poor measure. After all, the nature of power has changed greatly over the past two hundred years. Population size and iron and steel production were important indicators of power in the early 20th century, but today education levels and digital connectivity may be more indicative of a country's influence. Moreover, the CINC score underweights other factors important to international leadership (and in which democracies tend to excel), such as maintaining international alliance networks. Still, there is no other measure that covers such a long period of time for every country, so it has become the standard indicator employed by political scientists. For our purposes, it provides a quick and easy (if highly imperfect) snapshot of international power over the past two hundred years. So, the CINC rankings will not be the final word on this matter, but they are at least a useful place to start.

Political scientists also categorize states into the "major powers" and all other states.[3] According to the standard coding, the major powers since 1816 (the year in which that dataset begins) include: the United States since 1898; the United Kingdom since 1816; France from 1816 until 1940 and again after 1945; Germany (1816–1918, 1925–1945, 1991– present); Austria-Hungary (1816–1918); Italy (1860–1943); Russia (1816–1917, 1922–present); China (1950–present); and Japan (1895– 1945, 1991–present).

To analyze how a state's domestic political institutions affect its international power position, we now need a way to measure democracy. Here too, political scientists have a standard and widely used measure: Polity scores. As discussed previously, Polity scores measure a country's level of political openness on a continuum, which ranges from −10 (most autocratic) to +10 (most democratic).[4] Full democracies, such as the United Kingdom, receive a Polity score of +10. The most autocratic dictatorships, such as Kim Jong Un's North Korea, receive a −10. Other countries are somewhere in the middle. For example, the United States was scored a +10, Russia +4, and China −5. Positive six and above is the standard cutoff to qualify as a democracy in the modern international system.

Using these data to conduct some simple statistical analysis, we see that, on average, democracies possess more power than autocracies. Among all democracies (states scoring a +6 or above in the Polity scores) throughout this time period, 28 percent possessed at least 1 percent of the total power in the international system.[5] In contrast, only 20 percent of autocracies met that same threshold of global power possession.[6] The probability of observing these figures if there is in fact no difference between democracy and autocracy is less than one one-thousandth of one percent.[7]

Democracies are also more likely to rank among the "major powers." Sixteen percent of all full democracies in the data were categorized as major powers. This compares to only 7 percent of autocracies.[8] Again, this is a statistically significant difference.[9] Five of the seven major powers in 2017 (71 percent) were full democracies (scoring a perfect 10 out of 10) even though full democracies make up only about 15 percent of the observations in the data.

Finally, democracies are more likely to become the most powerful state in the system. If we count the United Kingdom in 1816 as a democracy, then democracies possessed the highest CINC score in 160 out of 190 (84 percent) of the years since 1816.[10] The United Kingdom possessed the largest CINC score until the 1890s, when it was overtaken by the United States, with the Soviet Union and China each breaking into the top spot for brief periods of time.[11] Democracies' near-stranglehold on global hegemony occurs despite the fact that, throughout this time period, democracies have been rarer than autocracies, making up only about 35 percent of all the observations in the data.

Turning to more sophisticated regression analysis that also controls for other factors that might shape national power, we get a similar result.[12] There is a positive and statistically significant relationship between a state's domestic political regime type and hegemony. The more democratic a country, the more likely it is to be the world's most powerful state. The substantive size of this effect is impressive as well. Shifting from the most autocratic to the most democratic regime type is associated with a twenty-five-fold increase in the probability of holding the top spot in the international system.

To put this finding in more concrete terms, what if China and Russia were to undergo a thoroughgoing transition to full democracy or the United States were to backslide into dictatorship? Given the above statistical models, we would predict that if China were to undergo a full transition to democracy in the future, the probability that it would be the most powerful state in the international system would increase twenty-fold. The consequences of complete democratization in Russia would be to increase more than eight times its chances of global hegemony. Contrariwise, a collapse of the democratic system in the United States and the rise of a dictatorship would make it twenty-five times less likely that Washington would hold the top spot.

Next, let us look at how the international distribution of power has changed over time for specific pairs of democratic-autocratic great power rivals: the United States and Russia from 1816 to 2007 (Figure 3.1) and the United States and China from 1860 to 2007 (Figure 3.2). (The U.S.-China analysis begins in 1860 because it is the first year for which data is available on China).

The figures show the change in the percent of world power held by each state over time, using the start date of the analysis as a common baseline.

Here we see visual support for the idea that democracies perform better on average than their autocratic counterpart in long-run competitions.

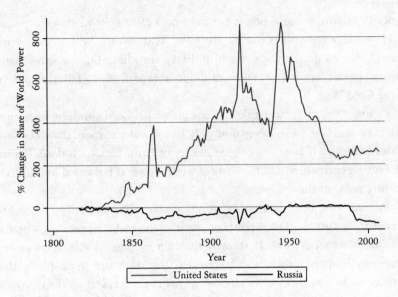

FIGURE 3.1 Change in Share of World Power, United States and Russia, 1816–2007

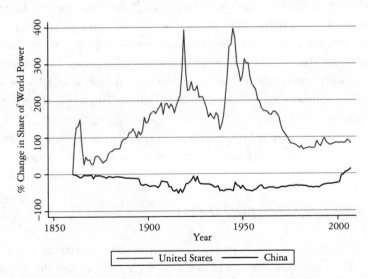

FIGURE 3.2 Change in Share of World Power, United States and China, 1860–2007

Note: This figure runs from 1860 to 2007 because 1860 is the first year for which the Correlates of War dataset reports data for China.

America's share of world power has been on a clear upward trajectory since 1816, with major spikes during the Civil War, World War I, and World War II, due to drastic increases in military spending. On the other hand, Russian power was flat for centuries and then experienced a falloff at the end of the Cold War.

Figure 3.2 shows that while Chinese power has been climbing upward in recent years, these gains have come only in the wake of more than a century of steady decline (China's so-called Century of Humiliation). Indeed, Beijing has only recently surpassed the share of world power it possessed in 1860, the starting point of the analysis.

In sum, this brief section examined quantitative evidence of the link between a state's domestic political institutions and its power position in the international system. It showed that, on average, democracies possess more power than autocracies. It revealed that they are more likely than autocracies to find themselves among the major powers and on the tippy-top of the global distribution of power. Finally, it also demonstrated that when comparing democratic and autocratic competitors from a common baseline and watching their power trajectories unfold over time, the trend lines favor democracies.

What about the idea that democracy affects power because it is linked to the intervening variables discussed in chapter 1 (economic, diplomatic, and military strength)? As a reminder, and as we saw in chapter 1, there is already a slew of statistical studies showing that democracy is correlated with economic growth, creditworthiness, trade openness, alliance size, alliance duration, alliance reliability, and military effectiveness. This work, therefore, has already been done for us.

Taken together, these findings provide quantitative support for the idea that democracies have a leg up in international political competition.

Turning to the Historical Cases

The statistical findings are certainly suggestive, but correlation is not causation. How does the democratic advantage play out in specific historical cases? To answer this question, the coming chapters will examine a series of democratic-autocratic great power rivalries from the ancient world through the Cold War.

Political scientists have devised standards to ensure that scholars do not cherry-pick historical examples to prove their argument, so please permit me to pause for a brief moment to consider why I study the following cases. Best practices call for scholars to select cases in order to ensure (to use social science jargon) "variation on the independent variable."[13] In other words, for this study, we need to look at both democratic and autocratic great powers and trace how their domestic political institutions affect their power trajectories and the outcome of great power competitions. Since democracies have been relatively rare historically, this narrows down substantially the number of cases we could possibly study. We begin, therefore, with the world's first democracy, Athens. We then continue to the world's first republic, Rome. Open government then vanishes for several hundred years only to return to the Italian Peninsula in the late middle ages and early Renaissance period. Many of the city-states of medieval and Renaissance Italy, such as Florence, experience regime changes from autocracy to democracy and back again, but Venice was the only major city-state to retain a republican form of government throughout this time period. It is, therefore, an obvious case to study. The Dutch Republic emerged as early-modern Europe's first republic.[14] It then passed its form of government to England at a time when there were few if any other open states in Europe. The United States then succeeded the United Kingdom as the world's leading great power democracy. These are the open great powers that will be studied in this book, along with their many rivals.

Some might argue that this book should also study history's most powerful autocracies, such as Genghis Khan and his Mongol Empire. The problem with this approach is that, throughout much of human history, autocratic states did not face off against democratic competitors. Autocracies can certainly do well against other autocracies, but to return to political science jargon, these rivalries do not provide variation on the independent variable. A study of why the Mongols were able to overthrow China's Jin dynasty would be interesting, but since they are both autocracies, it would not tell us anything about how democracies and autocracies stack up against one another, which is the focus of this book.

Others might argue that the book should study smaller democratic states, like Segesta in ancient Greece, or Israel and Japan in the modern world. But this is a book about great power competition. Moreover, the trajectory of these smaller powers is significantly shaped by the fate of their great power, democratic patrons. Segesta depended on Athens for diplomatic and military support, just as Israel and Japan rely on the United States today. It would be possible to study the Peloponnesian Wars or the Cold War exclusively through the eyes of Segesta or Japan, respectively, but it would be an indirect approach. The more straightforward route would be to simply study the democratic great powers of interest, like Athens and the United States. That will be the method followed in this book.

The historical studies that follow are ordered chronologically. We, therefore, begin at the beginning, in the cradle of democracy, with a study of ancient Greece.

CHAPTER 4 | Athens, Sparta, and Persia

A THENS WAS THE world's first democracy and it rose to become a leader of the Greeks, with a sphere of influence that stretched from North Africa to Crimea. It was a major trading and naval power and forged a formidable alliance of Greek city-states to defeat the mighty Persian Empire. It then fought a legendary series of wars against its oligarchic rival, Sparta, for ascendancy in Greece. In the end, Athens's form of direct democracy and decision-making through tyranny of the majority was its undoing. But not before Athens reigned as a liberal leviathan for nearly a century and showcased an enduring model for how other open states could acquire international power and influence.

The Greco-Persian Wars

The most powerful state of the Mediterranean at the beginning of the 5th century BC was the Persian Empire. Under the leadership of Cyrus the Great, Persia (centered on present-day Iran) became the world's first superpower. It had expanded to dominate existing civilizations and nomadic tribes and control all of the Middle East from Anatolia in the East to Afghanistan in the West.

The Persian Empire was an archetypical autocracy with a strong emperor at the center of the system and local satraps to govern over major regions and report to the emperor. Autocracies can do quite well in competitions with other autocracies, but it would soon meet a more serious competitor.

Its conflict with the Greeks began in 547 BC, when Cyrus conquered the Greek city-states on the Ionian coast (in present-day Turkey).[1] The Persians overthrew the existing governments and installed local tyrants loyal to the empire. The practice of great powers overthrowing regimes and installing ones more to their liking is far from a new phenomenon.

The Ionian Greeks did not welcome Persian subjugation and engaged in open revolt in 499 BC. Their uprising was supported by Greek city-states, including Athens, motivated by historical ties, a desire to support independent city-states, and to balance against Persia.

Just a few years earlier Athens had attempted a radical political experiment that would change the world. The city-states of Greece had long been ruled by kings or aristocratic oligarchies, but in 508 BC, the Athenian nobleman Cleisthenes became the "father of Greek democracy." In a dispute with a rival aristocratic faction for control of Athens, Cleisthenes enlisted the people on his side by offering them political power in exchange for support. He was successful, and the concept of democracy was born. The word "democracy" comes from the ancient Greek and literally translates as "people power." Cleisthenes followed through on his promises and established a revolutionary system of government. The most notable feature of Athenian democracy was the assembly, a body in which all adult, male citizens met, debated, and voted on political matters important to the city, including issues of war and peace.

Like other democracies throughout history, Athens became a major trading power. The harsh surrounding countryside was not well suited to most agriculture, but it was conducive to the production of wine and olive oil. Athens was also a leading producer of pottery and other crafts, which it traded from its port of Piraeus throughout the Mediterranean and as far away as the Black Sea in exchange for wheat and other basic foodstuffs. As a trading state, Athens came into contact with many foreigners, and it became a tolerant society with a significant portion of its population made up of foreigners from other parts of the Mediterranean.

With the backing of Athens, the Ionians succeeded in sacking Persia's regional capital at Sardis.

The Persian emperor, Darius the Great, sought revenge and put down the rebellion in Ionia before marching his forces on Greece itself. He hoped to subjugate Athens and expand his empire further to the East.

The Persian forces were victorious in several early battles, but suffered an unexpected defeat at the Battle of Marathon, just outside of Athens, in 490

BC. According to legend, a messenger ran the 26.2 miles from Marathon to Athens to announce the news of the surprising victory before dropping dead from exhaustion. It is this legend that is the inspiration for the modern marathon race.

Darius would pass away before he could send another military expedition, but his son, Xerxes, vowed to avenge his father's losses and subjugate Greece once and for all.

Xerxes did not move immediately, however, and this delay gave Athens time to prepare. When Athens struck a major silver vein at Larium shortly after the Battle of Marathon, the citizens debated what to do with their new-found wealth. They decided to use it to build a navy to protect their commercial interests and defend against rivals. Athens constructed two hundred trireme warships, rapidly transforming it into a major naval power. In addition, it sought to improve its geopolitical position by forming an alliance. In 481 BC, Athens worked with Sparta, the other major city-state of ancient Greece, and corralled roughly seventy of an estimated seven hundred Greek city-states into an alliance to resist the Persian invasion.

Sparta was an oligarchic war machine supported by a permanent under-class of slaves, the helots. While the helots worked the land, Spartan men prepared for war. Infants with imperfections were not permitted to live. Boys were taken from their families at a young age to be trained as warriors and to live in barracks and eat in communal mess halls. While luxury was flaunted in other parts of the ancient world, it was shunned in Sparta, where citizens lived, to coin a phrase, a "Spartan existence." Sparta was strictly closed to immigration, and foreigners were not permitted to stay.

The political system was an oligarchy, in which dual kings, from two separate royal families, served simultaneously as a check on one another.[2] Sparta also had an assembly of twenty-eight men, the Gerousia, made up mostly of members from the royal families. Spartan citizens were also permitted to elect five Ephors, who served in an executive role alongside the kings.

In 480 BC, Xerxes was ready to once again take on the Greeks, and he personally led a large invasion force. According to legend, Xerxes commanded a million-man army. This is likely an exaggeration, but even one hundred thousand men would have been enough to greatly outnumber the Greek forces.

The Greeks, however, were better trained and equipped. Indeed, this is the first example of a quantity-quality distinction we will see throughout history, with autocracies tending to rely on larger numbers of lower quality forces and democracies seeking to offset quantitative advantages with superior technology and training.

The Persian army included forces conscripted from its vast empire, some more motivated and skilled than others. The Persians relied heavily on archers and cavalry to attack and harass enemies into exhaustion from a distance while avoiding direct combat. The Persian army also included infantry, but they were armed with only wicker or animal-hide shields and short spears. This style of warfare worked well in the wide open Asian steppes, but was less well suited for the rocky terrain and tight quarters of the Balkan Peninsula.

The Greeks, on the other hand, had developed a revolutionary and effective, new style of warfare. Greek hoplite warriors were heavily armed with bronze shields, helmets, and body armor. They wielded long spears and fought side-by-side in tight "phalanx" formations. When one soldier fell, another in the back lines moved up to take his place. So long as the Greeks did not break ranks and could confront the enemy head on, they presented an insurmountable wall of bronze to an enemy. Unlike the indirect style of Persian warfare, the Greeks sought direct frontal engagements in which they attempted to engage and annihilate the enemy in a single, decisive battle.

Some military historians have pointed to these basic differences between the Persians and the Greeks as the beginnings of distinctive traditions of Eastern and Western styles of warfare, respectively.[3] The goal of the Eastern style of warfare is to use maneuver and deception to, as the ancient Chinese strategist Sun Tzu put it, "win without fighting."[4] By contrast, the Western style seeks to directly engage the enemy's "center of gravity" and fight a battle of annihilation.[5]

The Greeks understood, however, that, greatly outnumbered, they could not win against the full force of the Persian army. Instead, they cleverly planned to confront the invading Persian forces at Thermopylae in the summer of 480 BC. At this narrow pass between the mountains and the sea, the Persians would need to funnel their massive forces into a confined space, allowing the better-armed Greeks to take them on in smaller bits. Led by the Spartan king Leonidas and, according to legend, only three hundred Spartans and several thousand other soldiers, the Greeks held off the fearsome Persian army for over two days.

But, in one of the great betrayals of history, a Greek shepherd led a contingent of elite Persian forces, The Immortals, through a mountain pass to a position in the rear of the Greek army. The Persians surrounded the Greek forces and massacred them.

The way was clear for Persia to march uncontested to Athens, which it did and burned the evacuated Acropolis to the ground. Xerxes had nearly subjugated Greece. The last remaining step was to destroy Athens's formidable naval fleet.

The Greeks did not give up, however. While Thermopylae was a battle-field defeat, it was something of a moral victory as they learned that they could hold off a much larger Persian force with superior technology and strategy.

Later that year, in September 480 BC, the Greeks lured the Persian navy into the narrow straits of Salamis. In this time period, ships were armed with battering rams and naval warfare was conducted by ramming enemy ships to sink them or render them inoperable. In addition, when ships collided, marines would attempt to board the opposing vessels and fight in hand-to-hand combat against enemy sailors and marines.

Once again geography constrained Persia's quantitative advantage. In the narrow straits of Salamis, the large number of ships could not easily maneuver. The allied Greek navy was lying in wait. It rammed the Persian ships, sinking or disabling an estimated two hundred to three hundred Persian vessels and won a clear naval victory.

This was the turning point of the Greco-Persian Wars. Xerxes feared that with its newfound naval superiority, the Greeks might attempt to cut off his retreat, so he decided to return to Persia with the majority of his forces. He left behind his general Mardonius and the elite Immortal forces to winter in Attica with the goal of continuing the war against the Greeks when the fighting season resumed in the spring.

Instead, in August 479 BC, the Greeks won another victory over the Persians at the Battle of Platea. The very same day, the Greeks destroyed the remaining Persian ships in a victorious battle at Mycale.

This would mark a new phase in the conflict in which the Greeks would now go on the offensive into Persia. Ionian city-states once again rose up, and the allied Greeks intervened to support them. While Athens was eager to support the independent city-states of Ionia, many of which had been Athenian colonies, the Spartans were less motivated. They were satisfied with the ejection of the Persians from Greece. Moreover, the Spartans lived in constant fear of a helot slave revolt and could not sustain extended military campaigning away from home. As Aristotle wrote, the helots were "an enemy constantly sitting in wait of the disaster of the Spartans."[6] After forty days, Sparta needed to return home to quell unrest. In addition, Pausanias, a high-handed Spartan general who was suspected of colluding with the Persians, alienated many of the Greek city-states, which now strongly preferred Athenian leadership.

Sparta returned home, leaving Athens as the undisputed leader of the Greeks. In 477 BC, the remaining Greek allies met at the holy island of Delos to recommit to the alliance and establish the Delian League, with Athens at its head. From 477 to 449 BC, the Delian League, under Athens's leadership continued to bring the war to Persia, waging campaigns in present-day Turkey, Cyprus, and Egypt. The fighting ended in 449 BC. A peace settlement was reached in which the Delian League achieved its major goals. Persia agreed to grant autonomy to the Greek city-states of Ionia and never again to bring military forces into Greek territory or waters.

Following the Delian League's victory over Persia, Athens decided to maintain its system of wartime alliances. Rather than each and every city-state building separate armed forces, most allies simply paid a tribute that went toward building the Athenian navy. Many allies were pleased that their young men would not be going in harm's way, and the system allowed Athens to become the uncontested naval power of the Hellenic world.[7] The arrangement in some ways foreshadowed America's current system of extended nuclear deterrence in which Washington dissuades allies from building their own nuclear forces in exchange for the United States offering to provide them with a nuclear umbrella for their protection. The influx of funds would also allow Athens to support the arts and architecture, giving it status in its time and renown to the present day. In particular, the stunning temple complex at the Parthenon was built from 447 to 438 BC to honor Athens' patron goddess Athena, but it was also intended as a political symbol of Athens' triumph over Persia and of its leadership of the Delian League.

The act that more than any other symbolized Athens's consolidation of its international authority, however, was when the Athenian leader, Pericles, moved the Delian League's treasury from Delos to Athens in 454 BC.[8] By this point, Athens had asserted control over all of the Hellenic world with the exception of Sparta and its allies in the Peloponnesian League.

In sum, in just over fifty years after transitioning to a democratic form of government, Athens rose from being a small and unremarkable city-state in Greece to becoming the leading power in the Hellenic world. It co-led an alliance to defeat the enormous Persian Empire in open warfare. And it emerged from the conflict as the wealthiest polity in Greece, with the largest navy, and an alliance structure of hundreds of city-states and colonies spread throughout the Eastern Mediterranean (Figure 4.1).

Democracy versus Autocracy

Athens provides incipient support for the democratic advantage thesis. Athens was the world's first democracy, and it rose to become the most powerful force in ancient Greece for nearly a century.

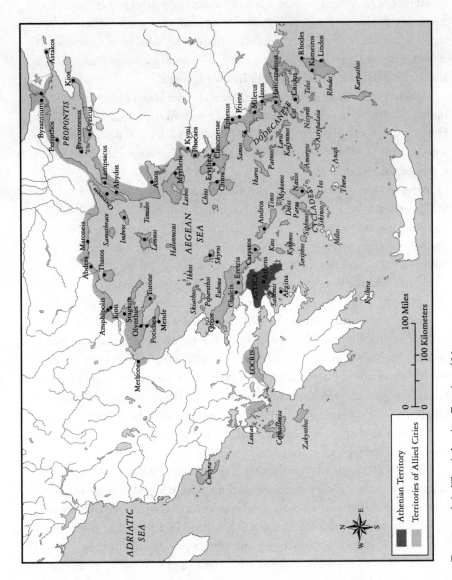

FIGURE 4.1 The Athenian Empire, 431 BC

Athens's open political system led to an open economic system. It possessed the most vibrant economy of ancient Greece, structured around international trade throughout the Mediterranean. It also benefited from a brain drain as talented Greeks immigrated to Athens to engage in trade and practice their crafts. Athens was fortunate to sit atop rich silver mines, but it took ingenuity to discover and systematically exploit that good fortune to construct a dominant naval force to protect its trading routes and defend itself. Athens's tribute system made it the financial center of ancient Greece, and it also facilitated commerce by issuing its own coinage.

Athens built a large alliance system, and this network of partners was sustained and strengthened after Sparta withdrew from the Greco-Persian Wars. It was also an innovator in foreign and defense policy. Alongside Sparta, it led the other Greeks to defeat Persia by employing clever strategy and tactics and superior technology.

Athens's soft power among the Greeks was boosted by its creativity in the arts and sciences as well. It bequeathed to human civilization arts and learning that enrich our lives today, including the architecture of the Parthenon, the poetry of Aeschylus and Sophocles, and the philosophy of Socrates, Plato, and Aristotle.

Athens and the Greeks were more open to enemy espionage operations as the incident at the mountain pass of Thermopylae exemplifies. But Athens did not appear to suffer from the other supposed weaknesses of democracies, such as an inability to mass resources or get tough in international affairs. When it perceived an existential threat from Persia, it poured its national wealth into building a powerful navy. And when the small island of Melos refused to join the Delian League in 416 BC, Athens had all Melian men killed and sold the women and children into slavery. As the Athenian delegation frankly explained, in international affairs, "the strong do what they will and the weak accept what they must."9

Some might argue that such merciless behavior abroad by Athens or other democratic powers shows that these nations were not truly devoted to democratic principles in all respects, but it is quite consistent with the central thesis of this book, which is that states governed by democratic government at home tend to be fearsome competitors on the international stage.

Persia and Sparta were plagued with some of the enduring problems of autocracies. Xerxes's invasion of Greece was certainly a bold and decisive action in which resources were massed toward a clear goal, but it was all in a losing effort. In addition, the Ionian Greeks and the helots did not like living under the respective thumbs of Persepolis and Sparta, and both powers had to constantly deal with uprisings. Athens, like many democracies since, actively intervened to exploit its opponents' domestic fragility. Sparta's decision to return home halfway through the war against Persia, motivated in part by concerns about domestic stability, is what allowed Athens to become the leader of the anti-Persia alliance.

The autocrats also suffered from clumsy diplomacy. Xerxes's invasion provoked a counterbalancing coalition of Greek city-states. And an overbearing Spartan general pushed allies into Athens's arms.

Athens's period of ascendancy, however, would not last forever, as the Greeks were about to turn on each other in the epic Peloponnesian Wars. As the historian Thucydides put it, "The growth of Athenian power, and the fear which this inspired in Sparta, made war inevitable."

Athens succeeded due its open system of government, but, in the end, fell due to its system of direct democracy. As discussed earlier, political theorists, like Machiavelli, celebrated open government, but denigrated direct democracy, such as that which prevailed in Athens, as tyranny of the majority that often produced poor decisions.

Most devastating to Athens's war effort was a strategic blunder chosen freely in the assembly: the decision to embark on the Sicilian Expedition in 415 BC to aid its beleaguered ally Segesta in its fight against its democratic rival, Syracuse.[10]

The failed Sicilian Expedition was the turning point in the war, and it was the result of all citizens in the Assembly voting on the number of ships to be sent to Sicily. Just imagine the chaos if the United States held an online referendum to select the proper U.S. force levels in Afghanistan.

Athens was also up against a capable adversary as Syracuse was also a democracy at the time. Indeed, the Sicilian Expedition may be an early exception to the well-known democratic peace theory, the idea that democracies do not tend to fight each other.

After years of fighting against a coalition made up of Sparta, Syracuse, and their other allies, including eventually Persia, Athens was defeated in 404 BC. Sparta engaged in regime change, overthrowing Athens's democracy and imposing a puppet oligarchy, known as The Thirty.

Still, although its hegemony did not last forever, Athens helped show the way for how open states can attain supremacy over autocratic rivals.

Intra-autocratic warfare among the remaining monarchies and oligarchies of the Eastern Mediterranean would continue for another century. After defeating Athens, Sparta was vanquished by Thebes, which in turn was brought down by Philip of Macedon and his son Alexander the Great. Alexander would go on to take control of all of Greece and dismantle the Persian Empire. He would also spread Greek culture from the Balkan Peninsula to the Indus River Valley, creating a new Hellenistic world.

As we will see in the next chapter, however, Macedon would itself fall to the next state to take up the mantle of democratic leadership, a polity that to the Greeks was nothing more than a small barbarian tribe somewhere north of Sicily: the Roman Republic.

CHAPTER 5 | The Roman Republic, Carthage, and Macedon

F OR CENTURIES, SCHOLARS have been fascinated with the question of how and why Rome rose from being a small kingdom on the Tiber River in central Italy to dominate the entire Mediterranean and become one of the most powerful geopolitical forces in world history.[1] The answer arrived at from scholars as diverse as Polybius, Machiavelli, and Montesquieu is that it was the institutions of the Roman Republic that were the source of its ascendance. After its transition to republican governance in 509 BC, Rome succeeded in defeating neighboring tribes to control the entire Italian Peninsula and setting it up for rivalry with the other great republican powerhouse of the western Mediterranean: Carthage. Rome destroyed Carthage in a series of three Punic Wars. Finally, it quickly dispensed with several autocratic kingdoms of the Hellenic world in the eastern Mediterranean, including Macedon.

In just a few short centuries, Rome found itself transformed into a superpower standing astride all of Western civilization.

Rome's Origins

Rome's early history is shrouded in myth. Rome's contemporary historians were not as careful as present-day scholars about separating fact from fiction. According to legend, Rome was founded either by Aeneas, the hero from the

Trojan Wars, or Romulus and Remus, twin boys suckled by a she-wolf. The latter story would have us believe that Romulus then killed his brother, set himself up as king, and named the city after himself. Needing women to populate the city, Romulus and his army went to war with the neighboring Sabine tribe and abducted their young females in the infamous "Rape of the Sabine Women."

What is known with a bit more certainty is that early Rome was overshadowed by its neighbors to the north, the Etruscans, and ruled over by monarchs of Etruscan descent.[2] While a monarchy, early Rome still possessed certain representative bodies, including a Senate. Over time, the monarchs ceded power and the kingdom was replaced by the world's first republican system of government. Indeed, the very term "republic" comes from the ancient Latin *res publica*, roughly translating as "public thing" or "public affair."

The apocryphal story is that the monarchy fell because a virtuous noblewoman, Lucretia, was raped by the son of the king and then committed suicide. The tragedy convinced the Romans to never again let the city be ruled by haughty and abusive monarchs. The truth is likely more prosaic with the monarchy gradually losing power to Rome's representative bodies.

Rome's republican form of government differed from Athenian direct democracy. Rather than an all-powerful assembly, authority in Rome was divided among three major branches of government. In addition, while citizens could still vote on important matters, more power was granted to elected representatives instead of the people themselves.

Two consuls, each elected for one year, were the chief executives of the republic and commanders in chief of the military. They oversaw a body of lower-level elected "magistrates" who carried out the acts of government. The Senate was the most important political body in the Roman Republic. Its membership included previous magistrates and they held their positions for life. The third body was made up of a number of various representative assemblies. All adult, male citizens were organized into a designated assembly in which they could vote on important matters facing the state, and their votes were aggregated into bigger groupings before being counted, similar in some ways to the U.S. Electoral College system for electing presidents.

The success of the Roman system would inspire many subsequent constitution writers, including America's founding fathers.

A major political cleavage in the early Roman Republic was the constant clashes between the upper classes, the "patricians," and the common people, or the "plebeians." This bitter "struggle of the orders" lasted from 500 to 287 BC, but ultimately resulted in greater equality and increased political power for the lower classes. Some ancient commentators criticized the constant tumult between the social classes in Rome, but others, including Machiavelli, argued that it was this constant tension that resulted in greater liberty at home and expanding power abroad. And expand Rome did.

The Conquest of the Italian Peninsula

Warfare was endemic, and Rome found itself in constant clashes with neighboring tribes, villages, and cities. Rome repeatedly came out on top in these early struggles and gradually started absorbing nearby territory on the Tiber River.

Rome and many other armies on the Italian Peninsula had adopted the successful phalanx style of warfare from Greece. Greek colonies in southern Italy (Magna Grecia) had brought this and other aspects of Greek culture to the Italian Peninsula. Some cities, however, still had disorganized armies that charged haphazardly at the enemy and were easily defeated. In 496 BC, Rome won an important victory over a combined grouping of Latin villages and tribes to the south, the Latin League, allowing Rome to establish itself as the leader of the Latins. Subsequent victories would incorporate other nearby tribes and villages, including Aequi and Volsci.

These victories would also serve as a template for Rome's future expansion. Rome was exceptionally skilled at expanding its international network of friends and allies. Rather than kill all the men and sell the women and children into slavery (as had happened during the Peloponnesian Wars, for example) Rome offered vanquished peoples the opportunity to become part of the Roman polity. In some cases, especially for nearby and culturally similar Latin tribes, people were granted full Roman citizenship. In other cases, defeated peoples were not allowed to vote, but they were given a broad set of "Latin rights," in exchange for an obligation that young men serve in the Roman military. Rome also established colonies in conquered territories, slowly Romanizing the Italian Peninsula. In still other cases, Rome signed mutual defense alliances with conquered states. These conquered nations were able to retain full autonomy domestically, but they agreed to outsource their foreign policy to Rome and to contribute resources, supplies, and manpower to the Roman army. In this way, the growing Roman Republic was less the homogeneous entity depicted on maps of the time period, and more a network of aligned polities centered around Rome. Indeed, at its height, there were over 150 separate treaties linking subjected political groups to the Roman capital.

This system provided Rome with a number of advantages. It gave conquered peoples a stake in Rome's future success. They were able to benefit personally from the spoils of Rome's many successful wars, including conquered land. And their allegiance gave Rome a growing and virtually unlimited supply of military manpower as its territorial holdings expanded.

In 396 BC, Rome was able to defeat the resilient Etruscans in an epic ten-year siege and capture their capital city of Veii, ten miles north of Rome.

Rome's growing influence in the north brought it into contact with the Gauls (Celtic tribes from present-day France) and one of the worst disasters in the history of the Roman Republic. In 390 BC, Rome suffered a devastating defeat when the Gauls invaded Italy and sacked Rome. With Rome weakened, some allies began to defect. Rome's eventual ascendance, therefore, was by no means preordained. Indeed, had the Gauls decided to stay and occupy Rome, the fledgling superpower may have been strangled in its cradle. Instead, the Romans bribed the invaders to leave after several months and, remarkably, Rome quickly recovered.

With the Etruscans and Gauls still relatively strong in the North, Rome turned its attention South. The Samnites were a confederation of rugged tribes who lived in the Apennine mountains and occupied much of south-central Italy. When the Samnites threatened a Roman ally, Capua, Rome came to its rescue. From 343 BC to 290 BC, Rome fought a series of three wars with the Samnites and eventually emerged victorious.

These were no easy victories, however. At the initiation of hostilities, the Samnites were numerically superior to Rome. In addition, the Samnites were able to enlist the support of other Roman adversaries, including the Etruscans, Gauls, and Umbrians, to join the fight. Moreover, the mountainous terrain was not conducive to the Roman phalanx style of warfare. It was difficult to keep the front lines straight and unified when climbing over mountainous terrain. Further, the phalanx had always lacked maneuverability and was vulnerable when attacked on its flanks.

After a series of early, humiliating defeats (including the Battle of Claudine Forks in 321 BC, in which the Samnites forced captured Roman soldiers to pass beneath yokes like beasts of burden) the Romans knew that something would have to change.

So, Rome's military leaders innovated. Instead of forces arranged in a single, straight line in the old, phalanx style, Rome developed the maniple: a number of smaller units that were arranged like the black squares on a checkerboard. Units were linked in a way that still presented a formidable front to the enemy, but spacing to the front, back, and sides of each unit also allowed greater maneuverability, especially in tough terrain.

The maniple formation was complemented with a new diversity in the types of military units. The *hastati* were the least experienced forces, and they were sent to the front to harass and wear down the enemy. They would then fall back and allow the more experienced *principes* to join the fray. This would often be sufficient to subdue Rome's foes, but, when necessary as a last resort, a third group of the most seasoned warriors, the *triari*, could be called in from the rear to finish the fight.

Rome introduced new weaponry into its ranks as well. Instead of a spear, as in traditional phalanx-style warfare, *hastati* and *principes* were armed with a javelin and a short sword. The javelin gave them a greater ability to attack the enemy from standoff distances and the sword allowed for quicker and more agile thrusting attacks in close quarters. The *triari* were still armed like hoplite warriors, with a spear in addition to the short sword. The maniples were supported on their flanks by cavalry. Rome also introduced more sophisticated weaponry for siege warfare, including advanced battering rams, siege towers, and artillery.

With their new and improved military forces, Rome eventually succeeded in pacifying the Samnites. In 290 BC, Rome captured the capital of Samnium and the vanquished Samnites sued for peace. They were forced to become Roman allies on highly unequal terms. Rome now controlled nearly all of central and southern Italy.

It was during the wars with the Samnites that Rome would build its first road system. This was done out of necessity to help ferry its troops back and forth across the Italian Peninsula. Over time, Roman roads would come to crisscross all of Europe, leading to the saying that "all roads lead to Rome." These sophisticated-for-the-time roads supported Roman troop movements, but they also greatly facilitated trade and communication—Roman roads were the world's first Internet—fueling economic growth within Roman territory. They also helped Rome to consolidate control of newly acquired lands and served as a visible symbol of Rome's imperial presence.

The Roman innovations that contributed to the vitality of its economy and the richness of Roman life did not stop with roads, however. Rome also invented aqueducts that brought water into cities and agricultural plots to sustain Rome's rapidly growing population. Other inventions and innovations included concrete, battlefield surgery, the incorporation of arches into architecture, sewage systems, and others. Rome also innovated in the arts and culture, including the architecture of the Roman Forum, the poems of Virgil, and intricate busts and tombs sculpted from marble and bronze.

After defeating the Samnites, Rome turned north, pursuing the Etruscans, Umbrians, and Gauls. It won an important victory in 283 BC at the Battle of Lake Vadimo, thus bringing much of north-central Italy also under Roman dominion.

The only portions of southern Italy not yet under Roman control were the Greek city-states in the toe and heel of Italy's boot. The most powerful of these polities was Tarentum (present-day Taranto), which had been founded centuries before as a Spartan colony. Tarentum was worried about Rome's rise and, in 282 BC, when Roman warships appeared in the Gulf of Tarentum, the Tarentines sunk them and declared war. The Tarentines then turned to Pyrrhus, the king of Epirus, for help. At the time, Epirus was a powerful city-state in Greece. Pyrrhus, who was the second cousin of Alexander the Great, dreamed of following the family tradition and establishing his own glorious record of military conquest.

Pyrrhus accepted the invitation and brought a large force, including war elephants, to southern Italy. In 280 and 279 BC, Pyrrhus won major battles against Rome, at Heraclea and Asculum, respectively, but at a steep price. They were bloody contests and Pyrrhus's forces were badly degraded. He famously remarked, "If we are victorious in one more battle with the Romans, we shall be utterly ruined."[3] Indeed, to this day, the term "pyrrhic victory" refers to a win that is so costly that it might as well have been a defeat.

Pyrrhus then debarked to Sicily in a bid to capture that island and make it part of his imagined empire. When that effort failed, he again returned to the Italian mainland to engage the Romans. At the Battle of Beneventum in 275 BC, the Romans killed two of his war elephants and captured the other eight, throwing Pyrrhus's army into disarray.

Conquering Italy had turned out to be harder than he had hoped, and Pyrrhus returned home to Greece, leaving Tarentum at the mercy of the Romans. Tarentum surrendered, and all of southern Italy passed under Roman control.

Thus, in a slow and gradual process that lasted just over two centuries, the Roman Republic went from being an insignificant kingdom on the Tiber River in 509 BC to controlling almost all of Italy by 275 BC. It was now a major regional power, which would bring it into increasing tension with the prevailing hegemon of the western Mediterranean.

The Punic Wars

In the 3rd century BC, the most powerful political entity in the western Mediterranean was not Rome, but Carthage. Carthage was founded as a

Phoenician colony and was located in North Africa at the site of present-day Tunis, Tunisia. Its series of epic wars with Rome are called the Punic Wars because the term "Punicus" was the Latin word for Phoenician. Carthage was a trading state and major naval power. It controlled the North African coast from present-day Libya to Morocco, southern Spain, Sardinia, Corsica, and the western half of Sicily.

Compared to Rome, we know relatively little about Carthage's form of government. It did, however, have many of the distinguishing features of a republic, including a senate made up of noblemen. At the same time, government was largely controlled by several wealthy merchant families. Historians, therefore, debate whether Carthage is better characterized as a republic or an oligarchy. Aristotle argued that "the Carthaginian constitution . . . inclines to oligarchy."[4] Still, it was more open than many other ancient states, such as the monarchies in the Hellenic world, and its relatively representative institutions may have contributed to its ascendance to a position of leadership in the ancient Mediterranean.

Rome and Carthage had previously enjoyed friendly relations. They had even signed several formal treaties, recognizing each other's respective spheres of influence. But as both polities grew in power, size, and influence, they began to bump up against each other, sparking tensions. With Rome moving down the Italian Peninsula and Carthage expanding northward in the Mediterranean Sea, the location of the first major flashpoint could have been predicted: Sicily. Athens and Sparta had sparred over control of Sicily two centuries before, and Rome and Carthage were now returning to the same arena to battle over the strategically located island.

The First Punic War began with a minor conflict between two Sicilian city-states, Syracuse and Messina. Two centuries after it had contributed to the defeat of Athens, Syracuse was still the most powerful state in Sicily, but by this time it had backslid into autocracy and was under the rule of a tyrant, Hiero II. Messina, a port town in the northeast corner of the island, was threatened by Syracuse and turned to distant and powerful neighbors for protection. In 264 BC, Messina sent messengers to both Carthage and Rome, begging for their intervention. Both saw an opportunity to expand their dominions into Sicily and accepted the invitation.

Carthage arrived first, but Rome continued with its forces knowing full well that doing so would likely lead to war with Carthage. Rome successfully defeated both Carthaginian and Syracusan forces at Messina and then marched to Syracuse, besieging and eventually conquering that once-indomitable city as well. Under the terms of the peace treaty, Syracuse became a Roman ally and agreed to provide money and manpower to Rome.

Rome and Carthage were now engaged in open warfare on the island of Sicily. Rome, the dominant land power, won a decisive battle at Agrigentum in 262 BC. Carthage was weaker on land, in part, because it hired mercenary armies, from Spain, Numidia, and elsewhere within Carthage's empire, to do its fighting. These hired hands were motivated by lucre, not patriotism, and they were less willing to die for their state than Rome's citizen-soldiers.

Carthage astutely decided to take the fight to sea, where it possessed the larger navy and more seasoned sailors, and it won some important early naval battles. To continue the fight, therefore, Rome needed to build a more effective navy. Rome quickly constructed over one hundred warships, but this was insufficient. Carthage had been a naval power for some time and it possessed the best ships and sailors in the world. It was difficult for Rome to outmaneuver Carthaginian ships and get into position to ram and sink them. So, Rome innovated. It devised a strategy for turning naval combat (where it was weak) into land combat (where it was strong). Rome invented the *corvus*, a large raised gangplank with a hook on the end. When approaching Carthaginian ships, Rome would drop the *corvus*, locking the two vessels together. Then, Rome's formidable foot soldiers would storm the enemy ship and engage in hand-to-hand combat. This tactic proved quite successful, allowing Rome to win several significant naval battles.

Meanwhile, back on the ground in Sicily, Rome continued to hold an advantage, but it struggled to fully subdue Carthaginian forces. This was, in part, because Carthage was led by an extremely capable general, Hamilcar Barca. The First Punic War would become the longest in Rome's history, with twenty-three years of continuous fighting.

In the end, however, the war came to a conclusion not for military, but for political reasons. A new oligarchic faction led by Hanno the Great came to power in Carthage that was less interested in pursuing the war in Sicily. They cut resources and supplies for the conflict, and Hamilcar Barca had no choice but to sue for peace in 241 BC. Under the terms of the peace treaty, Carthage paid a large cash indemnity and Sicily became a Roman province.

The First Punic War was an important milestone in Rome's rise. It was the first time that Rome acquired an overseas empire and it was also the first time that it turned a conquered land, Sicily, into a formal province under the control of a Roman governor.

Even though the war had ended, Carthage's problems had not. The large war indemnity meant that Carthage could not afford to pay its mercenary armies, leading to revolts throughout its empire. Rome stepped in to quell the uprisings in Sardinia and Corsica and, in so doing, also annexed those two major Mediterranean islands to its holdings.

For roughly two decades, the peace held between Rome and Carthage. But war resumed in 219 BC. The towering figure of the Second Punic War was Hamilcar Barca's son, and perhaps the greatest military genius in world history, Hannibal Barca. According to legend, Hamilcar forced his young son to swear that Rome would be his lifelong enemy. He more than fulfilled that promise.

Hannibal was Carthage's top military commander and was stationed in Carthaginian territory in the Iberian Peninsula. When Hannibal attacked Saguntum, a Roman ally in Spain, Rome declared war. In one of the most daring military moves in history, Hannibal responded by attacking Italy *from the north*. The Alps were thought to provide Rome with an insurmountable barrier of protection: the mountains were tall and icy, and too treacherous to cross with a large army. But Hannibal did just that, traversing the Alps with tens of thousands of men and dozens of war elephants. The dangerous conditions took their toll on Hannibal and his army, but he still arrived in northern Italy with surprising speed and a formidable force. He ambushed Rome in a number of surprise attacks that resulted in convincing military victories, including at Lake Tasimene in 217 BC.

Hannibal then marched virtually uncontested all the way down the Italian Peninsula. The mighty Romans had had enough and they decided to send an overwhelming military force, led by both of Rome's consuls, to crush Hannibal at Cannae in 216 BC. Instead, Hannibal once again routed the Romans, this time in what would become one of the most famous battles in world history. Recall that at the time, military doctrine called for straight lines of one's strongest forces centered and squared off against the enemy. Instead, Hannibal intentionally placed his weakest forces in the center of his line and the strongest forces on the flanks. He also bowed the center of his line outward toward the approaching Roman army. As the Roman army advanced, Hannibal's weak center forces fell back, and the Roman soldiers aggressively pressed ahead. Rome's advancing soldiers thought they were winning the battle, but, in the meantime, Carthage's stronger forces and cavalry on the flanks closed in on Rome's army from the sides and the rear. Soon, Rome was completely surrounded. Carthage hacked to death sixty-five thousand Romans, including two consuls, in three hours. Rome lost almost thirty times more men in a single afternoon than the United States lost during the entire nineteen-year-long-and counting war in Afghanistan. Hannibal's ingenious "double envelopment" strategy has served as a template for generals throughout the millennia, with U.S. General Norman Schwarzkopf invoking it as late as 1991 as inspiration for his battle plan in the First Persian Gulf War.

While Hannibal was tactically successful, his strategy was failing. He understood that Rome was not a homogeneous unit but a patchwork of alliances and he hoped that as he demonstrated Rome's weakness, its allies would switch sides. Some recently conquered polities in the south did come over to Carthage, but many remained committed to Rome. Remember that Rome had incentivized their loyalty. Hannibal were now stuck in southern Italy, surrounded by a hostile population, and he was able to receive only limited reinforcements from Carthage.

In addition, Rome developed a new, more effective military strategy: namely, do not fight Hannibal. Under the new Fabian strategy, developed by the consul Quintus Fabius Maximus Verrucosus, Rome avoided direct military conflict with Hannibal and resolved to wait him out.

At the same time, Rome counterpunched, sending its own daring military leader, Scipio Africanus, to attack Carthage. Scipio succeeded in defeating Carthaginian forces in Spain. He then brought an army to North Africa. Whereas Rome's alliances had been its greatest asset, Carthage's turned out to be its Achilles heel. Scipio succeeded in flipping Carthage's North African allies, the Numidians, and together they marched on the city of Carthage itself. Hannibal was hastily recalled from Italy to defend his city and was handed his first military defeat at the Battle of Zama in 202 BC.

Carthage was ruined.

Rome was famous for offering defeated opponents a bright future as members of the Roman Republic, but it showed no such mercy to its archrival. In the peace treaty that followed, Carthage submitted to harsh conditions. It agreed to turn over Spain as a Roman province. Numidia became a Roman client state. Carthage's own territorial holdings were reduced to only the city of Carthage itself. It was permitted to keep a tiny navy and no army, and its international disputes were to be submitted to the Roman Senate for arbitration.

For some in Rome, this was still not enough. For years, the Roman Senator Cato the Elder famously ended every speech, regardless of the subject, with the words, "furthermore, Carthage must be destroyed."[5] He would get his wish.

The Third Punic War began in 149 BC when Carthage engaged in military hostilities with the neighboring Numidians without first consulting Rome. Rome judged that this action violated the terms of their peace agreement and issued an extreme ultimatum that was little more than a pretext for war. Among other demands, Rome required Carthage to move the entire city ten miles inland. When Carthage refused, Rome besieged the city. After three years, Carthage fell. Rome sold the surviving Carthaginians into slavery, burned the city to the ground, and annexed the territory as the new Roman province of Africa.

Only a century before, Carthage was a leading power, and now it ceased to exist. In the same time period, Rome went from a rising upstart to hold exclusive dominion over the entire western Mediterranean.

Rome did not stop to revel in its victory, however. It was already knee-deep in a series of major military campaigns to subdue the Hellenic kingdoms of the eastern Mediterranean.

The Macedonian Wars

Since the time of Athenian glory, the Hellenic (or Greek) world had been the center of Mediterranean civilization. It was wealthier and perceived as more sophisticated than the West. To the Greeks and those influenced by Greek culture, Rome was something of a barbarian nation and not a subject of much interest or concern. But, suddenly, in less than a century, the entire Hellenic world would become absorbed as provinces within the mighty Roman Republic. How did this happen?

Polybius experienced this whiplash directly. He was a citizen in the Greek city-state of Megalopolis, a member of the Achaean League. Understanding Rome's rapid success is what motivated him to conduct his previously discussed monumental study on the history of Rome.

Following the death of Alexander the Great in 323 BC, the short-lived empire he created collapsed. Into the vacuum arose a number of Hellenized kingdoms. Every aspect of these polities, including their language, art, science, and literature, had been heavily influenced by Alexander the Great and Greek culture. This post-Alexander, Hellenic world in the eastern Mediterranean basin included the Kingdom of Macedon in northern Greece, Ptolemaic Egypt, Pergamum in present-day Turkey, and the Seleucid Empire in present-day Turkey, Syria, Iran, and Iraq. In addition, there were a number of other smaller Greek kingdoms and city-states organized into leagues on the Balkan Peninsula, including the Aetolian League, and the Achaean League.

Their initial contact with the expanding Roman Republic began in 215 BC, when Philip V of Macedon decided to align with Hannibal and Carthage during the Second Punic War. Watching Rome suffer a number of early battlefield defeats, Philip saw an opportunity to bandwagon with Carthage and join in on the spoils of victory. In response, Rome sent a small number of forces to the Illyrian Coast (present-day Croatia and Bosnia-Herzegovina) to skirmish with Philip's forces and keep him occupied while Rome fought Hannibal. With this objective achieved, Rome was ready to make peace in 205 BC. This brought an end to the First Macedonian War, with Rome taking possession of some territorial holdings in Illyria.

The Second Macedonian War sprang from a succession crisis in Ptolemaic Egypt in 204 BC. One of autocracies' greatest weakness is domestic political instability, especially during times of succession, and this plague afflicted Egypt when Ptolemy IV died, passing power to a five-year-old boy. The uncertainty over the future governance of the kingdom set off a destructive civil war.

Sensing an opportunity, Antiochus II of the Seleucid Empire and Philip V of Macedon colluded to divide Egypt between them. As part of the deal, they also signed a nonaggression pact. Philip V, alleviated from a possible threat from either the Seleucids or Egypt, used his free hand to also wage a war against the smaller Greek polities to his south and east.

Seeing no other alternative, these Greek polities, Pergamum and Rhodes, turned to Rome for assistance. The Roman Republic agreed to intercede on their behalf and issued an ultimatum against Philip V; cease aggression against Rome's newfound Greek allies, or else. When Philip V refused, Rome attacked. Macedon's army, still made up of hoplites fighting in phalanx formations, were overmatched by the Roman legions, with their advanced technology and operational concepts.

At a decisive victory at Cynoscephalae in 197 BC, for example, Roman officers took initiative on the battlefield. During the battle, the Roman right flank was pushing back the Macedonian line on its way to an easy victory. The battle on the Roman left flank was more evenly pitched, however, with Macedon even slowly gaining the advantage. Rather than add additional strength to a battle that was all but won on Rome's right flank, therefore, a small number of Roman maniples astutely doubled back and attacked the Macedonian right flank from the rear. The Macedonian forces were surrounded and ultimately crushed by Rome.

Philip V sued for peace again. He relinquished his conquered territory and agreed to become a Roman ally and to refrain from any further foreign interference.

Following this victory, at the Greek Isthmian Games in 196 BC, Rome announced a new ambitious policy of "freedom for the Greeks." Democracy promotion by democratic great powers is hardly a recent policy invention.

At the end of the first and second Macedonian Wars, Rome completely withdrew its forces, believing the peace it created would remain in its absence.

Instead, it left a power vacuum that the Seleucid Empire was eager to fill. The empire also had some help in this regard from an old Roman enemy: Hannibal. After the Second Punic War, Hannibal went into self-imposed exile. Rather than give up the fight, however, he simply went to work for the next great power with a chance of vanquishing his lifelong nemesis. As the Seleucids expanded into Egypt and Greece, Rome and its new Greek partners, including Philip V, grew worried. In response, Rome and the Greeks mobilized a large army and initiated the Seleucid War. History does not repeat itself, but it sometimes rhymes, and the first major battle was back at Thermopylae in 191 BC. This time the democracy won. Rome continued to pursue the retreating Seleucid army across the Hellespont, marking the first time Roman forces set foot in Asia. In the Battle of Magnesia in 190 BC, Rome again won a smashing victory over the overmatched Seleucid Empire. The Roman general at the helm was none other than the brother of Scipio Africanus, who from this point forward would go by the honorific, Scipio Asiaticus, conqueror of Asia. When Hannibal was later trapped, he elected to drink poison rather than give the Romans the pleasure of killing him. The Seleucid Empire was forced to abandon its recent Greek holdings. Rome established a new Roman Province of Asia in Anatolia under the control of a Roman client king. Once again Rome withdrew its forces at the end of the war.

It was only a few short years, however, before Rome would be drawn back into Greece in the Third Macedonian War. When Philip V died in 179 BC, his son, Perseus of Macedon, assumed the Macedonian throne. The new ruler was determined to chart an ambitious new course and resurrect Macedon's former glory. When Perseus aggressed against Rome's Greek allies, Rome once again came to their defense. After some initial success, Macedon's phalanxes were obliterated at the Battle of Pydna in 168 BC. Rome had had enough of Macedonian aggression, and it dismembered the kingdom and established four new republics, all client states of Rome.

Rome still could not rest, however, as instability on the Balkan Peninsula returned two decades later. The Fourth Macedonian War began in 150 BC, as an ambitious new politician, Andriscus, attempted once again to reestablish the Macedonian monarchy. Once again Rome intervened and once again Rome achieved an influential victory at the Second Battle of Pydna in 148 BC. Finally, in 146 BC, the same year that Carthage was destroyed in the Third Punic War, the Achaean League recklessly declared a suicidal war on Rome. Rome was in no mood to show mercy. It defeated the Achaean League and laid waste to its leading state, Corinth. Not taking any more chances, the Roman Republic divided Macedon into Achaea and Epirus, provinces under the direct control of a Roman governor.

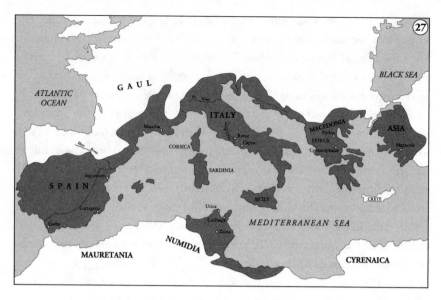

FIGURE 5.1 The Roman Republic, 100 BC

The entire Mediterranean basin from Spain to Asia Minor was now under direct Roman control (Figure 5.1).

Democracy versus Autocracy

The case of Rome provides substantial support for the democratic advantage thesis. Rome was the world's first republic, and it rose to become the most dominant state the world had ever seen.

Its innovative economy, including the introduction of roads and aqueducts, among other inventions, allowed Rome to fuel economic growth, facilitate trade and communication, and consolidate its territorial control.

The Roman Republic astutely managed its alliance relationships, giving conquered nations a stake in Rome's future success. Rome's adversaries were unable to break the bonds that tied Rome to its colonies, allies, and provinces. Its ability to incorporate talent from its empire contributed to its success. At the height of the Roman Republic, large portions of the Roman Senate were from outside the city of Rome and a Samnite was the head of the Roman military in the Punic Wars, only twenty years after the Samnites themselves had been defeated. To conquered lands, Rome was not a temporary overlord, but the new motherland.

On the field of battle, Rome was unmatched. Its robust economy and alliance system provided a strong base from which to conduct military operations. It was also a military innovator, developing new military strategies, technologies, and operational concepts, like the maniple system and the corvus. Rome's commanders possessed the autonomy and skill necessary to take initiative on the battlefield, such as at the Battle of Cynoscephalae. At the strategic level, Rome also showed sound judgment, including in the development and implementation of the Fabian strategy.

Rome does not appear to have suffered from the supposed weaknesses of democracies. It was certainly ruthless at times as it showed in its utter destruction of Carthage and Corinth. Rome also defied the expectation that democracies cannot achieve global mastery because they are unstable or unable to stick to a long-term plan. Rome enjoyed a stable form of government and charted a consistent strategic direction for centuries during its rise. In contrast, it was changing political circumstances and an inadequate political commitment in Carthage that led to Rome's victory in the first Punic War. And political succession crises in the East led to instability and changing foreign policy directions that led to the eventual defeats of Ptolemaic Egypt and Macedon.

Carthage was more open than most states in the ancient world, and it shared some of the strengths we see in democracies throughout history. It was a trading state and a major naval power. Its military generals, especially Hannibal Barca, were among the most innovative and effective in world history. These were some of the traits that allowed Carthage to become the most formidable challenger ever faced by Rome. Indeed, if one considers Carthage to be a republic, which is at least debatable, the Punic Wars would qualify as another early exception to the democratic peace theory.

Aristotle believed that Carthage was an oligarchy, however, and Carthage certainly possessed some of the traits and weaknesses characteristics of autocracies. It was relatively poor at cultivating reliable alliances and its supposed friends, the Numidians, turned on them when given the chance. And while Carthage displayed brilliant military tactics, its broader strategic judgement left something to be desired. Hamilcar fought successfully in Sicily, but he lacked the political support at home to emerge victorious. And his son, Hannibal, won military victories, but his strategy failed due to his inability to fragment Rome's alliances. Good strategists seek to array their strengths against an enemy's weakness, but Hannibal did the opposite: pitting Carthaginian weaknesses against Rome's greatest strength.

The other monarchies and oligarchies that stood up to Rome fared even worse. Rome patiently and systematically dismantled its rivals on the Italian Peninsula and made short work of the Hellenic kingdoms in the East. These states often got themselves into trouble when they threatened local rivals who then appealed to the Roman Republic for help. Weak states preferred subordination to Rome, over subjugation to autocratic powers. Realist international relations theory states that countries balance against, not bandwagon with, the most powerful state in the system. But the Roman case suggests that states bandwagon with democratic powers and balance against autocratic ones.

The Roman Republic was the undisputed leader of the Mediterranean for exactly one hundred years. Its international leadership did not last forever, however. Not because the Roman Republic was defeated, but because it experienced a regime change. In 49 BC, Julius Caesar became dictator eventually paving the way for his adopted son, Augustus, to turn the Roman Republic into an empire. The empire would remain the leading political entity on Earth for several centuries, but its vitality was gone. It was living off of the achievements of the Republic and it eventually succumbed to internal decay and external attack. Rome itself was sacked by barbarians in 410 AD and the end of the Empire is often dated to 476 AD.

Rome did not give way to a new global leader, but rather to an extended period of regional disorder, the European dark ages. For several centuries, ancient wisdom in the arts, literature, and science were largely lost in Europe. Democratic government was another casualty of this great forgetting of ancient ways. In these Middle Ages, autocratic political actors, such as Charlemagne in AD 800, temporarily managed to establish themselves as leading powers. And, indeed, autocratic powers can do quite well when not facing off against democratic competitors.

It was not until several centuries later that the old ways and modes were reborn, including the art of liberal hegemony, during the Italian Renaissance.

| The Venetian Republic, the Byzantine Empire, and the Duchy of Milan

THE VENETIAN REPUBLIC was one of the most open polities of the Middle Ages, and it found itself in strategic competitions with other rival powers, including the Byzantine Empire, Genoa, and the Duchy of Milan.[1] Like other dominant democracies before and since, Venice became a major trading, financial, and naval power and it was renowned for its shrewd diplomacy. In the end, Venice bested its rivals, even sacking the imperial city of Constantinople in AD 1204. At the peak of its power, the Venetian Empire's territorial control spanned from northern Italy, along the Dalmatian Coast, to much of Greece and Anatolia, including Constantinople, with significant influence in the Levant, North Africa, and the Black Sea. Our friend Machiavelli admired Venice as "excellent among modern republics."[2]

The Rise of Venice

Venice's founding can be traced to the collapse of the Roman Empire. With the Italian Peninsula beset by barbarian invasions, frightened Italians fled the mainland to find refuge in the lagoons and islands in the armpit of Italy on the Adriatic Sea. These island-dwelling, Veneti people grew more numerous and eventually established a new city-state in AD 5th century.

While the Roman Empire collapsed in the West, it remained intact in the East. The Eastern Roman Empire, or Byzantine Empire, had a capital in Constantinople and controlled the areas of present-day Turkey, Greece, and the southern Balkans. It also retained scattered holdings and nominal control over parts of the Italian mainland, including Venice. The Byzantine Empire was an autocracy, with the emperor sitting on top of the system as an absolute monarch, commander-in-chief of the armed forces, and head of the Church. The large empire was divided into smaller administrative units ruled over by appointed officials. To exert authority over the independently minded and geographically isolated peoples of the Italian lagoons, therefore, the Byzantine Emperor, appointed a duke (*doge*, in Venetian dialect) as Venice's ruler in 697.

In 726, Venice became a republic when, for the first time, Venice selected its own leader, Orso Ipato.[3] Ipato and other subsequent doges attempted to make the position a hereditary one, but those efforts were firmly and successfully resisted by the Venetians. The introduction of tribunes and a variety of advisory councils in the early years of the republic prevented the doge from consolidating power in a monarchical fashion.

Gradually, Venice came into its own. It began to build out from the islands to create an interlocking city of bridges, canals, fortifications, and ports, and transformed itself from a tiny fishing village into a seafaring nation and trading state. Venice was well suited to becoming a trading power. Its people were skilled sailors and shipbuilders. And its geographic location gave it easy access to the Mediterranean and direct inland routes to mainland Europe.

In 800, Charlemagne, king of the Franks and the Lombards, was crowned Holy Roman Emperor by the pope on Christmas Day. In 804, a pro-Frankish faction within Venice conspired with Charlemagne and invited him to take control of the city. He sent his son Pepin the Short on what turned out to be a fatal military mission. The Venetians withdrew behind their large, natural moat, and Pepin's navy was unable to navigate the treacherous lagoons without local guides. Instead, Pepin's forces encamped for months on the mainland, where they were ambushed and harried by Venetian forces. To add insult to injury, Pepin fell ill in the swampy conditions and withdrew his forces, only to die a few weeks later.

Grateful that Venice had helped fend off a major potential rival, and bowing to reality, Constantinople granted Venice greater autonomy and endowed it with special trading privileges within the Byzantine Empire. By this time, Venice enjoyed de facto independence. Its privileges expanded over time to eventually include allocation of territory and docks within the capital and a special, tax-free trading status.

In what would become a characteristic move and reflecting on Venice's diplomatic acumen, Venice even negotiated a trade agreement with its defeated enemy, striking a trade deal with Charlemagne's grandson, Lothair I, the Holy Roman Emperor, later in the 9th century.

Venice's desire to expand trade, however, bumped up against the dangers of pirates operating in the Adriatic Sea along the Dalmatian Coast, from present-day Croatia. Venice converted its maritime and shipbuilding prowess into naval capability. Over the course of a century, Venice succeeded in subduing the pirates. By the turn of the millennium, Venice gained possession of its first overseas holdings along the Dalmatian Coast and the doge added to his title, the Duke of Dalmatia. The Adriatic Sea was firmly in control of the people from the lagoon, and the northern portion was nicknamed the Gulf of Venice.

Like other dominant democracies, Venice enjoyed domestic political stability with a single republican form of government in control for nearly one thousand years, from 726 to 1797. Venice was nicknamed *La Serenisima*, the most serene, due to its domestic tranquility. In the 12th century, a Great Council was established that served as the central representative body of the Venetians. In addition to electing the doge, the council was responsible for passing laws, decreeing punishments, and granting pardons. The Great Council also elected all magistrates and members of other councils, which became increasingly numerous. The Council was dominated by wealthy families, but there was turnover and room for upward mobility, with new members added each year.

To prevent vote rigging, the process for electing the doge consisted of an almost-comically-complicated, ten-step procedure. First, the names of thirty members of the Great Council were drawn from an urn. Then, these thirty names were returned to the urn for another blind draw in which nine names were selected. These nine people would then nominate forty other members of the Great Council. These forty were reduced to nine and these nine would then put forward another twenty-five names. And so on, until, eventually, a single person was selected. And we think the U.S. electoral college is complicated.

To be sure, the Venetian Republic would not qualify as a full democracy according to modern standards. But it was more open than other states in this period. It was considered a republic by itself and its contemporaries, including Machiavelli. Significant political authority was vested in the Great Council and citizens enjoyed a wide range of liberties.

Venice's open political system facilitated an open economic system. It was an open and tolerant society, whose diverse inhabitants included numerous foreign traders from throughout Europe and the Mediterranean. Venice built on its trading advantages with clever economic innovations. The origins of capitalism can arguably be traced to the Venetian *commenda*. This was a kind of business partnership that lasted for a single voyage. Two men would enter into a contract in which one sedentary merchant would put up the capital for the trade and the other traveling merchant would accompany the goods to their destination and back. The two men would then split the profits or losses. The system facilitated upward mobility, as ambitious young men willing to travel on potentially dangerous voyages to deliver goods could become wealthy.

Aided by its special rights in the Byzantine Empire, Venice was able to dominate the trade in goods between the Middle East and Europe, including spices, silks, lumber, wheat, and salt. Venice became a "staple" port—most goods traded in the Mediterranean first passed through Venice for weighing and inspection before being sent off to their final destination. At its peak, Venetian trading routes stretched from the Black Sea, to the Levant, North Africa, southern Europe, and even to England.

Venice's most famous merchant and explorer was Marco Polo, whose mostly overland travels took him all the way to Peking, at the time the capital of the Chinese Mongol Empire, and back to Venice.

Venice also became a major innovator in manufacturing. In 1104, the Venetians fully appreciated how central shipbuilding was to their economic well-being and security, and they adopted a more strategic approach to mass-producing naval vessels. The Venetian Arsenal shipbuilding yards were established to standardize and mass-produce ships. The Arsenal was perhaps the largest industrial enterprise the world had seen until the Industrial Revolution hundreds of years later. With standardized designs and prefabricated and stockpiled parts, Venice could quickly repair damaged ships or build new ones from scratch. Indeed, with the Arsenal, Venice had the ability to build an entire galley warship in a single day.

Major financial innovations took place in Venice, and the Venetian Republic issued what may have been the world's first government bonds in 1164.[4] Although Venice was already wealthy, the government sometimes struggled to fund its outsized trade and foreign policy ambitions. In 1164, the government of Venice forced its citizens to fork over more money to the government, but the wealthy elites did not want to see their taxes increased, so the government promised to repay them over time from the streams of revenue coming in from the salt and grain trade. This *Monte Vecchio* system expanded and became more flexible and sophisticated, allowing for voluntary purchases of government debt in exchange for repayment with interest. The system helped Venice borrow large amounts of money to meet extraordinary expenditures, including for international warfare.[5] Venice was also quick to adopt financial innovations taking place in other Italian republics, including bills of exchange, double-entry bookkeeping, partnership contracts, and commercial courts.[6] Due to these innovations, Venice is often considered the world's first international financial center.[7]

A positive externality of Venice's ingenuity was in the arts, and it became a leading center of the Italian Renaissance, bequeathing to the world the architecture of St. Mark's Basilica and Palladio, the paintings of Titian, Tintoretto, and Bellini, and later, the music of Vivaldi.

Venice's economic power provided heft to its diplomacy, and it was known for its shrewd negotiating skills, turning broader alliances to its parochial ends and gaining favorable trading privileges, even with rivals.

Venice's maritime prowess and the shipbuilding capabilities of the Arsenal meant that it was a major naval power with one of the largest fleets of warships and transports in the Mediterranean. Naval warfare had not changed much since the ancient world and was still largely conducted by ramming enemy ships and/or attempting to board them for hand-to-hand combat. Ship technology had advanced somewhat, and triremes were replaced with Venetian galleys. These ships were larger and allocated multiple rowers to each oar. In addition, Venice incorporated projectile weapons into naval battles, including bows and crossbows, to be fired as enemy ships approached. Siege warfare was also important to Venice as, to control trading routes, it sometimes needed to subdue hostile coastal cities.

The Fourth Crusade

Venice's most rapid period of expansion took place during the Crusades in the 12th and 13th centuries. The Christian powers of Western Europe needed some way to transport large numbers of men to the Middle East, and Venice agreed to offer its large fleet for that purpose. In addition to payment and spoils of war, Venice capitalized on crusader victories by acquiring strategic port cities, further enhancing its naval control of the Mediterranean. In 1122, Venice attacked Tyre in present-day Lebanon and the peace deal resulted in Venice controlling one-third of the city in addition to territorial and commercial privileges. In 1123, Venice signed a treaty with the Kingdom of Jerusalem that granted Venetian citizens complete autonomy within the holy city. On its return from the Holy Land, the Venetian fleet attacked

Greek islands and territory, forcing the Byzantine Empire to also recognize Venetian control over, and trading privileges in, Greece.

In 1202, Venice played a leading role in the Fourth Crusade and, under the leadership of Doge Enrico Dandolo, redirected the overwhelming military power of the religious coalition to its own ends. As it ferried forces from Western Europe to the planned attack site in Egypt, it convinced its allies to stop off in Zara (present-day Zadar, Croatia) to help Venice subdue this renegade city on the Dalmatian Coast. Much to the dismay of the pope, the first battle of the Fourth Crusades was a Christian-versus-Christian affair, and the crusaders succeeded in capturing Zara and returning it to Venice.

Before advancing to the holy land, the crusaders were diverted once more. As is common in autocratic systems, the Byzantine Empire, Venice's onetime imperial overlord, was engulfed in a succession crisis. The emperor, Isaac II Angelos, had been deposed in a coup by his brother, Alexios III Angelos. Isaac had been deeply unpopular and, like other Byzantine rulers before him, had financially weakened the empire by exploiting the state treasury for personal enrichment and to buy political loyalty.

This ouster did not sit well, however, with Isaac's son, Alexios IV Angelos. Alexios IV conspired with the crusaders. He promised them that in exchange for help in toppling his uncle and returning his father and himself to the throne, he would provide financial and military support to the crusaders from the Byzantine treasury.

This was attractive to crusaders, but it was doubly attractive to Venice, in no small part due to its growing rivalry with the Byzantine Empire. The empire was worried about Venice's growing power and, in the 12th century, it began to curtail Venice's commercial privileges in Constantinople. In addition, it started showing preferential treatment to Venice's rivals in Italy, the other maritime republics of Pisa and Genoa. This enraged the Venetians, and conflicts of interest among these rival Italian trading states led to several bouts of civil unrest in Constantinople. From Venice's point of view, therefore, it would be convenient to have a friend on the throne in Constantinople.

Venice and the crusaders, therefore, agreed to assist Alexios IV, and, once again, the crusade was hijacked for intra-Christian warfare. And, once again, as we have seen throughout history, an open power, the Venetian Republic, engaged in an act of regime change against an autocratic rival.

In July 1203, the crusaders laid siege to Constantinople, forcing Alexios III to flee. Isaac II and his son, Alexios IV, were declared co-emperors. But Alexios IV was unable to make good on his promises to repay the crusaders because there were insufficient funds in the depleted imperial treasury. Moreover, Isaac II and Alexios IV lacked popularity at home and held only a tenuous grip on power. In January 1204, the aged Isaac II passed away. In February, Alexios was strangled to death by a rival nobleman who declared himself emperor.

The upstart emperor refused to pay the crusaders, and in response, in April 1204, the crusaders sacked Constantinople. They raped and pillaged. They burned large portions of the city to the ground. They destroyed art and looted large stores of wealth.

In the aftermath of the war, the Byzantine Empire was dismembered and three-eighths of its territory passed to the Venetian Republic. Venice's territorial acquisition included part of the capital city of Constantinople itself, in addition to the strategically important islands of Crete, Corfu, Rhodes, Negroponte, and Cephalonia.

Venice was now a major power in the eastern Mediterranean. It negotiated to expand its trading privileges in the region. It signed trade deals with the sultan of Egypt in 1208 and the Mongol Empire in 1221.[8] It also opened new trading routes into the Black Sea and the Sea of Azov, founding new colonies and trading ports, including Tanais in modern-day Russia.

Venetian-Genoese Wars, 1256–1381

Having subdued its major rival to the east, Venice turned its attention to the west. It may come as no surprise that some of Venice's most formidable challenges came from other open states. Venice was the most powerful trading state of this time, but it was not the only one. There were three other "maritime republics" in late-medieval Italy, including Amalfi, Pisa, and Genoa. Like Venice, they possessed republican governments and excelled in trade, finance, and naval warfare.

In still more historical evidence against the democratic peace theory, these open states were about to square off in an extended rivalry for the control of Mediterranean trade. In 1135, Amalfi was sacked by Pisa, and it never retained its former glory. In 1284, Genoa won the Battle of Meloria over Pisa, hastening Pisan decline and establishing Genoa as the preeminent naval power in the Tyrrhenian Sea. Genoa had qualified, therefore, for the championship match against Venice. (Amalfi and Pisa are sought-after tourist destinations today, suggesting that some of today's most charming sites are the places that were wealthiest centuries ago, but subsequently fell from power).

From 1256 to 1381, Venice and Genoa fought a series of naval battles for control of the Mediterranean. The engagements stretched from Sardinia in the West to as far as Crimea in the East. In 1380, Genoa made a daring attack on the city of Venice itself in the Battle of Chioggia.

The Battle of Chioggia was marked by military innovation. Genoa succeeded in seizing Chioggia, a small port town within the Venetian Lagoon. From that point, Genoa had planned to launch an attack on downtown Venice. But Venice cleverly sunk barges laden with stones behind the Genoese ships. This trapped the Genoese vessels in the Venetian lagoon and prevented the arrival of reinforcements. In addition, in a historical first, Venice employed effective shipboard gunnery.[9] It mounted cannons on ships and pounded the Genoese positions in Chioggia. The cannon fire collapsed a Genoese fort, killing their commander, Pietro Doria. Battered and starving from the blockade, Genoa sued for peace. Genoa was expelled from the Adriatic Sea and shortly thereafter it lost its independence to neighboring land powers, France and then Milan.

Venice, in contrast, emerged victorious. It was able to pay off its debts, use the Arsenal to rebuild its navy, and maintain its independence and status as a major Mediterranean power.

The Great Italian Wars, 1423–1559

Venice reasserted its maritime control over the eastern Mediterranean, but it faced new threats from the Italian interior. Under Duke Gian Galeazzo Visconti, the Duchy of Milan had expanded in the late 1300s to occupy most of the Po River Valley, including Verona, Vicenza, Piacenza, and Padua, a city that lay just twenty-four miles west of Venice. In addition, Milan was stabbing south into the Romagna and Tuscany. Florence, at this time under the rule of the Medici princes, was also concerned about Milan's growing ambitions. Venice saw common cause with Florence, and its diplomats struck an anti-Milan alliance. From 1423 to 1454, the major powers of Northern Italy fought a series of four wars, the Lombardy Wars. The wars saw Venice conduct its first major ground campaigns, which included sending naval ships inland up the Po River to support its forces and to take on Milan. Venice won a critical battle at Maclodio, in Brescia, just outside of Milan in 1427. The wars resulted in a major shift in the balance of power in northern Europe. The Peace of Lodi in 1454 drew the boundary between the Duchy of Milan and the Republic of Venice at the Adda River, less than twenty miles east of central Milan. The peace held for forty years, and this time period, on the eve of the Italian Renaissance, may have represented the height of Venice's power. Its empire included most of northern Italy (Venice's *Stato da Terra*) its sprawling maritime possessions in the Adriatic, Aegean, and Ionian Seas (*Stato da Mare*), and commercial and geopolitical influence in the Levant, North Africa, and the Black Sea. Venice was likely the wealthiest city on Earth at this time, and its population was second only to Paris.[10]

In a desperate attempt to improve Milan's position in its intra-Italian rivalries, Ludovico Sforza, duke of Milan, enlisted France's help. In what must be one of history's clearest examples of rash autocratic decision-making, Sforza invited Charles VIII, king of France, to invade Italy with a large army in 1494. Charles VIII eagerly accepted Sforza's entreaty and marched into Italy. But, instead of helping Milan, he claimed it for itself. With a few brief exceptions, Milan would never again regain its independence, as it was passed from one major European power to another.

Machiavelli was an eyewitness to France's invasion of Italy. He was only twenty-five years old at the time, and the event had a profound effect on his views of international politics. Machiavelli noted of Ludovico's decision, "being defenseless makes you contemptible. This is one of the disgraces from which a prince must guard himself."[11]

The French did not stop with Milan, however. Instead, they marched virtually uncontested to southern Italy, where they sacked Naples.

In response, Venice employed its legendary diplomatic prowess to form a counterbalancing coalition against France, the League of Venice. The League included most of the city-states of northern Europe (including Milan) and the papacy as well as external powers concerned about French aggression in Italy, including England and Spain. The Battle of Fornovo, fought near Parma in 1495, pitted Venice against France. The bloody battle forced the French army to abandon its plunder and to retreat from Italy.

This was the opening salvo in the Great Italian Wars that raged in Italy from 1494 to 1559. The brutality and double-dealing in these wars would inspire Machiavelli to write his infamous treatise, *The Prince*. Still, as we saw previously, Machiavelli admired the Venetian Republic. More than once it seemed to be on the verge of utter ruin. Yet, each time, Venice was able to forge constructive alliances and repeatedly snatch victory from the jaws of near-certain defeat. Throughout the Great Italian Wars, the Venetian Republic was the only Italian state able to stand up as a peer to the larger nation-states forming in northern Europe. Unlike Milan and other Italian city-states that lost their independence in this state-formation process, Venice retained its independence and its republican form of government until the invasion of Napoleon in 1797.

Democracy versus Autocracy

The Venetian Republic was a prototypical example of a dominant democracy. It grew from a series of villages in a lagoon into a sprawling Mediterranean Empire (Figure 6.1). While we often refer to Venice as a "city-state," political scientist Daniel Nexon has argued that it would be better understood as a "city-empire."[12] Governors appointed by Venice ruled over subjected communities in far-flung Venetian colonies and trading ports.

The Venetian Republic was a trading power and the world's first global financial power. It had inclusive economic institutions that facilitated upward mobility.[13] It was an open trading state, dominating commerce in the eastern Mediterranean; it also attracted ambitious merchants from throughout the Mediterranean to live and trade in Venice, contributing to the city's economic vitality. Venice innovated economically, introducing the world to large-scale industrial production at the Arsenal, early versions of a limited liability company in the *commenda* system, and public debt through the *Monte Vecchio*.

Venice skillfully advanced its diplomatic interests. It signed trading agreements with friends and former enemies alike. It also built effective alliances, harnessing the Crusades to achieve its geopolitical interests, including against the Byzantine Empire. And it took the lead in uniting other major powers against France under the League of Venice in the Great Italian Wars.

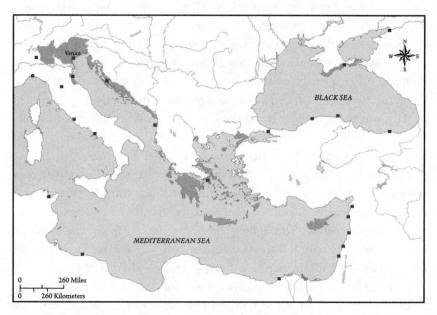

FIGURE 6.1 The Venetian Empire, 15th Century

Militarily, its strong economic and manufacturing base and its sprawling commercial interests led it to build the world's most dominant navy. Venice was also an innovator militarily, becoming arguably the first state to mount cannons on warships, among other ingenious tactics in the Battle of Chioggia. It took down a string of major power autocracies in battle, including Charlemagne, the Byzantine Empire, the Duchy of Milan, and France. It also defeated its democratic rival, Genoa, for maritime control of the eastern Mediterranean.

At the same time, Venice does not appear to have suffered from theorized democratic disadvantages. Granted, it was open to foreign interference, as the early incident with a Venetian faction colluding with Charlemagne demonstrates. But it was also capable of pitilessness in warfare and, indeed if anything, it could have shown more decency in the sacking of Constantinople. The government was able to mobilize resources toward important projects that enhanced national greatness when it counted, including the ship-building efforts at the Arsenal. Further, Venice seems to have devised a clever grand strategy and stuck with it for hundreds of years.[14] It leveraged its geographic position to become a trading power. It acquired strategic holdings along the coasts of its trade routes without biting off more than it could chew. Moreover, it supported its trade-centric strategy with naval power and cordial diplomatic relations.

Its rivals, on the other hand, were not as fortunate. Genoa flourished following the dominant-democracy model; its republican form of government helped it to become a dominant financial and trading power with a potent navy. It lost the Battle of Chioggia to Venice due largely to some late-stage military innovations on Venice's side, but the outcome of that battle and of the Venetian-Genoese rivalry more broadly could have conceivably gone either way.

Venice's autocratic rivals faced more structural deficiencies. The Byzantine emperors robbed the state treasury for their own purposes, undermining economic development. Moreover, Byzantium fell to Venice in the end because of the Achilles heel of autocracies: domestic political instability and crises of succession. Venice seized the opportunity to conduct regime change, sack the city, and claim much of the empire as its own.

The Duchy of Milan revealed poor autocratic decision-making. Sforza's decision to invite France to invade Italy was certainly bold, top-down, and decisive. It also cost his state its independence.

In sum, the rise of the Venetian Republic provides additional support for our democratic advantage thesis. And, indeed, so does its decline. A perfect storm of factors came together to conspire against Venice. It was plagued by repeated outbreaks of the Black Death. As a trading state, Venice was exposed to outside money, goods, ideas, peoples, and, unfortunately, diseases. The plague hit Venice several times over the centuries, but an outbreak in 1630 is thought to have killed off up to one-third of Venice's entire population.[15]

In addition, Venice faced a new geopolitical challenge in the East. The Ottoman Turks succeeded in building an empire that brought together most of the territory of the former Byzantine Empire. In 1453, Mehmed the Conqueror captured Constantinople, and the Ottoman Empire slowly encroached on Venetian possessions and threatened its trade routes. Venice held its own and won some stunning victories, including the naval Battle of Lepanto in 1571, but, still, the Ottoman Turks slowly chipped away at Venice's influence in the eastern Mediterranean.

Perhaps the most important cause of Venice's decline, however, was self-inflicted. In 1296, Venice weakened its greatest source of strength, its open system of government, with *La Serrata*, or the closure of the Great Council. From this point forward only noble families, recorded in a Golden Book, were eligible for seats on the Great Council. This closed off an important path for upward mobility that had been an engine for Venice's growth.[16] Venice remained a republic and more open than cotemporary rivals, but from the 14th century onward it became more oligarchic and lost some of its previous vibrancy. It was able to coast on its previous accomplishments, but, much like the Roman Republic after its transition to empire, Venice faltered in part because it changed the institutions that had propelled it to greatness.

Finally, Venice was affected by the opening up of new trade routes. In 1492, Christopher Columbus sailed the ocean blue and discovered a new world. With European traders able to circumnavigate Africa to reach Asia and the opening up of transatlantic trade, Venice was no longer at the center of global trading networks. States along the Atlantic Ocean were best able to exploit these new realities. The dictatorships were first out the gate, but they were quickly surpassed by democratic rivals, led by the Dutch Republic.

| The Dutch Republic and
the Spanish Empire

G ALLE IS A UNESCO World Heritage site on the southwest coast of the
island of Sri Lanka in South Asia. It is a charming seaside town, with
narrow and windy cobblestone streets. It sits on top of a peninsula that juts
out into the Indian Ocean, enveloped on nearly all sides by steep walls that
crash down into the crystal blue waters below. The town is filled with shops
and restaurants and is just a short drive away from long, sandy beaches with
good surf. It is no surprise that today Galle is one of the most popular tourist
destinations in Sri Lanka. But it was once a fiercely guarded colonial fort of
the mighty Dutch Republic. From here, the Dutch acquired exotic spices,
like black pepper, cinnamon, and turmeric, for trade back in Europe.

At its peak in the 17th century, the Netherlands possessed many such
colonial outposts. In the span of less than a century, from 1581 to 1648,
the Dutch Republic went from a tiny polity in northern Europe to a global
empire that stretched from the Americas to Africa and Asia.[1] It ruled the
high seas, dominated international trade, invented the stock market, and
revolutionized modern warfare, defeating the once-mighty Spanish Empire.
Its path to power was simple: it followed the recipe of the liberal leviathans
that had preceded it. But this outcome was far from preordained.

Persecution under the Spanish Empire

In the 16th century, the Hapsburg Empire was Europe's foremost power. Charles V inherited the thrones of what had been several kingdoms, brought under the rule of a single person: the Holy Roman Empire, the Netherlands, Southern Italy, Austria, and Spain and its colonial holdings in the Americas. Under Charles V, more of Europe was combined under a single ruler than at any time since Charlemagne in AD 800. As he neared the end of his life, however, his empire was split, with the Holy Roman Empire and Austria going to his brother, and the Spanish Empire passing to his son Philip II in 1556.

Spain and Portugal had been the early beneficiaries of the opening up of new trade routes in the late 1400s and early 1500s, and both possessed colonies outside of Europe. Spain was growing rich from the mining of gold and silver in the Americas following its conquest of the Incas and the Aztecs. And Portugal had colonies in South America, Africa, and Asia. These Iberian powers were rivals and competed for overseas possessions and trade routes for decades, but, in 1580, Philip II inherited the throne of Portugal and merged them into a single empire.

Philip II ruled as an autocratic, divine-right monarch. This was the age of the Counter-Reformation, and Philip II was an ardent Catholic. Among his foremost priorities was enforcing religious purity among his subjects. He continued and intensified the Spanish Inquisition that had been started a century before. Jews, Muslims, and Protestants were banished from Spanish territory. Those that remained were subject to arrest, imprisonment, torture, and execution. To flee the persecution in Spanish-controlled areas, many of these minority groups fled to more tolerant societies in the north, including the Low Countries.

The "Low Countries" were a collection of seventeen small duchies and countries in present-day Netherlands, Belgium, and Luxembourg. They took their name due to their low elevation on the Rhine river delta along the coast of the North Sea. (This is also the root of the name for the modern-day country of the Netherlands, because it is located in the "nether" or "low" lands). In the 1400s, these polities, which included Holland, Zeeland, and Flanders, were ruled by the dukes of Burgundy. To ease in the management of these tiny statelets, the dukes established a "States General" assembly in which representatives from the various provinces would get together to discuss matters of common importance and receive edicts from the dukes.

The Low Countries were incorporated into the Holy Roman Empire in 1477, and Charles V and Philip II sought to bring them more fully under their control. In 1549, Charles V announced the Pragmatic Sanction, which unified the provinces into a single administrative entity under the crown's authority. Under this system, a regent appointed by the crown lived in the Low Countries and ruled in close collaboration with local nobles.

Philip II continued efforts to centralize his authority, provoking a backlash from the local inhabitants. But even more troubling to his subjects were his determined efforts to enforce religious orthodoxy and to strictly prosecute heresy. While the Low Countries were still predominantly Catholic, they were more tolerant than other parts of Europe. They were heavily involved in trade and they were, therefore, more accustomed to dealing with peoples of different backgrounds and religions. Its population also included many followers of the new protestant religions, including Lutheranism, Calvinism, and Anabaptism, that had sprung up since Martin Luther had nailed his theses to the church door just a half century before. In addition, many of the Jews who had been persecuted during the Inquisition had fled north, settling in the larger cities of the Low Countries, such as Antwerp and Amsterdam.

Like other autocrats, Philip II was able to impose a top-down strategy, but without societal backing, his plans met resistance. Local nobles in the Low Countries, led by William of Orange (also known as William the Silent) petitioned the crown to allow for religious freedom, but they were rebuked, with an advisor to the crown dismissing them as nothing more than "beggars." (Later Dutch rebels would appropriate the name with pride, referring to themselves as the *Geuzen*, or Beggars.) In response to the religious persecution, a popular uprising began in 1566, with Dutch protestants defacing and destroying Catholic religious sites in the "Iconoclastic Fury," or *Beeldenstorm*.

Philip II sent in the high-handed Duke of Alba, "the Iron Duke," to restore order. Alba promptly set up a "blood court" and executed up to one thousand people accused of involvement in the uprising. Many others fled the country to avoid persecution.

In exile, William of Orange and other disaffected nobles planned a military campaign to unseat Alba. William was a Catholic and, at this point, still loyal to Philip II. But he wanted greater autonomy and tolerance for the Low Countries. He hired several mercenary armies and invaded from different directions, but his forces were defeated handily by the Spanish. In the Battle of Heiligerlee in May 1568, however, the rebels won their first victory and this date is often considered the beginning of the 80 Years' War for Dutch independence, or the Dutch Revolt.

The Dutch Revolt

In 1571, resentment against the crown intensified when Alba imposed a large tax on the States General. Spain had been increasing taxes on the relatively wealthy Netherlands for years to fund its participation in wars in Italy and against the Ottoman Empire. Along with the increasing centralization and religious persecution, the heavy taxes further fueled anti-Spanish sentiment.

The Dutch were already a burgeoning trading power with a large fleet of commercial vessels conducting a brisk trade in timber in the Baltic region. Dutch private vessels joined the rebellion and began conducting attacks on Spanish naval craft. In 1572, these Dutch "Sea Beggars" won a surprising victory against the Spanish, taking the coastal city of Brielle. For the first time the Dutch rebels succeeded in taking and occupying territory formerly controlled by Spain.

This stunning success sparked anti-Alba uprisings throughout the Netherlands and, in the provinces of Holland and Zeeland, more cities fell into rebel hands. Later that year, William of Orange was named the official leader of the rebels, taking the title of Governor-General and Stadtholder of Holland, Zeeland, Friesland, and Utrecht.

But the empire struck back. Over years of wanton destruction now known as the "Spanish Fury," Alba and his forces reclaimed rebel cities and showed no mercy on the vanquished. Spanish forces sacked a string of towns from 1572 to 1579. After raping, pillaging, and looting their way through Mechelen in 1572, Alba bragged to Philip II that his forces did not leave even a single nail in the walls. In the same year, Philip II burned Naarden to the ground and killed all but a handful of its inhabitants.

The empire's barbaric approach gave the rebels even more incentive to fight. Why surrender if all you have to look forward to is annihilation?

In the Siege of Leiden in 1573, the Dutch held out for months against insurmountable odds. In a brilliant military maneuver, William of Orange broke the Spanish siege by destroying the city's dikes. The surrounding fields were flooded, washing away Spanish forces. The Sea Beggars sailed in to relieve the starving population. The event is still celebrated annually in Leiden with a feast of herring and white bread, the same provisions brought by the rebel forces.

By this point, Spain was facing economic difficulty. Unlike in the commercially minded Low Countries, Spanish nobles flaunted their status by living lives of leisure. Even nouveau-riche merchants did not stay active for long. Instead of reinvesting in their businesses, they bought titles and land and retired in order to mimic the lifestyles of the nobles. The influx of silver and gold from the new world helped finance Spain's wars, but it also caused economic problems. It gave Philip II few incentives to devise a more efficient means of raising taxes and crowded out the development of other aspects of the Spanish economy. Indeed, nobles were exempt from taxation entirely. In addition, the massive influx of gold and silver caused inflation that hurt Spain's working classes and exports, leaving Spain with a constant trade deficit.[2] With Dutch Sea Beggars and other foreign privateers attacking and capturing Spanish specie shipments from the new world, Philip was in trouble.

In 1575, Spain declared bankruptcy. The crown was unable to pay its army, and the troops mutinied. This only added to the Spanish Fury, as unpaid Spanish troops looted and pillaged Dutch towns in anger. In 1576, they sacked Antwerp and massacred an estimated eight thousand people in three days. The catastrophe led to the decline of Antwerp's long-standing position as the leading city in the Low Countries and paved the way for the later rise of Amsterdam.

Opposition to Spanish brutality helped to temporarily unite the previously fractious Dutch provinces. In the 1576 Pacification of Ghent, the seventeen provinces of the Low Countries agreed to fight together against the Spanish in order to protect religious tolerance. Only three years later, however, the ten more heavily Catholic southern provinces split from the group, declaring their continued allegiance to Spain. This divided the provinces, with the seven northern provinces forming the Union of Utrecht in continued opposition to Spain. This split had an important effect on contemporary geography. These United Provinces formed in the Union of Utrecht would eventually became the independent Dutch Republic and, later, the Netherlands. The Catholic provinces of the Spanish Netherlands in the South eventually formed the core of present-day Belgium and Luxembourg.

The United Provinces in the North had had enough of titular Spanish rule. In the 1581 Act of Abjuration, the rebels declared their secession from Spain. Not yet imagining that they, a small set of provinces, might possibly be qualified to rule themselves, they sought other European monarchs to become their masters. None of these arrangements worked out for a variety of reasons, however, and the United Provinces became independent largely by default. The Dutch Republic was born.

Many inhabitants of the Low Countries preferred the freedom of the Dutch Republic to Spanish tyranny, and people voted with their feet and fled north. The population of Antwerp fell dramatically in the late sixteenth century, while the population of Amsterdam soared.

This new Dutch Republic became the first free republic of early modern Europe. The seven provinces each sent representatives to the legislative body, the States General. Each province had a single vote and a veto in the legislature. This meant that major decisions, including on war and peace, were arrived at by consensus. According to law, the provinces were equal, although Holland was by far the wealthiest and most influential of the bunch. In the Dutch Republic, as in Venice, the capitalists and merchants were able to interact with the government far more equally than other states, as the overlap between the two classes was significant.[3] This helped to facilitate the development of inclusive economic institutions. The chief executive of the system was the stadtholder. This person was appointed by the provinces and served as the commander of chief of the armed forces and held sway over government appointments.[4]

Autocracies have a hard time accumulating power without provoking counterbalancing coalitions, and Philip II had made plenty of enemies throughout Europe. In addition to the Dutch Republic, Spain was also at war with England, France, and the Ottoman Empire in the late 16th century. These states were happy to see Spain's troubles with the Dutch. England, in particular, decided to openly aid the rebel forces.

England was an irritant to Spain for other reasons as well. Its pirates, like Sir Francis Drake, raided Spanish shipments from the new world. Moreover, England was a Protestant power and an obstacle to Philip II's efforts to impose Catholicism on the rest of Europe.

In 1588, Philip II attempted to deal a game-ending blow to England. He sent the mighty Spanish Armada of over one hundred ships with a plan for regime change. He would overthrow Queen Elizabeth I and her Protestant government and set up a Catholic government that would better suit his preferences. Instead, the expedition of the Spanish Armada ended in utter disaster. A combined English and Dutch fleet defeated the Spanish. The Dutch fleet blockaded the Low Countries and prevented Spanish ships from linking up with reinforcements on the ground in the Spanish Netherlands. In addition, the English sent "fire ships" into the Spanish fleet that burned some Spanish vessels and disoriented others. In its retreat, the Spanish Armada was then caught in a violent storm. Almost half the Spanish ships and most of its sailors were lost.

In 1584, William of Orange, who by this time had converted to Protestantism, was assassinated by a Spanish loyalist. Following his death, his son, Maurice of Orange, was elected stadtholder and took command of the Dutch forces. Maurice is often credited with ushering in a military revolution in modern Europe, as the first to fully exploit the benefits of firearms on the modern battlefield.[5] A majority of the Spanish infantry were still armed with pikes—not that different from the spears of the ancient Greeks. In contrast, Maurice equipped the majority of his forces with muskets. To increase their rate of fire and to protect musketeers while reloading, he introduced a system of volley fire. The frontline soldiers would fire their weapons, then retreat to the rear of the formation and reload. The next line of soldiers would step forward and fire before retreating themselves, and so on. This system generated a steady stream of fire on the enemy and protected the reloading musketeers from enemy attack. To work, however, the system required clear doctrine and constant drilling, which Maurice also introduced. Soon, the repeated steps of marching, firing, countermarching, reloading, etc., became second nature to his forces. Constant practice required more professional standing armies and a move away from the temporarily hired mercenaries that had been the standard practice in previous centuries. Maurice was ridiculed at first for attempting this unorthodox method of warfare, but it proved to be so effective that it was eventually copied throughout the rest of Europe.

Throughout the 1590s, Maurice conquered and fortified most of the important cities of the Dutch Republic still contested by the Spanish. While the war would continue for another half century, from this point forward, the homeland of the Dutch Republic was never again in danger.

Maurice's more ambitious forays into the Spanish Netherlands, however, were thwarted. Having fought to a standstill, the two sides agreed to a Twelve Years' Truce in 1609. The agreement was signed in The Hague and mediated by the English and the French. The purpose was to create the time and space to negotiate a more lasting peace. It was a major milestone in the history of the Dutch Republic, as it was, for the first time, officially recognized as an independent state by other major powers.

The Dutch Golden Age

The Dutch Republic would use these dozen years productively and ushered in what has become known as The Dutch Golden Age. The Dutch Republic was an open and tolerant society, and it benefited from a massive brain drain. Skilled migrants, including protestants and Jews, persecuted in the Spanish Empire and elsewhere in Europe, found refuge in the Dutch Republic. During the revolt, over 10 percent of the population of the southern Low Countries migrated to the north to escape Spanish brutality, including a large proportion of the south's banking and merchant class.[6] These new arrivals greatly contributed to the economic vitality of the fledgling republic.

Like other open states, the Dutch Republic became an economic innovator. It dug canals, which allowed for the rapid transportation of goods and passengers. Democracies tend to be more open to international trade, and the Netherlands was no different. For years, the Low Countries had engaged in trade in timber and other products in the Baltics and the rest of northern Europe. To up their game, the Dutch invented a new form of ship, the *Fluyt*. While other maritime powers, like Portugal and Spain, built ships that did double-duty as both cargo vessels and warships, the Dutch designed a ship optimized for trade. It was cheaper to build and operate, and carried much more cargo. The Dutch became the world's most efficient traders and by the 1590s, they began challenging Portuguese trading routes in the "Spice Islands" of Southeast Asia. At this time, Dutch cargo capacity was at least double that of both Spain and England.[7]

One of the most important innovations of the Dutch Republic, however, was the creation of the world's first corporation, the *Vereenigde Oostindische Compagnie* (VOC), often translated into English as the Dutch East India Company. The VOC was created in 1602, when several rival trading companies merged into one. The States General granted it a monopoly on Dutch trade in Asia. To secure its trading routes, the VOC possessed the right to use force and establish ports and colonies. The VOC soon became a dominant force in global trade. Its logo was a globally-recognized trademark, and the VOC served as a model for subsequent global businesses. Its commercial activities greatly contributed to the Dutch Republic's global empire. In 1621, the States General also created the Dutch West India Company, *Verenigde Westindische Compagnie*, (WIC) in a bid to match the VOC's success and to compete for trade in the Americas.

The VOC motivated the Dutch Republic to innovate in another way: to invent the world's first stock market. Previous trading expeditions, as we saw in Venice, were set up for a single voyage with a small group of investors who could recoup their investment when the expedition ended. Now, with the VOC, there was a larger company meant to operate permanently. Some of the investors did not want, or could not afford, to have their funds in the company tied up indefinitely. They wanted to sell their share of the firm and, in 1602, a stall was set up in the Amsterdam's harbor market to do just that. Shares were made available to the public and were traded alongside fish and other commodities. As demand for the shares increased with the success of the company, speculators realized they could profit simply by buying and selling shares. New financial practices (including some that we might assume were more modern innovations) such as trading in derivatives and short selling, were created within months. Indeed, in 1637, the Dutch Republic also gave the world its first speculative bubble in "tulip mania" as prices of the then-exotic flowers were bid up to astronomical levels only to quickly come crashing back down. Fortunately, this early financial crisis did not have a noticeable impact on the power and wealth of the rising Dutch Republic.

The States General also followed in the footsteps of Venice and offered government bonds for sale in this market. Buying Dutch debt was a safe investment. Dutch politicians themselves were major investors, and as Paul Kennedy explains, they had a strong interest to ensure "the principles of sound money, secure credit, and regular repayment of debt [were] upheld."[8] The market spread government debt across a larger section of the population, and even foreigners began investing in Dutch bonds. The high demand for Dutch debt meant that the States General only needed to pay low (~4 percent) interest rates to attract investors.[9] This allowed the States General to raise large amounts of money without dramatic tax increases.[10]

Amsterdam soon became the center of global finance. The Bank of Amsterdam, established in 1609, was arguably the world's first central bank. Foreign traders relied on institutions in Amsterdam for currency exchange and to facilitate trade with other countries. As late as 1763, London merchants, for example, went through Amsterdam for trade with Russia.[11]

In contrast, the Spanish monarchy had to offer much higher interest rates to attract investors, up to 20 percent. This imposed additional financial strain on the feeble Spanish economy, and the overstretched Spanish Empire repeatedly defaulted on its debt in 1575, 1596, 1607, 1627, 1647, 1652, 1660, and 1662.[12]

The Netherlands was likely the wealthiest and fastest-growing country in the world at this time. It is estimated the GDP per capita in the United Provinces was at least double that in Spain, and its economy was growing at double-digit rates.[13]

Amsterdam also enjoyed significant soft power as its freewheeling model facilitated developments in the arts and sciences. Today, many remember this period for the Dutch Masters, such as Rembrandt, Johannes Vermeer, and Jan Steen. Philosophers and writers working in Amsterdam at the time included monumental figures in the history of human thought, including Rene Descartes, Hugo Grotius, and Baruch Spinoza.

To protect its growing commercial interests, the Dutch built a large military. In the mid-1600s, the Netherlands possessed one of the largest armies in Europe, with 110,000 men under arms compared to only 70,000 in Spain.[14]

In the same time period, Dutch Admiral Michiel de Ruyter brought the military revolution, started by Maurice on land, to sea. By this time, galleys were eliminated in favor of the man o' war. Navies followed Venice's lead in arming ships with cannons, and sails replaced oars as the main power source. But early naval gun battles, like the Battle of Lepanto between Venice and the Ottoman Turks in 1571, were chaotic frays. Ruyte designed rational operational concepts that maximized the technology's potential, operating ships in carefully orchestrated formations and concentrating firepower on the enemy. The stronger naval presence was created just in time as the war with Spain was about to resume.

The Thirty Years' War

The Twelve Years' Truce broke down due to intractable disputes over religion and trade. The Dutch were willing to offer Catholics the freedom to practice their religion in the Dutch Republic, but the Spanish were unwilling to grant similar rights to Protestants in the Spanish territories. In addition, the two sides disagreed over international trading routes. While the Dutch had signed the Twelve Years' Truce with Spain, it did not have a similar agreement with Portugal (which, as the reader will recall, was also under the control of the Spanish crown at the time). The Netherlands exploited this loophole and the downtime during the Truce to enhance its trading position at the expense of Portugal's overseas empire.

In 1603, the VOC seized a Portuguese trading ship and its prized cargo. The Portuguese protested, but the Dutch defended their actions. Dutch jurist Hugo Grotius formulated his ideas about the freedom of the seas in response to this incident, and his views still influence international maritime law to this day.[15] Later that year, the Dutch established their first overseas trading colony in Indonesia and Batavia (present-day Jakarta) was named the capital of the Dutch East Indies. The Dutch and Portuguese clashed over Goa in 1604, Mozambique in 1607, and Malacca in 1615.

In 1621, the 80 Years' War formally resumed. It merged into the broader Thirty Years' War (1618–1648), also a war primarily between Protestants and Catholics raging across the rest of Europe. On land, the Dutch captured several cities from the Spanish Netherlands, including Maastricht. But efforts to take the more important cities in the South, such as Brussels and Antwerp, were repulsed. Contrary to Dutch expectation, the people of the Spanish Netherlands did not rise up and greet them as liberators. By this time, the population was thoroughly Catholic and content to be ruled by the Spanish crown.

Rather, the major action in this second phase of the war was over Spain and Portugal's colonial empires. In this theater, the war was decisively decided in the Netherlands' favor. In 1624, the Dutch East India Company established a colonial outpost on Formosa (present-day Taiwan), and in 1642, they took the entire island from Spain. In 1638, a small group of islands in the Indian Ocean was seized from Portugal and renamed Mauritius, in honor of Maurice of Orange. In 1640, the Dutch established their foothold in Galle (the city described in the beginning of this chapter), and in 1658, they succeeded in claiming all of Ceylon (present-day Sri Lanka). In 1648, the Dutch took Malacca (in present-day Malaysia). This was an especially important gain for the Dutch, because the Malaccan Straits serve as an important choke point for all Asian trade. The conquests of the Dutch East India Company were rounded out in 1663, when they took the Malabar Coast of India from Portugal.

As the VOC was making hay in the East, the WIC, was doing the same in the new world. In 1624, it established a colony in North America to serve as a fort and fur-trading post. This port of New Amsterdam would later become a small town we know today as New York City. In the same period, the WIC established a colony at Portugal's expense in Brazil to engage in the lucrative sugar trade. It also gained other possessions in South America and the Caribbean including Suriname, Aruba, and Curacao. The Dutch Republic also got into the slave trade. It took Luanda in present-day Angola from Portugal in 1640 and conquered the Portuguese Gold Coast (present-day Ghana) in 1642. In 1652, the Dutch established the Cape Colony in present-day South Africa.

This was the beginning of the end for Spain's attempts to subdue the Dutch, and things came to a head in the Battle of the Downs in 1639. With France's entry into the Thirty Years' War, Spain could no longer transport forces over land into the Spanish Netherlands. It, therefore, looked to reinforce its ground forces by sea. When they anchored at the Downs, near the English Chanel, the Dutch navy engaged them in battle, winning a conclusive victory and forever ending Spain's status as a naval power.

Autocracy's greatest weakness is domestic political instability, and the Spanish Empire was no different. In addition to the Dutch Revolt, Philip II's successor, Philip III, had to put down two additional uprisings. Spanish Catalonia revolted against the crown in 1640. Inspired by this example, Portugal decided it was time to reclaim its independence from Spain. These uprisings would end with Spain losing Portugal and ceding parts of Catalonia to France.

In 1648, the broader Thirty Years' War came to an end with the Peace of Westphalia. This peace settlement is often considered the foundation of the modern nation-state system. After fighting over religion for nearly a century, the countries of Europe agreed to the principles of sovereignty and territorial integrity. Nation-states would have the power to determine matters within their own borders, such as the practice of religion, without external inference.

More importantly for our purposes, Spain and the Dutch Republic also made their peace in the related Treaty of Munster. The agreement granted the Dutch Republic independence. The Netherlands emerged stronger from the conflict as arguably the wealthiest and most powerful country in the world, with a global empire and possessions across Asia, Africa, and the Americas. The outcome was a humiliating defeat for Spain. It had lost territory in Europe and around the world, and was no longer a major naval power.

Democracy versus Autocracy

The story of the Dutch Republic's revolt against Spain provides significant support for the democratic advantage theory. The Dutch Republic rose from a collection of small polities under the rule of another empire to become an independent nation with a global empire of its own (Figure 7.1). Consistent with the democratic advantage thesis, the Dutch Republic's open model of politics was a major reason for its rise to power. Its inclusive economic institutions facilitated economic growth. Tolerance created a massive influx of talented migrants that contributed to its human capital. Like other open states, it became a leader in global trade. Its most impressive economic innovations, however, were in finance. Amsterdam succeeded Venice as the capital of capital. It was the home of the first modern corporation, stock market, and central bank.

Diplomatically, it was able to amass power and wealth without provoking resistance. It also succeeded in enlisting outside help, including from England and France, in its cause against Spain. Contrary to claims that democracies cannot persist in any grand design, the Dutch Republic remained laser-focused on its war with Spain for eight consecutive decades and eventually came out on top.

In military matters, the Dutch Republic's large economic base supported its military power. The Dutch Republic possessed the world's largest navy and one of the largest armies. It repeatedly defeated the Spanish and the Portuguese as it gained independence and established a global empire. It was also a military innovator. The Dutch Republic ushered in a revolution in military affairs, designing coherent operational concepts for the new and disruptive gunpowder revolution on both land and sea.

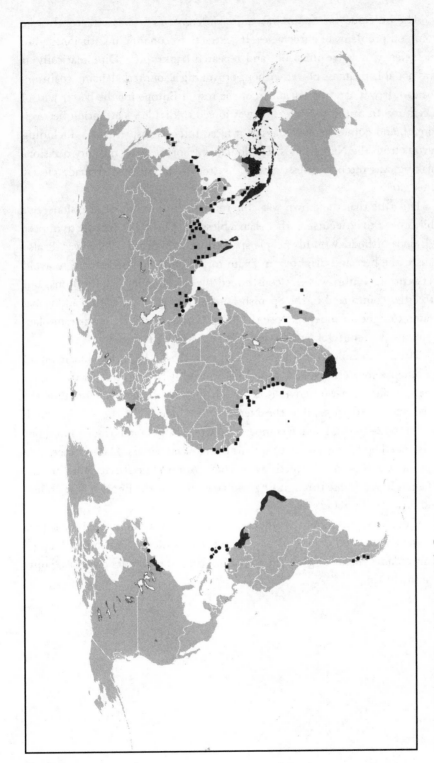

Figure 7.1 The Dutch Empire, 17th Century

The outcome for Spain was quite different, as it was afflicted by the common problems of autocracies. Its extractive economic institutions led to inefficiency, massive inflation, and repeated bankruptcy. Diplomatically, it was not able to amass power without provoking a counterbalancing coalition; instead, it was at war with much of the rest of Europe for the better part of a century. In military matters, it was forced to divide its attention between foreign and domestic challenges as it faced internal insurrections, including revolts from the Netherlands, Catalonia, and Portugal. Its military decision-making was often heedless, as the disaster of the Spanish Armada clearly illustrates.

It is true that the crown was able to make big, top-down decisions, but this proved to be a curse, rather than a blessing. Philip II's crusade to impose religious orthodoxy on his people sparked a costly decades-long war. It also caused the best and brightest in Spain to flee north to Amsterdam to avoid persecution. Philip was not constrained by moral or legal inhibitions, but atrocities committed in the Spanish Fury merely gave the Dutch additional reason to fight for independence. If Philip II had a strategic long-term plan, a supposed strength of autocracies, it is not clear what it was.

The Dutch Golden Age lasted throughout the 17th century, but it would not endure forever. For, just across the English Channel, there was another small, seafaring nation envious of Dutch success. As a monarchy, England tried and failed to subdue the Netherlands. Indeed, in the Anglo-Dutch Wars (1652–1674), London competed to wrest away Dutch trade routes, but only ended up losing a series of embarrassing naval battles. In one remarkable episode, the Raid on the Medway in 1667, Admiral de Ruyte sailed up the Thames River, broke through England's defenses, lit the English fleet on fire, and captured England's flagship.

If England was going to compete successfully, it would need to do things differently. It would need a new and better system. So, London copied Amsterdam's model of global domination, right down to its domestic political institutions.

| Great Britain and France

I F YOU CAN'T beat 'em, join 'em. And then beat 'em. That was England's philosophy when it came to the Dutch Republic. London was envious of Amsterdam's success, so it adopted its successful model, including its: political system, economic innovations, vast trading network, overseas empire, and even its leading family. The path to global ascendancy was not easy, however. On its way to the top, Britain had to square up against some of the most well-known dictators in world history: Louis XIV, Napoleon Bonaparte, and Adolf Hitler. Yet, each time, this small island in the North Atlantic managed to come out on top over its authoritarian, continental rivals. By the 19th century, Great Britain had surpassed the Netherlands as the wealthiest country on Earth and possessed the largest global empire the world has ever seen.

England's Origins

The territory that became England was populated by indigenous Celtic tribes before it was conquered by the Roman Republic in AD 43. Several centuries after the collapse of the Roman Empire, Alfred the Great emerged as England's first Anglo-Saxon king, in AD 871. English kings always had to deal with powerful and independently minded nobles, and, in 1215, the Magna Carta was signed, planting the seeds for subsequent political democracy. The Magna Carta limited the king's powers, enshrined nobles' rights, and created a forum for discussions between the king and his subjects. The

French word for talk is *parler*, and the new institution was referred to as the parliament.

In 1337, a dispute over the rightful heir to the French throne led to the Hundred Years' War with France. As soon as the dust settled, the English royal family went to war with itself over control of the English crown. This War of the Roses lasted from 1455 to 1487. The Tudor line led by Henry VII emerged victorious. In order to avoid future bloodshed and to have in place a clear successor, Henry VIII, Henry VII's son, badly wanted a male heir. When he and his wife, Catherine of Aragon, failed to produce one, he sought a divorce, but the Catholic Church would not allow it. He suddenly found himself a convert to the new Protestant religious movement that was more open to such things. In 1533, he established a new Church of England, separate from the Catholic Church, setting England on a collision course with Spain and other Catholic powers on the European continent. Henry eventually had a son, but it was his daughter Queen Elizabeth I (r. 1558–1603) who became one of England's most influential leaders.

England was still a relatively poor country compared to its counterparts on the European continent, including the Spanish Hapsburg Empire, the Dutch Republic, the Venetian Republic, and France. To gain hard currency, Elizabeth authorized pirates, like Sir Francis Drake, to raid Spanish ships for gold and silver. England was envious of the overseas empires of its rivals, and in the early 1600s, it established outposts in the Caribbean and North America, including Jamestown in the Virginia colony, named after Queen Elizabeth, "the virgin queen." These spots were selected because they were available; the more promising territories in South America had already been taken.

In 1642, England descended back into civil war, but this time over the powers between the king and parliament. The parliamentarians emerged victorious, but their military leader, Oliver Cromwell, exploited the victory to set himself up as a dictator, the self-proclaimed "Lord Protector" of England. In 1652, England turned to international opponents, squaring off against the newly independent Dutch superpower. As we saw in the last chapter, this did not go well for England.

England was endlessly striving, but it just could not seem to compete with its continental rivals—until the Glorious Revolution.

The Glorious Revolution

In 1688, the English were having yet another dispute over who should be the rightful ruler of the country. Some were concerned that the sitting king,

James II, would return the country to Catholicism. This faction turned to James II's daughter, Mary, for help. Mary had left England to marry William III of Orange, the great-grandson of William the Silent, and the stadtholder of the Dutch Republic. The anti-James coalition asked William and Mary, who were both Protestants, to come back to England, push out James II, and rule England themselves. They agreed. William brought a large army across the English Channel, fought a few skirmishes with James II's forces, and succeeded in conquering the country. He and his wife assumed the titles of King William III and Queen Mary II of England.

This episode is often referred to as a "Bloodless Revolution," or the "Glorious Revolution," but it can be seen as the Dutch Republic's most important military victory over an autocratic rival. In an example of 17th century regime change, the Dutch invaded England, overthrew the king, and set up a new, more open system of government.

William of Orange brought more than the silverware with him to London. He transported Dutch institutions as well. In 1689 a Bill of Rights was passed that established Parliament—much like the States General in Amsterdam—as the supreme ruling body of England and circumscribed the power of the king. In addition, the Bill provided for the individual rights and liberties of English citizens. From that point forward, England was ruled as a constitutional monarchy, avoiding the monarchical absolutism present on the European continent. Over time, the monarch's powers were limited and those of parliament increased. The Glorious Revolution, therefore, marks the beginning of greater political democracy in England.

With freer political institutions come free economic institutions. In 1694 the Bank of England was established, and it began issuing public debt. Like the Netherlands, the British had set up a monopoly to conduct overseas trade, the British East India Company. In the second half of the 17th century, it issued public stocks for the first time, becoming a publicly traded company, like the VOC. In 1698, the first exchanges of stock began taking place in London coffee houses. Later these activities were moved to the Royal Exchange building, which had previously been a market for selling alcohol and exchanging other commodities. Also at this time, merchants and financiers interested in British shipping began meeting at Edward Lloyd's coffee house in London. In 1691, a group of businessmen there formed a group to offer insurance for maritime trade, and Lloyds of London was born. The financial revolution had come to England, and it would eventually pave the way for London to overtake Amsterdam as the center of global finance.

England was also emerging as a major trading and colonial power. It possessed colonies in North America and the Caribbean and had been vying with the Dutch for control over trade in Asia. After the Glorious Revolution, with William of Orange leading both countries through a personal union, the navies and trading routes of the two powers merged in a way that benefited England over the long run. An agreement was reached in which the Dutch Republic was allowed a monopoly on the spice trade, but England was given control of the textile trade with India, setting up a fort and factory in Madras. England soon built a more powerful navy to protect its trading routes.

England would need this bolstered economic and military strength because it was about to enter into a century-long competition with a newly ascendant autocratic power on the European continent.

The Wars of Louis XIV

As the Hapsburg Spanish monarchy declined in power, Louis XIV of France was there to take its place. France acquired territory from Spain and the Holy Roman Empire in the Thirty Years' War, the War of the Devolution (1667–1668), and the Franco-Dutch War (1672–1678). Louis XIV, the "Sun King," was the epitome of the absolute, divine-right monarch. He centralized power and undermined the independence of the nobility by forcing them to come and live with his royal court at Versailles, which had been enlarged from a hunting lodge into a grand palace in the second half of the seventeenth century. He also enforced religious conformity and essentially eliminated France's remaining Protestant minority. Many of these persecuted Protestants fled to the Netherlands and England. Louis XIV accurately described France's political institutions at the time when he famously said, "L'état c'est moi"—"the state is me."

Louis XIV's France was the largest land power in Europe by this point, and he harbored hegemonic ambitions. He attempted to build on his gains from previous wars by grabbing more territory from Spain and the Holy Roman Empire, the latter of which was also fighting a war against the Ottoman Empire in the East. The Sun King also aspired to use military force against England to overthrow William, and re-install a Catholic monarch, James II, on the English throne. War began in 1688 when Louis XIV invaded the Holy Roman Empire.

France's aggressive foreign policy and England's alliance-building skills, however, combined to form the basis for a counterbalancing coalition that ultimately stymied France's expansion and contributed to England's rise. International relations theory suggests that democracies are more likely to cooperate and the English and the Dutch, the most open states in Europe at the time, both led by William III, were partners in this decades-long fight with the French. In addition, William III managed to persuade the Holy Roman Empire, Spain, and other smaller states to join in this "grand alliance" against France. This War of the Grand Alliance (1688–1697) saw fighting all along France's various borders and also in Ireland, Scotland, and North America. The conflict was one of positional warfare with nations jockeying for control along fortified lines with few decisive battles. The major contests were sieges of cities in the Spanish Netherlands. The Spanish Netherlands was an important theater because it lay between France and the Dutch Republic and was also a desirable geographic staging area for France's planned descent on England. In 1692, France succeeded in taking Namur, roughly thirty miles south of Brussels. But in 1695, the Grand Alliance took it right back. The war ended in stalemate with France making some minor territorial concessions and formally recognizing William III as the legitimate king of England.

The same basic conflict would resume several years later in the War of the Spanish Succession (1701–1714). When King Charles II of Spain died without an heir, the throne was set to pass to the grandson of Louis XIV, who saw an opportunity to greatly expand his kingdom. Concerned that all of France and Spain might be united into a single hegemonic entity, England once again used its alliance-building acumen and deep financial resources to resurrect the Grand Alliance. Once again, France was no match for a combined counterbalancing alliance of most of Europe's major powers.

France ended the war in a weakened position. Louis XIV managed to install his grandson on the Spanish throne, but only on the condition that the young king would renounce any and all claims to control of France. Louis XIV was also forced to give up conquered territories in Italy and the Spanish Netherlands. Finally, the war was costly for France. France suffered a deep financial decline that was exacerbated by "the inherent unreliability of a government dominated by an absolute monarch."[1] Among other poor financial practices, Louis XIV would "threaten dealers in the foreign exchange and public debt markets with prison and professional proscription for pricing financial instruments on a realistic but unfavorable basis."[2] By war's end, France's debt had multiplied seven-fold.

Britain, on the other hand, emerged from the conflict in the best position of any of the combatants.[3] The balance of power on land had been stabilized, British dominance at sea went unchallenged, and the Protestant succession of the Glorious Revolution was recognized by the major European powers. Britain gained colonial holdings in North America from France, including Newfoundland and Acadia. In addition, London took Gibraltar, a major strategic position to control trade between the Atlantic Ocean and the Mediterranean Sea. Moreover, Britain was the only major contestant that was able to effectively finance its war efforts. It convinced "a large and diverse number of individuals to hold" its debt and this success was mostly "due to British institutions."[4]

Louis XIV died in 1715 without realizing his goal of European ascendance, and Britain emerged as the world's preeminent commercial and maritime power. This is the year in which political scientist William Thompson codes Great Britain as becoming the leading state in the international system.

During the war, in 1707, England received another boost to its power and influence when the parliament of Scotland voted in the Acts of Union to merge with England and form a united Great Britain. The two countries had been ruled by the same king since the 1603 Union of the Crowns, when King James I inherited the thrones of both kingdoms. From this point forward, Great Britain would be a single political entity, ruled by the parliament in London.

The British-French rivalry soon resumed, but this time in the new world. In 1754, George Washington started what was arguably history's first world war. In the 17th and 18th centuries, France established a colonial presence in North America. Beginning north along the St. Lawrence River, France founded Quebec (1608) and Montreal (1611). The French then worked their way down the Great Lakes and Mississippi River basin to the west of the British colonies along the coast, establishing outposts in Detroit (1701) and as far south as New Orleans (1718). Britain and its American colonies became concerned, however, as France started encroaching on British holdings by moving eastward up the Ohio River Valley. When France attempted to build a fort on the forks of the Allegheny and Monongahela Rivers, a British colonial unit led by George Washington attacked.

This was the beginning of the Seven Years' War (1756–1763). The conflict between Britain and France over American colonial possessions eventually drew in every major European power and saw fighting in Europe, the Americas, Africa, and Asia. The end result was a major victory for Britain and another defeat for France. France's navy was completely destroyed. It ceded nearly all of its colonial holdings in the Americas, giving Britain control of all of North America East of the Mississippi River. The conflict also effectively ended French ambitions in India and paved the way for Britain's future control of the subcontinent. Britain also gained French colonial outposts in Senegal and the Gambia in Africa.

The fort that started the conflict was named after Britain's victorious prime minister William Pitt, and the area is still known to this day as Pittsburgh.

Britain succeeded in this global war in no small part because of its ability to finance massive defense expenditures, but by the end of the conflict its treasuries were drained, and it attempted to raise taxes on its colonial settlements in the Americas to help pay for the victory. This led Britain's thirteen colonies in the Americas to revolt in the American War of Independence (1775–1783). France eagerly aided the rebels in war against their rival, and the loss of the American colonies was a major setback to Britain's rising global influence. But the setback was only temporary, as Britain was in the midst of launching an economic revolution that had the most profound effect on human standards of living since the domestication of plants and animals in 10,000 BC.

The Industrial Revolution

From roughly 1760 to 1830, Britain was the central locus of the Industrial Revolution. Machines supplanted humans as the primary means of manufacturing. Steam engines and water power replaced humans and animals as the primary power source. New processes produced larger quantities of cheaper iron and steel. The Industrial Revolution made Britain the wealthiest country on Earth (surpassing the Netherlands in per capita wealth in 1780) and set the stage for continued economic growth worldwide.

Some have argued that Britain benefited from the Industrial Revolution due to dumb luck; that, for example, it was blessed with a natural abundance of coal. But a closer look suggests the revolution was the direct result of Britain's institutions. Open states tend to be more innovative, and decades before the Industrial Revolution Britain generated innovative new farming methods, such as crop rotation, that greatly increased agricultural productivity. This "agricultural revolution" increased Britain's food supply and population and allowed large numbers of people to move from the countryside to the cities to work in factories as a new industrial labor force. Additional British innovations followed that turbocharged the revolution, including the invention of James Watt's steam engine and new methods for producing iron. Finally, large amounts of capital were needed to finance the building of new machines and factories, and Britain sat on an abundance of capital, due to its role as the world's financial center. In sum, it is no accident that the Industrial Revolution occurred in a country with an open political and economic system and not elsewhere.

The French Revolution

Meanwhile, as Britain's economy was booming, France's was suffering. Paris was deeply indebted from its expansive foreign policy, including its support to the American War of Independence. Unlike Britain, it was unable to float large loans at affordable rates of interest. So, the monarchy attempted to raise taxes on its already suffering masses.

The commoners, the Third Estate, were outraged by the economic oppression. They were also inspired by Enlightenment ideals and the examples of successful democracy in the United Kingdom and the United States. In 1789 they rioted and published the Declaration of the Rights of Man and of the Citizen. In 1792, a new French Republic was proclaimed, and King Louis XVI and his family were executed in 1793.[5]

Other European monarchs were horrified by this violent revolution and feared they might be next. Soon France was at war with the rest of Europe. The French Revolutionary Wars (1792–1802) were in large part an ideological clash between the new ideals of republicanism spreading throughout Europe and the entrenched interests of the old monarchical regimes. In short, it was, at least initially, a clash between democracy and autocracy.

Republics are better able to harness the energies of a population toward international expansion and the early French republic was unleashed on Europe. In 1793, the French Republic introduced the most important military revolution since the introduction of gunpowder: the *levée en masse*. Able-bodied men between the ages of eighteen and twenty-five were conscripted for the French army. Early modern Europe saw limited warfare between mercenary or small standing armies, but the *levée en masse* would introduce the world to total war. France amassed what may have been the largest army ever created, with over one million men at arms. In addition, the early French Republic benefited from the soft power of republican ideals. Its soldiers were motivated to fight for liberty and democrats throughout Europe were inspired by the French revolution and welcomed France's armies into their homelands to overthrow monarchical overlords. Aided by mass conscription and revolutionary fervor, France managed to conquer major parts of Europe and beyond. At the end of the War of the Second Coalition, France conquered, controlled, or had installed dependent "sister republics" in the Low Countries, Italy, parts of Prussia, Switzerland, and Egypt, and regained the Louisiana territories in the Americas. French attempts to invade Great Britain, however, were thwarted.

The French Republic had, in a few years, achieved more on the battlefield than the French monarchs, including Louis XIV, had produced through decades of constant warfare.

The French Republic was greatly aided in its revolutionary wars by the brilliant exploits of a young artillery officer, Napoleon Bonaparte. Napoleon and other officers were given the freedom to take initiative on the battlefield, and he introduced innovative, new tactics that are still studied in military academies to this day.

In November 1799, however, Napoleon took France on a fateful turn for the worse. He seized his newfound status as a French war hero and, exploiting domestic political turmoil in Paris, carried out a coup d'état to establish himself as a dictator. By 1804, he was declared emperor of France. The republican phase of the war and of France's rapid ascent would soon come to an end.

The Napoleonic Wars

Napoleon continued to wage war against much of the rest of Europe. The gains made during the period of the French Republic meant that Napoleon started from a strong position. He nearly managed to establish lasting hegemony over all of Europe, but Britain proved to be an implacable foe. Britain used its growing industrial and financial power to its advantage. It invested in its naval power, greatly increasing its number of warships. Napoleon suffered major naval defeats to British Admiral Lord Nelson at the Battle of the Nile (1798) and at the Battle of Trafalgar (1805). In the Battle of Trafalgar, Lord Nelson introduced ingenious new operational concepts that confused and overwhelmed France's ships of the line. This prevented an invasion of Britain and gave London uncontested control of the high seas. Moreover, the inexhaustible British treasury allowed it to generously fund anti-French forces throughout Europe.

Perhaps the greatest cause of the decline of Napoleonic France was an autocratic own goal; in 1812, Napoleon made the fateful mistake of invading Russia. Russian forces sought to avoid direct battle with Napoleon and continually withdrew, using scorched-Earth tactics to prevent Napoleon's forces from living off the land. Napoleon eventually marched victoriously into Moscow. But he had not yet defeated the Russian army, and Russian Tsar Alexander I refused to surrender. With winter approaching, Napoleon could not continue the fight or attempt to occupy all of Russia, so he had no choice but to retreat. The Russian winter, the lack of supplies, and guerilla ambushes from Russian forces took a devastating toll. Of the half a million French forces that invaded Russia, it is estimated that only twenty-five thousand or so survived.

The other European powers, buoyed by Napoleon's retreat, rejoined the war. Napoleon fought until the bitter end, but he never recovered from the Russian disaster. On April 6, 1814, Napoleon abdicated and was exiled to the island of Elba. Remarkably, he escaped from the island the very next year and raised a new army. But he was defeated yet again by a combined British and Prussian army led by the British Duke of Wellington at Waterloo in June 1815.

Following Napoleon's defeat, the victorious powers set up the Concert of Europe system to maintain a balance of power among the major powers on the continent, including France, Prussia, Austria, and Russia. The stability on the European continent freed Britain to establish itself as the world's dominant commercial, maritime, and colonial power.

Pax Britannica

The period from the end of the Napoleonic Wars until World War I is often known as the *Pax Britannica*, or British Peace. Britain's economy boomed as it experienced a "Second Industrial Revolution." Britain introduced more inventions, including the railroad, the steamship, and the telegraph, which allowed cheaper transportation and communication and set the stage for the first era of globalization. The mechanization of production, especially in textiles, earned Britain the nickname "the workshop of the world." Its mass production of goods allowed it to become a major exporter. British GDP roughly doubled in the 19th century.[6]

Like other open states, Britain also innovated in the arts and sciences. In the 18th and 19th centuries, it produced cutting-edge thinkers, such as David Hume, Adam Smith, and John Stuart Mill; painters, including Thomas Gainsborough, William Hogarth, and Joshua Reynolds; novelists, such as Charles Dickens and the Brontë sisters; and poets, including Tennyson and Keats.

(It must be admitted that France's artistic achievements were quite impressive under autocratic rule, including the Palace of Versailles, the painting of Boucher and David, and the philosophy of Voltaire. However, the high point of French art was in the Belle Epoch under the French Third Republic, which gave us Monet, Degas, Gauguin, and Matisse, among others.)

Britain's global empire continued to expand. In 1788, Australia was settled as a British penal colony, and prisoners were sent there for decades until its leading city, Melbourne, grew to become one of the largest cities in the world. Ireland was formally merged with Great Britain to form the

United Kingdom in 1801. In 1840, the British signed a treaty with local Maori chiefs and New Zealand also became a British colony.

During the French Revolutionary and Napoleonic Wars, Britain worried that France's occupation of the Netherlands might also give it control over the Dutch Empire. Britain, therefore, seized the Cape Colony in South Africa, Mauritius, and Ceylon, including Galle, and incorporated them into its own empire instead. Britain's victory in the French Revolutionary and Napoleonic Wars won it territory previously occupied by France, including Malta and several Caribbean islands. The East India Company added territory in Asia, including Singapore (1819), Malaysia (1824), and Burma (1826). In 1839, the Opium Wars opened China to trade and gave Britain the city of Hong Kong as a colony and trading port. In 1858, India was formally added as the "crown jewel" of Britain's overseas empire.

Britain and Russia engaged in a "great game" competition over control of central Asia, but the latter was badly defeated by Britain, and its new ally France, in the Crimean War (1853–1856), leading to an agreement on British and Russian spheres of influence in the region.

With Africa as the only major continent still largely untouched by imperialism, the European powers raced to establish control in a "scramble for Africa" in the late 1800s. Britain would add to its colonial possessions: Egypt, Sudan, Somaliland (Somalia), Kenya, Uganda, Tanzania, Bechuanaland (Botswana), Seychelles, Northern and Southern Rhodesia (Zambia and Zimbabwe), Southwest Africa (Namibia), Gambia, Sierra Leone, Nigeria, Gold Coast (Ghana), Nyasaland (Malawi), Basutoland (Lesotho), and Swaziland.

In addition to its formal empire, Britain's economic and naval dominance gave it significant control, an "informal empire," over many nations around the world.

France, now also a republic, expanded its overseas empire in the late 1800s, gaining Algeria, French Indochina in Southeast Asia, and significant holdings in Africa. But, following the Napoleonic Wars, France was never again in a position to challenge for global mastery.

On the other hand, by the early 1900s, Britain was the most powerful political entity the world had ever seen. It possessed the world's largest economy, undisputed naval primacy, and a vast global empire.

Democracy versus Autocracy

The Anglo-French rivalry provides significant support for the democratic advantage theory. It is unlikely that Britain's remarkable expansion could have happened under any other form of political system. Inclusive institutions fueled British economic growth. Its open political system made British debt an attractive investment and led London to take the title of center of global finance from Amsterdam. This ability to raise debt gave Britain an inexhaustible source of funds to finance its wars for military spending and aid to allies. Democracies tend to be more open to wealth-enhancing international trade and Britain became the world's leading commercial power and trading state. It was also the center of other world-changing economic innovations, including the agricultural and industrial revolutions, which made Britain the wealthiest nation on Earth.

Britain also proved to be an effective alliance and counter-hegemonic coalition builder in the War of the Grand Alliance and even in the darkest hours of the Napoleonic Wars. Unlike Paris, under both Louis XIV and Napoleon, London was able to amass power without provoking counterbalancing coalitions.

Britain's economic base and commercial interests facilitated its rise to possess the world's most dominant naval force. And its military commanders, including the Duke of Marlborough, the Duke of Wellington, and Admiral Nelson proved to be innovative and effective on land and sea.

France, on the other hand, began this period as one of several great powers on the European continent, and it finished about where it started. Its extractive economic system under the Bourbon kings did not lead to rapid economic growth and, instead, contributed to financial decline, revolution, and regime collapse. Its financial system suffered under autocratic rule and this hindered its ability to finance its repeated wars.

France's most explosive growth in geopolitical power, from 1789 to 1798, occurred while France was a Republic. Democracies are more innovative, and it was during this time that it introduced the world to a revolution in military affairs with the *levée en masse*. Its soldiers were motivated to fight for republican ideals and conquered populations welcomed them as liberators. France's greatest collapse in power, on the other hand, occurred after it returned to dictatorship under Napoleon. There is no doubt that Napoleon's domination of Europe was remarkable and had things gone slightly differently, he might have just succeeded in becoming emperor of the world. But dictators tend to make poor decisions, and Napoleon made a doozy—getting his entire army caught in Russia in the winter. There were other mistakes as well, including a costly invasion of Spain and a stubborn refusal to accept reasonable peace offerings from Austrian foreign minister Klemens von Metternich. Napoleon's bid for mastery ended much like Louis XIV's: defeat in international warfare and regime disintegration.

In sum, following the Glorious Revolution in 1688, Great Britain experienced a remarkable explosion in its wealth and power. In a century and a half, it went from being a small and relatively poor island in the North Atlantic to becoming the most powerful state in the history of the world with a globe-spanning empire.

Its place in the global pecking order would not go unchallenged, however. For other major powers had benefited by copying Britain's model of industrialization, and some of them were steadily cutting into Britain's commanding lead. One of them was of particular concern, a revisionist autocratic power, looking to claim "its place in the sun."

CHAPTER 9 | # The United Kingdom and Germany

I N OUR LAST chapter, we left the United Kingdom as the most powerful empire the world had ever seen. But, after nearly two centuries of ascendancy, it was about to be challenged by an autocratic Germany growing in the heart of Europe. The two clashed in World War I, and the United Kingdom (UK) emerged victorious and with its largest-ever territorial expanse, expanding its empire into the Middle East. World War II took a harder toll on the UK, but, again, with the help of its navy, its financial power, and its democratic allies—and in no small part to the heedless decision-making of its autocratic rival—it once again prevailed.

The Rise of Germany

Germany did not become a unified state until the late 1800s. During the time of the Roman Republic, the territories of present-day Germany were inhabited by barbarians just outside of Rome's grasp. Throughout the Middle Ages, Germany was under the rule of the Holy Roman Empire, beginning with the reign of Otto I in AD 962. Following the cataclysmic Thirty Years' War in 1648, the Empire was weakened and it was dissolved altogether during the Napoleonic Wars. Prussia emerged as the most powerful German state over the course of the 18th and 19th centuries, and in 1871 it succeeded in reunifying disparate German-speaking entities, including Saxony and Bavaria, into a single great power: the German Empire.

Germany's unification led to a major shift in the European balance of power. Suddenly, there was a large and powerful new state in the center of Europe. In addition, Germany had adopted the practices of industrialization from the UK, and its economic growth was firing on all cylinders. The United Kingdom and other European powers took note of this rising juggernaut.

Prussia's capital, Berlin, became this new German state's seat of government and Prussia's king, Kaiser Wilhelm I, the new emperor of Germany. The German Empire was a constitutional monarchy, with the kaiser at its head and an elected parliament and government to run day-to-day affairs. Some might assume that the German Empire was a democracy because it had a legislative body. But, in fact, Kaiser Wilhelm and his chancellor, Otto von Bismarck, held ultimate authority over most matters, including foreign and defense policy. Unlike in the United Kingdom, parliament was far from supreme. Indeed, according to the widely used Polity measures, Germany was scored +1 (nondemocracy) on the eve of World War I and the United Kingdom a +8 (democracy).

The kaiser was aided in his rule by the shrewd advice of Bismarck. Indeed, his "Iron Chancellor" is often considered among the greatest statesmen of all time. Bismarck was the driving force behind Germany's unification, and he understood that a newly powerful and geographically central Germany was a potential threat to all of its neighbors. He worked constantly to reassure potential rivals of Germany's benign intent. Bismarck pursued a peaceful foreign policy, and his foremost goal was to prevent an alliance between France and Russia that would leave Germany surrounded.

Near the end of Bismarck's term and after, however, Germany adopted a more bellicose stance toward the world.[1] In the 1880s Germany participated in the Scramble for Africa, over Bismarck's objections, and assembled the third-largest global empire (after the UK and France). Present-day Cameroon, Rwanda, Burundi, Togo, Namibia, and parts of Nigeria, Tanzania, and Ghana, came under Berlin's control, as well as several islands in the Pacific and a trading post in China. Then, in 1888, Kaiser Wilhelm I died and his grandson, the 29-year-old Kaiser Wilhelm II, took power later that year. This young man was not content to keep German power under wraps, and he was eager for Germany to step up and claim its "place in the sun." Indeed, this now-common phrase was actually coined by his government to describe Germany's new and more ambitious foreign policy. He dismissed the too-cautious Iron Chancellor and replaced him with a man more supportive of his expansionist vision, Leo Caprivi.

To support his ambitious foreign policy, Kaiser Wilhelm II dramatically increased German defense spending. Germany possessed the largest army on the European continent, but Wilhelm also wanted to challenge British naval superiority. His investments in this area ignited a major Anglo-German naval arms race.[2] Beginning in 1898, Germany began rapidly building up its fleet of surface ships.

The United Kingdom responded by innovating. It developed a revolutionary next-generation surface ship, the Dreadnought. The Dreadnought was steam powered, making it the world's fastest battleship. It was also the first ship with a "main battery" of guns, which tripled the available firepower of previous warships. Germany, however, was soon able to copy the UK's model, building dreadnoughts of its own.[3]

Germany's aggressive new foreign policy provoked the exact counterbalancing coalition that Bismarck had worked so hard to forestall. In 1894, France and Russia, fearing Germany's rise, formed an alliance. In 1904, the United Kingdom signed an alliance with its onetime rival, France, and, in 1907, a separate convention with Russia. This overlapping set of alliance arrangements formed a Triple Entente against Germany. For years, Germany had been aligned with the Austro-Hungarian Empire and Italy in a Triple Alliance of its own. The battle lines of World War I were drawn.

World War I

The Austro-Hungarian Empire was attempting to hold together a fractious, multiethnic polity. On June 28, 1914, a Serbian nationalist, Gavrilo Princip, assassinated the heir to the Austro-Hungarian throne, Archduke Franz Ferdinand, in Sarajevo. Princip and his secret society, the Black Hand, dreamed that the Slavic portions of the Austro-Hungarian Empire could break away and join with Serbia to form a larger and independent all-Slavic state. The assassination prompted the Austro-Hungarian Empire to demand vengeance against Serbia, which it believed sponsored the attack. Vienna consulted with its German allies about how best to respond. Kaiser Wilhelm II famously issued a "blank check" for Austria-Hungary to do as it saw fit. Vienna issued an unreasonable ultimatum to Serbia and, when Serbia refused, Austria-Hungary declared war. Russia, bound to Serbia by Slavic ethnic ties, threatened to intervene. To show that it was serious, Moscow began mobilizing its military against Austria-Hungary. Recall that Germany was aligned with Austria-Hungary and would be implicated in any war between

Russia and Austria-Hungary. Berlin tried and failed to persuade Moscow to back down.

Sensing an impending two-front war against both Russia and Russia's treaty ally France, Germany decided to strike first. It had an off-the-shelf plan to deal with this long-feared, two-front war problem. The Schlieffen Plan imagined that Germany would first quickly defeat France in the west and then pivot to fight Russia in the east. On August 2, 1914, it invaded Luxembourg on its way to France. World War I had begun.

Scholars vigorously debate the causes of World War I. Many describe it as a war that no one wanted; they see a series of miscalculations gone terribly awry in a complicated world with many great powers enmeshed in entangling alliances.[4] More recent accounts see it basically as a war of German aggression launched by a young kaiser bent on world domination.[5] In either case, it became the largest and bloodiest war the world had ever seen.

At the outset, many anticipated the war would be over quickly. Military strategists thought that new and deadly technologies, like the machine gun, would provide a quick victory to whichever side attacked first.[6] Instead, all sides became bogged down in trench warfare in which the front lines barely moved over the course of years of fighting. The basic battle tactic was to charge one's forces through a no-man's land of trenches, barbed wire, and artillery barrages, straight into the machine-gun fire of the dug-in enemy. These charges often proved futile, but resulted in some of the deadliest battles in human history. At the Battle of the Somme, in 1916, for example, over one million men were killed and injured over the course of several months.

To break the stalemate, the combatants tried all manner of tactics, but nothing seemed to work. They employed chemical weapons in an attempt to clear the other side's trenches. The British and the French also tried a new technology, armored tanks, but they did not prove to be decisive.

In October 1917, Russia was beset by a revolution that overthrew the monarchy and brought to power communist revolutionaries. Preoccupied by this civil war at home, Russia withdrew from the war. It soon became clear that the war would be decided on the stalemated Western Front.

At sea, the British navy dominated. Despite spending vast sums on the arms race, Germany never reached naval parity with the UK, and its battleships remained bottled up in port for most of the war. Germany used its U-Boat submarines to attack British commercial vessels in an effort to disrupt British trade and weaken it economically. In 1915, Germany adopted a policy of unrestricted submarine warfare in which it sank civilian ships of its enemies or those trading with them without warning. The kaiser anticipated that this would likely bring the United States into the war at some point, but he decided that the benefits of bleeding British commerce were worth it. Germany sank several commercial ships with Americans on board, including the *Lusitania*. To add insult to injury, the United States learned from the infamous Zimmerman Telegram that Germany had attempted to prod Mexico into invading the United States. These developments provoked Washington to declare war in April 1917.

By 1918, Germany was exhausted and financially drained after four years of fighting. The United Kingdom was still able to raise debt to pay for its war efforts and it reasserted control over the high seas with new military technologies. British depth charges were employed, for example, to sink German U-Boats. Moreover, the adoption of new ground warfare tactics, such as concentrated firepower, and cover and concealment, helped to break through the stalemate of trench warfare.[7] But nothing may have been more important than the arrival of large numbers of fresh American troops.

In the Hundred Days Offensive of the summer of 1918, the Allied forces continually punched through German lines. Germany engaged in tactical retreats and fought rear-guard actions, but it soon became clear that this was all being done in a losing cause. The kaiser abdicated on November 9, and two days later, at 11 am (the eleventh hour of the eleventh day of the eleventh month), an armistice was reached, bringing World War I to a close.

The peace that followed was enshrined in the Treaty of Versailles.[8] Germany accepted responsibility for the war, handed over nearly all of its overseas empire, and was forced to demobilize its armed forces and pay steep war reparations.

The United Kingdom, on the other hand, emerged from the war with its largest-ever territorial expanse, picking up colonies from the defeated Axis powers, including the Emirate of Trans-Jordon (including present-day Israel, Palestine, Jordan, and parts of Syria and Iraq) from the Ottoman Empire. It also gained Cameroon, Togo, and Tanzania from Germany. After World War I, the British Empire covered roughly 25 percent of the Earth's land mass (Figure 9.1).[9]

The United States was also a major victor of World War I. While on paper, the United States possessed the world's largest economy at this time, it was not yet willing to step up and play a global leadership role. Indeed, U.S. President Woodrow Wilson championed the cause of a League of Nations at the Paris peace talks, but the U.S. Senate refused to ratify the agreement. It preferred that the United States retreat to isolationism on the other side of the Atlantic.

The twenty years between 1919 and 1939 are now referred to as the "interwar years."[10] Many had hoped that World War I would be the "war to end

FIGURE 9.1 The British Empire, 1921

all wars," but it was just the first part of a continuing conflict between an autocratic Germany and its democratic rivals. Many historians see much contingency in the interwar years.[11] Had the allies been more forgiving in their terms after World War I, or had Hitler been a better painter and decided not to go into politics, World War II might have been avoided. But international relations scholars see more fundamental dynamics at play.[12] The rise of one power and the decline of another often leads to major-power war. In this telling, World War I and II were the same war, with a twenty-year half-time in between.

World War II

The buzzer to start the second half sounded in 1933, when Adolf Hitler was appointed chancellor of the Weimar Republic in Germany. Within a year, he had succeeded in turning Germany into his personal dictatorship. Hitler harbored repellent racial ideas about the purity of the German race and how his nation had been weakened by Jews and other foreign influences. He desired "lebensraum," territory into which the German nation could expand. Hitler violated the terms of the Versailles Treaty and rearmed the German military.

In 1938, building on popular support to build a "Greater Germany" for German-speaking peoples, he peacefully annexed Austria. He then pressed to have the German-speaking areas of Czechoslovakia, the Sudetenland, incorporated into Germany. At the Munich Peace Conference in September 1938, the United Kingdom and France agreed to give Germany the territory, with British Prime Minister Neville Chamberlain boasting that, by appeasing the dictator, he had achieved "peace in our time." Instead, in March of 1939, Hitler went ahead and invaded and occupied the rest of Czechoslovakia in violation of the Munich agreement.

Fearing that Poland may be next, the UK and France promised to defend Poland. But Hitler was not deterred. As he said, "Our enemies are little worms. I saw them at Munich." Instead, Hitler signed his own pact—this one with the Soviet Union's dictator, Joseph Stalin. In this Molotov-Ribbentrop Pact, signed in August 1939, the two dictators agreed not to attack each other and to divide the rest of Eastern Europe, Poland and the Baltic states, between them.

In September 1939, Hitler followed through and invaded Poland. Days later, the UK and France were finally ready to stand up to Hitler's aggression. They declared war on Germany, and World War II began.

With his eastern flank secure due to his agreement with Moscow, Hitler could focus on Western Europe. In the Spring of 1940, he struck. Unlike in World War I, Germany this time succeeded in taking France and the Low Countries with amazing rapidity. Tanks and aircraft had been used in World War I, but the Nazis combined them into a new blitzkrieg style of warfare that went over and around the French defenses. Benito Mussolini in Italy hopped on Hitler's bandwagon and invaded France. By June, German troops were marching down the Champs-Élysées.

Hitler, now in control of most of Western Europe, turned his sights on knocking the United Kingdom out of the war. In July, German air forces began conducting raids on London and the Royal Air Force (RAF) defended the city. Until this point, wars had been conducted on land or sea, but the Battle of Britain was the world's first true aerial battle. While London was devastated in the Blitz of German bombing runs, Hitler failed to defeat the RAF, or force London to surrender. This was a turning point in the war; for the first time, Hitler's advance was stalled.

Stymied in the West, Hitler turned his appetites back East. The fact that he had signed a nonaggression pact with the Soviet Union proved not too great an obstacle to his ambitions for world domination and, in June 1941, he stabbed his ally in the back. Hitler invaded Russia in Operation Barbarossa. Nazi forces made impressive advances early and nearly succeeded in taking Moscow. But Russia held on.

Hitler was now knee-deep in the Russian heartland and winter was coming. Hitler was so confident going into the conflict that he did not even provide his troops with adequate winter clothing. As temperatures dropped to −35 degrees Fahrenheit, Nazi troops suffered frostbite and froze to death. Some slaughtered their horses to fashion makeshift fur coats. Meanwhile, they were facing properly outfitted Soviet troops used to surviving the Russian winter. By December 1941, in increasingly nasty weather, the Soviet Union turned the tide at the Battle of Moscow and began the long process of pushing the Nazis out of Russia. Hitler had not learned from Napoleon's blunder. It is even more surprising because in *Mein Kampf*, Hitler had written that fighting a two-front war was the worst possible mistake a military leader could make.

If things were not going poorly enough for Hitler, later that same month, he picked a fight with a rising superpower. The United States had wanted to avoid the conflict raging in Europe. It was willing to play the role of the "arsenal of democracy" and provide weapons to the UK in the lend-lease program, but fighting Nazis was a step too far. This would all change on December 7, 1941.

As Germany was marauding in Europe, imperial Japan was doing the same in Asia. It had taken parts of China and Southeast Asia in search of natural resources and to create a Japanese empire, under the banner of the "Greater East Asia Co-Prosperity Sphere." In response to its invasion of French Indochina, the United States put in place a complete oil and gas embargo on Japan. The sanctions threatened to economically strangle the resource-poor island. The Japanese emperor was on the horns of a dilemma. He could back down and accept the return to a little Japan. Or, he could escalate in an attempt to get the United States to acquiesce to his designs for Asian hegemony. He calculated that U.S. society was soft and that it did not have the stomach for a prolonged war in Asia. If he could just bloody America's nose, Washington would back down and Japan could have its way.

On December 7, 1941, in a "a date which will live in infamy," Japan conducted a sneak attack on the U.S. naval base at Pearl Harbor, Hawaii.[13] The United States proved to be a sleeping dragon, not a paper tiger. And now it was awake. The United States declared war on Japan the very next day.

At this point, it is conceivable that the United States could have stayed out of the war in Europe. But, on December 11, Hitler, perhaps foolishly, declared war on the United States. Washington immediately returned the favor.

The democracy-autocracy showdown was now set, with the free nations of the United States, the United Kingdom, and France (and the autocratic Soviet Union) on one side, and Nazi Germany, fascist Italy, and imperial Japan on the other.

In early 1942, the Allied powers set their strategy. There would be three more years of hard fighting, but it would be a repeated story of Axis retreats in the face of Allied advances. In February 1943, German forces surrendered at Stalingrad, losing what may have been history's bloodiest battle with upward of 2 million men killed in less than six months. In May 1943, the Allied powers defeated the Axis powers in North Africa. In June 1943, the Allies began the strategic bombing of Germany. As in the Peloponnesian and Punic Wars, Sicily returned to center stage of great power competition. In July 1943, the Allies conducted an amphibious invasion of the island and began the march up the Italian Peninsula. Mussolini was ousted from power, and the new Italian government surrendered, switched sides, and declared war on Germany.

D-Day came in June 1944. The Allied powers conducted the large-scale amphibious invasion of Normandy to take occupied France back from Germany. Paris was liberated in August. In late 1944, the Soviet Union pushed German forces back in Eastern Europe, through Poland, Romania, and Serbia.

A similar story was playing out in the Pacific. In 1942, the United States defeated Japan at the Battle of Midway. In 1943, Japan lost the Battle of Guadalcanal. From 1943 through 1945, the United States and its allies conducted the "island hopping" campaign to retake strategically important islands from Japanese occupation. In 1944, strategic bombing of Japan began, leading to the devastating firebombing of Tokyo.

In early 1945, Germany itself was invaded from both east and west. By April, American and Soviet forces were shaking hands at the Elbe River in Germany. Hitler committed suicide in a bunker below Berlin later that month, and, in May, Germany offered its unconditional surrender.

The Allies called on Japan to follow suit. The emperor refused. On August 6 and 9, 1945, the United States introduced the world to the ultimate instrument of military force, dropping nuclear weapons on Hiroshima and Nagasaki. Japan surrendered on August 15.

After six years of fighting, World War II had come to an end. The world's leading democracies, the United Kingdom, France, and the United States, came out on top, as did China and the Soviet Union. The leading autocracies of the early 20th century, Nazi Germany, fascist Italy, and imperial Japan, ceased to exist altogether. Instead, they were refashioned in the image of their conquerors. Within a few years, West Germany, Italy, and Japan were democracies formally allied with the United States.

Democracy versus Autocracy

The Anglo-German rivalry once again supports the democratic advantage thesis. Germany clearly lost. The result in this case was due as much to autocratic vices as to democratic virtues. Theory suggests that autocrats, surrounded by few if any trusted advisors, engage in heedless decision-making, and Kaiser Wilhelm II and Hitler demonstrated this tendency in spades. At the broadest level, not only did they start world wars that they lost badly, these wars also ended their regimes.

But poor decision-making can be seen at more fine-grained levels as well. Kaiser Wilhelm II decided to engage in a costly naval arms race in a capability that proved useless in the war. His *Weltpolitik* provoked the rest of Europe into lining up against him. His blank check to Austria-Hungary placed his fate in the hands of a vengeful emperor in Vienna. Most importantly, an incautious war plan, including unrestricted submarine warfare forced a reluctant United States to enter the war.

Hitler also started a world war that he lost. He wasted resources on an evil pet project, the Holocaust, which could have been productively directed toward the war effort. Had he stopped at controlling Western Europe, he might have succeeded, but he needlessly invaded Russia and declared war on the United States.

It should also be noted that Japan's decision to bomb Pearl Harbor is literally the textbook example of poor autocratic decision-making.[14]

The German military proved to be highly effective on the battlefield and more innovative than most autocracies, developing modern ground tactics at the end of World War I and blitzkrieg warfare on the eve of World War II. Still, tactical success could not compensate for strategic blunders and Germany's inability to contest Britain's naval supremacy was a handicap in both wars.

Germany successfully industrialized and enjoyed a strong economy, but its relative financial weakness proved to be a liability, as Britain was able to raise funds to finance its war efforts, while Berlin financially exhausted itself.

The UK displayed some of the typical strengths of democracies in its rivalry with Germany. It possessed one of the world's largest economies and it was the center of global finance. Its ability to raise cheap credit was critical to sustaining its war effort. It forged effective alliances with other states, including Russia, France, and especially the United States. America's participation was decisive in winning both wars, and this dominant democracy chose to intervene on behalf of democrats and the UK and not Germany's dictators. London was a dominant maritime power and was never seriously contested on the high seas. It also innovated militarily with the *Dreadnought*, and its democratic ally, the United States, invented nuclear weapons.

A supposed democratic weakness is undue legal and moral constraints. But Hitler's villainy did not seem to help, but led to a Holocaust that undermined his war effort. Moreover, the democracies matched tough measures with tough times, including the firebombing of Dresden and Tokyo and the use of nuclear weapons to end the war.

Both sides, not just the autocracies, were able to mobilize massive resources toward national goals. The United Kingdom, for example, spent roughly 50 percent of its GDP on defense at the height of World Wars I and II.[15] And the United States launched a crash program to invent and deploy nuclear weapons in a few short years.

One democratic liability, the limited capactiy to take bold and decisive action, was highly salient in this conflict. As Hitler engaged in early territorial conquests, the democracies dithered. The United Kingdom and France were unwilling to contain his expansion and instead preferred to appease him. Even as Hitler nearly succeeded in conquering all of Europe, America stayed on the sidelines. It took a direct attack on American soil to prompt the United States to enter the fray. As Winston Churchill said, "You can always count on the Americans to do the right thing after they have tried everything else." Still, despite their tardy start, the democracies eventually stepped up to the occasion and prevailed handily in the end.

Although the UK was on the winning side, it was devastated by World War II and no longer in a position to play the role of global leader. Moreover, with some American prodding, it voluntarily ceded almost all of its overseas empire in the years following the war. Many expected that the United States would again retreat back across the Atlantic into its isolation. Instead, Washington was finally willing to assume the mantle of democratic global leadership.

| The United States and
the Soviet Union

O TTO VON BISMARCK famously said that "God has special providence for fools, drunks, and the United States of America." Divine providence may not have hurt, but it was America's domestic political institutions that transformed a smattering of British colonies in North America into, first, an independent nation and, then, a global superpower with a network of allies and partners spanning six continents. The United States faced off against the Soviet Union for a half century during the Cold War. But Washington possessed the better institutions, and the stress of the competition caused Moscow's autocratic political system to collapse altogether.

In the post–Cold War period that followed, Washington deepened and expanded the *Pax Americana*, and spread unprecedented levels of global peace, prosperity, and freedom. For the first time since ancient Rome, a single superpower so overawed any potential competitors that great power rivalry itself came to a temporary halt.

The Rise of the United States

The United States benefited from the open political institutions that Britain seeded in its soil and it improved on them. Its founding fathers, inspired by Polybius, Montesquieu, and others, established a republican form of government with checks and balances among separate, but co-equal branches of government. The U.S. Constitution went into operation in 1789. Rather than a hereditary king as the chief executive as some had advocated, the Americans settled on a new presidential system of government. The people vote for the president and representatives in an assembly, the U.S. Congress. A separate judicial branch reviews laws and ensures their consistency with the constitution. The U.S. Bill of Rights, the first ten amendments to the constitution, grants American citizens a wide range of political and civil liberties. Polity scores the United States as a democracy throughout its history.

After ejecting its British overlords, this new democracy rapidly expanded in North America and then beyond.[1] Thanks to Britain's victory in the Seven Years' War, the United States already possessed most of North America east of the Mississippi River. Then, the young nation preyed on the possessions of the European powers in North America as they were busy destroying each other in the Napoleonic Wars. In 1803, President Thomas Jefferson took advantage of Napoleon's financial troubles and bought much of France's territory west of the Mississippi at bargain-bottom prices in the Louisiana Purchase. In the War of 1812, the United States basically tried and failed to take British Canada. But, in 1818, London ultimately ceded to the United States all of its territories below the 49th parallel, marking the contemporary border between Canada and the United States. (In 1846 that border was extended to the Pacific Ocean to also give the United States the Oregon territories). President James Monroe purchased Florida from a financially weary Spain in 1819. Then, in 1823, he issued his "Monroe Doctrine," warning European powers against imperial aggrandizement in the Western Hemisphere.

The United States' first major showdown with an autocracy was not with a European power, but with state-sponsored pirates in North Africa. To protect is commercial interests in the Mediterranean, the United States founded its navy and won the Barbary Wars from 1801 to 1815. There were also challenges on its southern border. In the early-to-mid 1800s, Mexico was dominated by a warlord-turned-dictator named Antonio López de Santa Anna. The Republic of Texas declared independence from Mexico in 1836 and soon sought annexation to America. Ten years later, shortly after Texas became a U.S. state, Mexico attacked. After two years of fighting, U.S. forces occupied Mexico City and the conquered nation acknowledged U.S. control of Texas and ceded the territories of New Mexico and California.

The United States nearly tore itself apart in a civil war from 1861 to 1865, but it soon recovered. The United States also continued the conflicts, started by early European settlers, against Native American tribes. These American Indian Wars lasted until the early 20th century and resulted in expanded territorial control for the United States and the assimilation, destruction, or removal to reservations, of the native peoples. Washington prevailed in the Spanish-American War in 1898 and won Cuban independence and overseas colonies in Guam, Puerto Rico, and the Philippines.

In the meantime, America's economy was booming. Without a landed aristocracy as in the old world, many of America's political elites came from the commercial and financial classes and they had incentives to set up rules conducive to business. The United States adopted the practices of the Industrial Revolution from Great Britain and shifted from an agrarian to an industrial economy. Canals, steamboats, and then railroads connected the country's major metropolitan areas, facilitating transcontinental trade and a division of labor. Immigrants flooded into the United States from around the world searching for a better life, and their major entry point into the new world, New York City, became a hub of frenetic business activity. America's open system also buzzed with creativity and began spinning off transformative inventions, including Thomas Edison's light bulb in 1879, the machine gun in 1884, the assembly line in 1901, and the airplane in 1903.

The United States also adopted successful financial innovations from London and Amsterdam. The U.S. government issued its first bonds in the revolutionary war and the "Buttonwood Agreement," signed under a buttonwood tree on Wall Street in New York City, set up America's first stock market in 1792. Money flowed into the market from overseas investors looking to make returns on the United States' flourishing railroad industry.

The period from 1870 to 1900 is known as America's "Gilded Age," and, indeed, by the 1890s, the United States had surpassed the United Kingdom as the world's largest economy.[2]

But the United States was not yet a geopolitical force outside of North America. It was the wealthiest country in the world, but it lagged behind European powers in other major indicators of military and diplomatic strength through the early 1900s.[3]

As we saw in the last chapter, the United States was dragged reluctantly into World War I and World War II. To win those global conflicts, it transformed its economic capabilities into military might, but U.S. leaders from George Washington onward had always warned about becoming entangled in Europe's rivalries. After World War I, U.S. leaders decided to return home and many expected the same outcome in 1945.

But with the rise of an autocratic great power threatening to dominate Europe and undermine democracy and capitalism globally, retreat no longer seemed like an acceptable option.

The Cold War

World War II destroyed the erstwhile major powers of Europe and left two superpowers standing on both ends of the European continent.[4] In the beginning, there was some hope that the United States and the Soviet Union might actually become partners. After all, they had been allies in World War II, and their armed forces were left occupying much of Europe and Asia. In a series of wartime summits at Tehran, Yalta, and Potsdam, U.S. and Soviet leaders decided that they would be responsible for rebuilding the nations under their control at the end of the war (Western Europe, Japan, and South Korea for the United States, and Eastern Europe and North Korea for the Soviet Union) and that they would allow free elections to choose the new leaders of the occupied countries.

The partnership was quickly torn asunder, however, when the Soviet Union's dictator, Joseph Stalin, failed to live up to his postwar summit commitments. Instead of allowing elections, he installed communist puppet regimes in Albania, Bulgaria, Czechoslovakia, East Germany, Hungary, Poland, Romania, and North Korea. Former British prime minister Winston Churchill decried this new "Iron Curtain" falling across Europe in a speech at Westminster College in 1946. The European portion of this "communist bloc" solidified into the Warsaw Pact alliance in 1955. China became Moscow's formal ally in 1950 after Mao Zedong and his Communists emerged victorious in the Chinese civil war.

Stalin's decision to take over Eastern Europe was motivated in part by understandable security concerns; Russia had been invaded from the West multiple times before, and Soviet control of Eastern Europe would provide a buffer zone between Russia and potentially hostile forces in the West.

But there were ideological motives as well. The Soviet Union was a Communist dictatorship, and its leaders believed that they would lead the way in spreading communist workers' revolutions to every nation on Earth. (Polity scored the Soviet Union as a an autocracy throughout the Cold War). Moscow was hostile to the Western system of capitalism, and it supported communist political parties in Western Europe and worldwide. Moscow would eventually succeed in inspiring communist takeovers in Cuba, Vietnam, and elsewhere.

It was not at all clear how the United States would respond to this challenge. Many in the United States wanted to come back home. But this would have left the Soviet Red Army as the dominant military power in Europe. If the United States had withdrawn its forces, Europe could have been vulnerable to Soviet domination. The United States had just fought a world war to prevent Europe from being dominated by a hostile autocratic power. Moreover, the spread of communism would threaten democratic forms of government around the world, including potentially in the United States itself.

Washington ultimately decided it shouldered the responsibility for making the world safe for democracy. In 1946, a midcareer State Department official, George Kennan, sent a "long telegram" coining the term that would become American strategy for the next half century: "containment."[5] The United States would seek to contain Soviet expansion by pushing back against aggressive Soviet policies with economic, political, and, if necessary, military might. Consistent with the central theme of this book, Kennan believed that the Soviet Union's autocratic system contained fundamental flaws and that, if its expansion were contained, it would eventually collapse under the weight of its own inherent contradictions.

The democracy versus autocracy showdown was set.

As part of this strategy, the United States and its democratic allies built the world that we inhabit today.[6] At the end of World War II, the United States possessed almost half of world GPD and its military occupied major parts of Europe and Asia. Washington, like Moscow, could have sought a formal empire. Instead, it built an international system that resembled its domestic political model, with international institutions that gives all members, regardless of their wealth and power, representation and voice.

In the security realm, the United Nations (UN) was founded in 1945 to provide a forum for major powers to discuss geopolitical differences without resort to warfare. The North Atlantic Treaty Organization (NATO) was established in 1949. While American power gives Washington significant influence, the Alliance formally works by consensus, giving even the smallest members a say in the exercise of American power. The founding members included the Western powers that had been victorious in World War II or had been occupied by Allied forces: Belgium, Canada, Denmark, France, Iceland, Italy, Luxembourg, Netherlands, Norway, Portugal, the United Kingdom, and the United States. Later, West Germany, Greece, Turkey, and Spain joined the group. The United States also signed formal defense pacts with friendly states in Asia, including Australia and New Zealand (1951), Japan (1954), the Philippines (1951), Thailand (1954), and, after the Korean War, South Korea (1953).

As a liberal leviathan, the United States sought to create an open economic system based on the free flow of goods and capital across borders. The framework for this globalizing order was drawn up by the United States and its allies at a resort in Bretton Woods, New Hampshire, in 1944. Instead of subjugating vanquished nations, like Germany and Japan, the United States rebuilt them. The United States aided the devastated nations of Europe through the Marshall Plan. The World Bank and the International Monetary Fund (IMF) were set up with the goal of helping battered nations rebuild and reintegrate into the global economy. Washington also helped itself and its allies grow rich by encouraging free trade policies. The General Agreement on Tariffs and Trade (GATT), later to become the World Trade Organization (WTO), ratcheted down trade barriers and enmeshed the free world in international commerce. This post–World War II global economic arrangement is often referred to as the "Bretton Woods System."

Throughout its sphere of influence, the United States promoted democratic institutions and encouraged people to select their own leaders. New democracies were set up in Germany, Japan, Italy, and elsewhere. Washington also sought to counter communist infiltration in Western Europe, the United States, and around the world.

With the exception of the United Nations, the Soviet bloc did not participate in these institutions of the free world, and Cold War hostilities prevented the development of a United Nations that could bridge the divide. The world was, therefore, divided into two rival blocs and spheres of influence with very little interaction between them. On one side was the liberal world order led by the United States. On the other side was the communist bloc under the leadership of the Soviet Union. Both sides saw the other as a threat not just to their national security, but to their very way of life.

The superpowers competed throughout the world to convince neutral and nonaligned countries to join their side. They squared off in constant proxy conflicts in every major world region, including in Korea (1950–1953), Congo (1960–1965), Vietnam (1955–1975), Afghanistan (1979–1989), Nicaragua (1981–1990), and elsewhere. The United States supported democratic and capitalist forces (or at least anti-communist forces) and the Soviet Union backed communist (or at least anti-American) factions.

In addition, the superpowers played dangerous games of nuclear brinkmanship. The United States invented nuclear weapons in 1945 and the Soviet Union quickly followed suit in 1949. Nuclear weapons ushered in a revolution in military affairs. The high cost of nuclear warfare deterred major power war, but it gave rise to a new kind of military contest: the nuclear crisis. In these high-stakes games of nuclear chicken, both sides raised the risk of nuclear Armageddon in the hope that the other side would back down before things spun out of control. In the Berlin Crisis (1958–1961) and the Cuban Missile Crisis (1962), the United States achieved its basic goals, maintaining its presence in the first case and forcing a withdrawal of Soviet missiles in the second.

Soviet leaders concluded that American nuclear superiority aided U.S. victories, and they vowed to close the gap.[7] The superpowers arms-raced for advantage. By the mid-1970s, the Soviet Union was catching up. Impending Soviet nuclear parity helped to persuade U.S. President Richard Nixon and his national security adviser and Secretary of State Henry Kissinger that it was best for the United States to seek an off-ramp from the competition. They negotiated a "détente" with their ideological rival and locked in quantitative nuclear parity in a series of arms control agreements, beginning with the Strategic Arms Limitation Talks Agreement (SALT) I in 1972.

By the late 1970s, many Americans even feared that the Soviet Union was pulling ahead in the Cold War competition.[8] The Soviet Union had achieved a remarkable level of industrialization and growth through state-led planning, while the U.S. economy was suffering through an oil crisis and "stagflation." The United States had failed in Vietnam, and the "domino theory" predicted that additional countries would also fall to communism. In 1979, Washington lost an ally in Tehran, and U.S. diplomats were held hostage for over one year. In that same year, Moscow invaded Afghanistan, showing that it was still intent on further expansion. Moreover, the U.S. Committee on the Present Danger warned that the Soviet Union was gaining a quantitative edge in several important military capabilities. Indeed, the Correlates of War CINC scores, widely used by political scientists to measure national power, ranked the Soviet Union as the most powerful country in the world in the 1970s.

In fact, however, the cracks in the Soviet system were already beginning to show. The Soviet alliance system had always been held together by coercion, not attraction. Moscow had to use military force to keep its allies from defecting. When the people of Berlin had a choice between communist East Berlin and democratic West Berlin, they voted with their feet and fled to the West. Moscow had to build the Berlin Wall in 1961 to physically trap them inside the Soviet empire. Anti-Soviet uprisings took place in Hungary in 1956 and again in Czechoslovakia in 1968. The Warsaw Pact mobilized to crush the dissidents. Indeed, the Warsaw Pact's most notable military engagements during the Cold War were invasions of its own members to keep them in line. When the Soviet Union and China found themselves in a border dispute in 1969, Moscow threatened nuclear war against its "ally."

The Soviet Union's troubles extended beyond diplomacy. It was struggling to keep up economically. America's open system allowed it to harness the nation's vast potential and actualize it into global leadership. Throughout the 1970s and 1980s, roughly 25 percent of the world's economic activity occurred within U.S. territory. The U.S. economy provided the perfect cocktail for radical economic innovation. The United States produced a consumer economy and a standard of living that was the world's envy, including among those living behind the Iron Curtain. American wealth also contributed to American soft power. Rock and roll, Hollywood, and Coca-Cola were aspects of American popular culture admired around the world.

U.S. growth and vitality was also aided by brain drain, as the world's sharpest minds fled autocracy in Europe during the World Wars and the Cold War to find freedom in the United States. Indeed, the United States was able to build the nuclear weapons necessary to win World War II due to help from foreign scientists who immigrated to the United States. Henry Kissinger, an architect of America's Cold War strategy, was a German-Jewish émigré. New York became America's business capital in part because it was the port of debarkation for hard-working immigrants looking to strike it rich in the new world.

Like other liberal leviathans in the past, the United States also became the center for innovation in the arts and sciences. Leading artists, writers, musicians, and scientists working in the United States in the twentieth century included: Jackson Pollock, Andy Warhol, Ernest Hemingway, F. Scott Fitzgerald, William Faulkner, Arnold Schoenberg, John Cage, Albert Einstein, and James Watson. Some leading artists, including Mark Rothko, Marc Chagall, and Igor Stravinsky, fled their homeland in the Soviet Union for better lives in the United States.

In contrast, the Soviet Union's autocratic form of government had profoundly negative effects on the nature of the Soviet economy. Centralized power resulted in a centralized, planned economy. Moscow's planners were able to generate high rates of industrialization and economic growth in the short term through forced industrialization. According to official Soviet statistics (which were likely exaggerated), the Soviet Union's annual growth rate was 14 percent in the 1920s and 10 percent in the 1950s.[9] As theory would lead us to believe, however, a planned economy cannot deliver sustained high rates of economic growth over the longer term. As Acemoglu and Robinson explain, "you can move someone to a factory, [but] you cannot force people to think and have good ideas by threatening to shoot them."[10] Without market competition, managers had little incentive to be efficient or turn out high-quality products and workers had scant motivation to put in a hard day of labor. In sum, human planners are simply not as efficient as the free market in allocating goods and services.

Moscow's imperative to compete with the United States meant that there were always resources for military expenditures, but this led to a "hypermilitarized" economy that crowded out investment in the commercial sector.[11] In 1985, during the vaunted Reagan military buildup, U.S. military spending only accounted for 5.9 percent of U.S. GDP.[12] The Soviet Union spent almost the same aggregate amount, but from a much smaller economic base, meaning that defense expenditures made up a whopping 17 percent of GDP. All of these factors operated as brakes on Russian economic development. Indeed, by the end of the Cold War, it could barely provide for its own people. As the old joke had it, people pretended to work and the state pretended to pay them.

Finally, despite quantitative parity and even advantages in some areas, the Soviet Union was not the United States' equal at the highest levels of technological-military competition. The Soviet Union beat the United States into outer space with the Sputnik satellite test of 1957. But this "sputnik moment" lit a fire under Washington that elevated the funding of basic science and research and development to become a foremost priority. The United States landed a man on the moon a decade later and never looked back.

Similarly, in the nuclear arms race, arms control agreements locked in quantitative parity, but Washington continued to outpace Moscow with qualitative advantages. The United States developed stealth aircraft, precision-guided munitions (PGMs), and network-centric warfare.

The United States also excelled in antisubmarine warfare.[13] The sine qua non of nuclear deterrence is the possession of a secure, second-strike capability. A country must be able to ride out an enemy nuclear attack and retain enough surviving warheads to retaliate with a devastating second strike. The best way to ensure one's nuclear weapons survive is to place them on submarines at sea. An enemy might be able to launch a massive nuclear attack against one's missile silos, air bases, and naval bases, but tracking down submarines in the Earth's vast oceans is a difficult task.

Except the United States succeeded in doing just this time and time again.[14] The United States became so skilled at tracking the Soviet Union's nuclear submarines that Moscow gave up and adopted a "bastion strategy." In other words, instead of sending its nuclear submarines into the deep ocean they simply submerged them near their own coastline. They were safe for a while. But then, the U.S. Navy became skilled at holding Russian submarines at risk in their bastions too. The Soviet Union rightly feared that they lacked a survivable nuclear deterrent.

And things were only about to get worse for Moscow. The Cold War military competition was about to kick into high gear. In 1981, President Ronald Reagan entered office. He was determined to overturn "détente," challenge the nation he called an "evil empire," and develop a strategy to "roll back" communism around the world. Of greatest concern in Moscow, however, was Reagan's promise to make nuclear-armed missiles obsolete through the development of a Strategic Defense Initiative (SDI) missile defense system. While Reagan's Star Wars system was little more than a distant dream at the time, Moscow's leaders understood that they would not be able to keep pace with the United States in an increasingly sophisticated strategic arms race.

Given its weakening position across the board, the Soviet leadership decided that changes were needed if Moscow was going to continue to compete. In 1985, the new Soviet Premier Mikhail Gorbachev announced a new policy of *Glasnost* (openness) and *Perestroika* (restructuring). The intention was to selectively incorporate political and economic reforms to reboot Communism for a new era. Instead, it was the beginning of the end. The talk of new political and economic liberalization created new expectations and hopes among subjugated peoples. Unlike his predecessors, Gorbachev was unwilling to use military force to crack down on democratic movements in Eastern Europe. A mistake at the Berlin Wall border crossing in 1989 led a guard to allow people to begin crossing freely and, suddenly, the Wall came crashing down. Two years later, the mighty Soviet Union itself disintegrated into fifteen newly independent states.[15]

The Post–Cold War World

Following the end of the Cold War, many predicted that, with the Soviet threat removed, the U.S.-led order would dissolve as well.[16] NATO would disband and great power rivalry would return among the major powers of Western Europe. Instead the United States only further expanded its influence.

America's formal alliance system grew. Former countries of the Warsaw Pact, and even the constituent states of the former Soviet Union, rushed to join America's camp. NATO was enlarged to include Poland, Hungary, and the Czech Republic in 1999; Bulgaria, Estonia, Latvia, Lithuania, Romania, Slovakia, and Slovenia in 2004; Albania and Croatia in 2009; and Montenegro in 2017. At the time of writing, Bosnia and Herzegovina, Georgia, North Macedonia, and Ukraine were additional aspiring members.

Throughout time, great powers have attempted to promote their own domestic political systems as models to others, but no country achieved more success in this regard than the United States in the 1990s and 2000s. Many saw the U.S. model of open markets and politics as the only legitimate form of government, and democracy and capitalism spread around the world. Former communist countries were incorporated into the global economy for the first time and levels of international trade and investment hit record highs. Freedom flourished as well, with more people were living under democratic forms of government than any time in world history.

At home, America's open economic model continued to generate radical innovations and bursts of economic growth. The Internet revolution of the 1990s and 2000s, for example (sometimes referred to as the Third Industrial Revolution), transformed the way people live and work around the world.

This is not to say that the post–Cold War world was problem free. Washington and its allies continued to face lower-order security challenges from ethnic conflict, weapons proliferation, and terrorism. In addition, autocratic regional powers, or "rogue states," like Iraq, Libya, Iran, and North Korea, actively challenged the U.S.-led order. Russia and China, while not outright enemies, never became the "responsible stakeholders" Washington had hoped for. In addition, following the terrorist attacks of 9/11, the United States embarked on controversial wars in Iraq and Afghanistan and struggled in difficult counterinsurgency campaigns. Finally, the global financial crisis in 2008 took some of the shine off the American economic model.

Still, following its Cold War victory, for a twenty-five-year period from 1989 to 2014, the United States stood alone as the world's sole and undisputed superpower. It was the wealthiest country on Earth with roughly 25 percent of global GDP. Roughly one-quarter of the nations in the world were formal U.S. allies (Figure 10.1). Finally, the United States possessed the only superpower military with global power-projection capabilities. According to Paul Kennedy, "Nothing has ever existed like this disparity of power. Nothing."[17] The United States is "the greatest superpower ever."

Democracy versus Autocracy

The rise of the United States of America provides strong support for the democratic advantage thesis. The United States grew from a small collection of colonies under the British Empire to an independent nation and then an unmatched global superpower. As U.S. Secretary of State Madeleine Albright described it, by the 1990s, the United States had become the world's "indispensable nation."

Like other dominant democracies, the United States adopted inclusive institutions that facilitated economic growth and helped it to become the world's largest and most dynamic economy. The United States advanced a system of open trade and investment globally that contributed to U.S. and global economic development. America's liberal market economy produced radical economic innovations, including the digital revolution. The United States was able to benefit from a brain drain as the best and the brightest from around the world flocked to its shores. New York became the global financial capital as Wall Street matched or surpassed the City of London as a center of global finance. U.S. Treasury bonds became the world's safest investment.

In the diplomatic sphere, the United States built a rules-based international order that gave its allies a say and channeled American hard power into institutional predictability. Its global system of alliances allowed Washington to project military force around the world and contributed manpower, resources, and legitimacy to U.S. diplomatic efforts. Its soft power helped it to win the Cold War because, simply put, people living in the Communist Bloc were more attracted to the U.S. model than to their own governments. In even more evidence that states bandwagon with, not balance against, democratic great powers, the U.S. alliance system grew along with American power (Figure 10.1).

America's economic and financial strength allowed it to finance the world's most powerful military. Its military innovations, including stealth, PGM, and missile defenses, surpassed anything Moscow could imagine and contributed to the Soviet Union's capitulation without firing a shot.

Granted, the United States fought and lost in wars to smaller powers and some of these conflicts, such as Vietnam and Iraq, are widely considered to have been mistakes. Still, unlike Napoleon or Hitler, the United States avoided fighting and losing a disastrous major power war.

Democracies supposedly flail when it comes to selecting a grand plan and sticking to it, but the United States settled on an effective grand strategy of deterrence and containment of the Soviet Union and vigorously prosecuted it for a half century. Despite the supposed fractiousness of democracies, fighting communism enjoyed widespread bipartisan support for decades.

For the Soviet Union, the outcome was very different. It was able to sustain growth early, but its centralized, planned economy was unable to compete over the long haul. It massed resources to industrialize and then to build a superpower military and nuclear arsenal. Its state-led model, however, proved less effective than a market economy at producing sustained economic growth. Further, it lacked the economic base and the ingenuity necessary to keep up with the United States in technological innovation and the strategic-military competition.

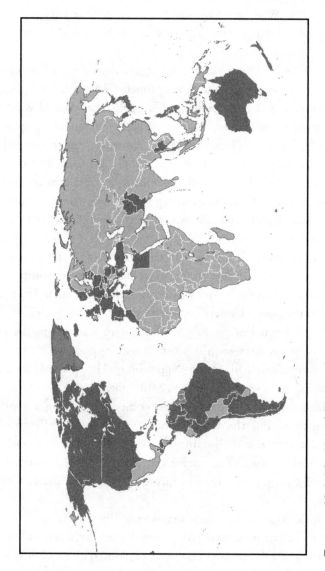

Figure 10.1 The United States and Its Allies, 2019

Moscow was able to pull levers and make things happen, but many of the resulting policies, such as "forced collectivization," were ideologically driven disasters.

The Soviet Union was certainly more ruthless than the United States. Joseph Stalin, for example, may have been history's greatest mass murderer. It is estimated that he killed tens of millions of his own people through the execution of political prisoners, forced labor in work camps, and starvation from misguided economic policies. It is hard to see, however, how this kind of barbarism aided Moscow in its great power competition with the United States.

Perhaps the Soviet Union's greatest vulnerability was its lack of soft power. It could only keep allies by shutting them behind walls or crushing them under the treads of tanks. Subjugated people within the Soviet Bloc caught glimpses of life in the West, and they liked what they saw. They switched sides as soon as they got the chance.[18]

Many hoped that the collapse of the Soviet Empire would be a step toward a "Europe whole and free" and that Russia might become a fully fledged liberal democratic member of the West. But, it was not to be. After a half-hearted attempt to implement political and economic reforms in the 1990s, Moscow returned to its autocratic roots.

In 2000, the Russian people elected a former KGB officer, Vladimir Putin, as president. He called the collapse of the Soviet Union the "greatest tragedy of the twenty-first century."[19] In Putin's mind, the Cold War never ended. His team was merely behind. And he was determined to even the score.

PART III | The Democratic
Advantage Today

| The Russian Federation

R USSIA MAY POSE the greatest near-term national security threat to the United States and its allies. It does not have a large economy, but it does possess the capabilities and the intention to cause great damage to U.S. and allied interests. The United States, therefore, must, therefore, take this challenge seriously. But Russia has a key vulnerability: its domestic political institutions. So long as it continues to be ruled by President Vladimir Putin, or another similar dictator, Russia will not be able to mount a serious challenge to U.S. global leadership.

Russia Resurgent

The modern Russian state traces its origins to Kyivan Rus.[1] Founded by Vikings from northern Europe and local Slavic populations, Kyivan Rus was a kingdom on the Dnieper River near present-day Kyiv from the 9th to the 13th century AD. Over time, Russia developed into a major Christian polity with a capital in Moscow. Powerful tsars (the Russian word for Caesar), like Ivan IV, Peter I, Catherine II, and Nicholas II, helped to modernize Russia and transform it into one of the major European powers. Since the early modern era, therefore, Russia has always been a great power.

Until the Cold War, however, Russia had also always been a weak great power. Unlike Britain, France, Spain, or Germany, it never vied for European hegemony or a global empire. But the Western European great powers destroyed themselves in the world wars of the 20th century, leaving the tsars' descendent, the Soviet Union, as the major land power in Europe.

Following the collapse of the Soviet Union and the end of the Cold War, many in the West hoped that Russia would become democratic and capitalist and a cooperative participant in a functioning rules-based, international system.[2] Russia adopted the trappings of democracy, such as elections, and introduced reforms to open its market. The democratic institutions and economic reforms never quite stuck, however, and the 1990s were a time of disillusionment among many in Russia. In addition, the end of the Cold War was followed by resurgence of nationalist and ethnic conflicts around the world, and Russia was not spared. Moscow fought a bloody war against its restive, majority-Muslim province of Chechnya. Hopes that the end of the Cold War would radically transform Russian standards of living did not materialize, and, by 2000, the Russian people were ready for a new direction. They elected the former director of the KGB, the Soviet Union's intelligence service and secret police, as their president.

Putin is vilified in the West, but he has enjoyed genuine popularity at home.[3] Many Russians admire his strongman style of leadership. Booming commodity prices in the 2000s contributed to the growth of Russia's export-dependent economy, and Putin rallied support through nationalist sentiment by reasserting Russia's role as a great power in international politics.

Putin's foremost goal is to reestablish Russia as a great power and to ensure that no important global security matter can be decided without Russia at the table. Correspondingly, Putin acts whenever he can to insert Russia into global security affairs and to limit the United States' ability to flex its muscles on the international stage.

Putin also views the spread of Western liberal democracy as a threat to his rule and to Russian civilization. After all, if democracy comes to Moscow, he is out of a job. He aspires, therefore, to prevent countries on his border from becoming full-fledged members of the West; to stop the United States and the West from overthrowing dictators as it has done in the past in Serbia, Afghanistan, Iraq, and Libya; to weaken and divide NATO to prevent these nations from combining against him; and to discredit democracy as a form of government around the world.

He moved cautiously toward these goals initially, as Russia's military and economy were still weakened by mismanagement and the end of the Cold War.

When neighboring Georgia began accession talks with NATO, however, Putin decided he could wait no longer. America's rival and expanding alliance system was closing in around him to include countries that had been core parts of Russia's former empire. After all, even Stalin himself was Georgian. In 2008, Putin invaded the small state to his south. Rather than take and hold the entire country, Russian forces occupied the provinces of Abkhazia and South Ossetia, invalidating Georgia's bid for NATO membership. (NATO rules require that states are ineligible for membership if they have ongoing border disputes, perhaps creating a moral hazard for Mr. Putin.)

In 2014, Putin invaded yet another country. This time it was his neighbor to the west, Ukraine, with a similar goal: to prevent the country from becoming a member of the European Union and NATO. He seized Crimea and continues to attack and occupy parts of eastern Ukraine. These actions put discussions about Ukraine's NATO membership on hold, as few Western European leaders are eager to sign up to a military alliance with a country actively at war with Russia.

For many, this event marked the return of great power competition. For the first time in decades, the map of Europe was redrawn at the barrel of a gun. American hegemony had lasted for twenty-five years, from 1989 to 2014, but now there was another powerful state willing to use large-scale military force to achieve its objectives.

Putin's aggression extended beyond Russia's near abroad. In the next year, 2015, Putin intervened in the Syrian civil war to prop up his long-time security partner Bashar al-Assad. Putin feared that the West would once again use instability in the Middle East as a pretext to intervene, overthrow a dictator, and install a democratic form of government. Russian intervention made sure that Moscow would be at the table when the future of Syria was decided.

The Soviet Union had been expelled from its foothold in the Middle East in the 1970s, when its former Arab proxies reached peace deals with Israel, but Putin's bold action in Syria reestablished Russia as a major Middle Eastern power broker. Even close U.S. partners in the region, like Israel, have recognized the need to pursue constructive relations with Moscow in order to secure their interests in Syria.

Putin has also flouted global conventions. Contrary to long-standing international norms banning the use of weapons of mass destruction (WMDs), Putin backed Assad as he gassed his own people in the Syrian civil war. In addition, Putin carried out his own chemical weapons attack in Europe in March 2018. In that month, Russian operatives used a nerve agent to assassinate a former Russian spy in England and also killed and sickened several innocent bystanders.

Under Putin, Russia has also worked to undermine democracy and court pro-Russian politicians in the West. Putin is conducting influence operations throughout Europe seeking to undermine faith in democracy, bring to power pro-Russian political forces, and to weaken and divide NATO. Russia is spearheading anti-liberal efforts in Europe and has close relations with ruling governments and opposition parties with populist bents.

Russian disinformation campaigns, including through its state media television channel Russia Today (RT), sow confusion about Russian misbehavior. Disinformation can be effective even if it does not persuade anyone of Moscow's view, so long as it causes just enough doubt that reasonable people believe the situation is too complicated to draw a clear conclusion.

Russia is using its size and geographic proximity to the Baltic states to pipe in pro-Russian propaganda, including nostalgic Soviet-era songs, in the hope of winning loyalty among Russian-speaking populations in these countries. Russian investors have also bought up real estate in Montenegro to make NATO's newest member economically dependent on Moscow.

In 2016, Russia intervened in the U.S. presidential election itself. The fact that an outside power could meddle in American democracy and possibly affect the result was a major wake-up call to many about the scale and scope of the Russian threat.

Putin is also projecting Russian influence into other world regions. In 2019, as much of the world united to force Nicolás Maduro to step down from power in Venezuela, Putin intervened to prop him up, even sending Russian troops to the country.[4] Moscow has increased its military influence in several African nations, with arms sales, security cooperation, and training to Burkina Faso, Central African Republic, Libya, Sudan, and others.[5] Russia is also growing closer to China, conducting military exercises in Asia and the Baltic Sea with the world's other autocratic great power.[6]

Perhaps the greatest threat posed by Russia, however, is the risk of World War III. While not likely, the probability may be greater now than at any time since the most dangerous periods of the Cold War. Putin could try to rerun his playbook from Ukraine, but against a NATO member, like Estonia, Latvia, or Lithuania.[7] As noted previously, there is little doubt that Russia could capture these capitals in just a few days.[8]

If Putin succeeded in such an effort, this would be a double victory for him. He could simultaneously reestablish his sphere of influence over the countries, while breaking NATO. As it showed in Ukraine, Russia has a sophisticated military strategy for carrying out these kind of campaigns, known as "next generation" warfare.[9] Russia has spent heavily on military modernization to support this strategy, showing where its priorities lie.

If Russia were to conduct such an attack, the United States would have no choice but to intervene to protect its formal treaty allies, but this would mean war with Russia. And since the United States and Russia are both nuclear powers, the whiff of split atoms would waft over any such conflict. Indeed, Russia's "escalate-to-de-escalate" nuclear doctrine explicitly threatens to use nuclear weapons in the early stage of any conflict with the West under the belief that Western leaders do not have the stomach for nuclear war and would choose capitulation over nuclear escalation.[10] This assessment is eerily similar to imperial Japan's mistaken belief that the United States would simply back down if attacked at Pearl Harbor. Even if the NATO-Russia conflict of interest never escalates to nuclear exchange, Russia's threat to do so contributes to day-to-day nuclear coercion of the United States and its NATO allies.

In sum, over the past decade, Russia has gone from a quiescent power licking its wounds to a major competitor, challenging U.S. interests, its democratic system, and even threatening nuclear war. So just how serious is the Russian challenge? To answer this question, we must begin with the fundamentals and examine Russia's domestic political institutions.

Putin's Tyranny

Russia is a relatively weak great power in part because it is, and always has been, an autocracy. Vladimir Putin is a tyrant. Russia has often been ruled by strongmen and occasionally a strong woman, like Catherine the Great. Communism was meant to be a democratic system in Marx's conception, but Lenin was not sufficiently patient to wait for democracy, so his "vanguard" imposed a centralized economy led by a Marxist-Leninist autocratic government. When that failed miserably, Russia experimented with open government in the 1990s, but it did not last long. Since his election in 2000, Putin has slowly, but deliberately dismantled the vestiges of democracy in Russia.

Putin has repeatedly asked the Duma, the Russian parliament, to change the constitution to grant him more power. In 2004, he was given the authority to appoint regional governors, centralizing power and making regional governments dependent on the person of the Russian president. After ruling Russia for two consecutive four-year terms from 2000 to 2008, he took a turn as prime minister as his hand-picked successor, Dmitry Medvedev, rotated into the presidency. By 2012, however, Putin was back in the top office. His rubber-stamp Duma extended the president's term from four to six years. In 2018, he won re-election for his fourth term as Russia's president with 77 percent of the vote—a whopping winning percentage that is not characteristic of a free and fair election.

Rather, Putin rigs elections to ensure victory. Opposition candidates are routinely disqualified on flimsy charges and numbers are fudged in Putin's favor. In one colorful example from the 2004 presidential elections, Putin won 50.6 percent of the vote in Chechnya and 85.4 percent of the vote in Ingushetia, despite leading repressive wars against those breakaway provinces. As political scientist M. Steven Fish writes, "The outcome, if accurate, represented either a magnificent spirit of forgiveness or an intriguing display of masochism on the part of people whose homes had been decimated by a military campaign associated closely with Putin himself."[11]

Putin has also set about to systematically eliminate any political opposition. When Putin's political party, United Russia, was founded in the early 2000s, it was the third-largest party in the country behind the Liberal Democratic Party and the Communists. In the most-recent presidential election, United Russia held 75 percent of the seats in the Duma. And the remaining seats go to parties that are allowed to exist only to provide Russia a minimal fig leaf of democracy.

His political opponents have a tendency to wind up dead or in jail. Mikhail Khodorkovsky, a successful Russian businessman, had political aspirations in the early 2000s, but, sensing a threat, Putin had him jailed for ten years on trumped-up charges of fraud. Khodorkovsky is now living in exile in London and is a vocal Putin critic. Sergei Magnitsky was not so lucky. Magnitsky was a Russian tax accountant who accused the Russian state of corruption. In 2008, he was arrested for no apparent reason and died in police custody less than a year later.

Boris Nemtsov lasted a bit longer. He was a successful Russian politician in the 1990s and, after Putin's election in 2000, frequently and prominently criticized Putin. In 2015, he was found dead on a bridge near the Kremlin with four bullet holes in his back. Indeed, dozens of prominent Russians have suffered mysterious deaths or disappearances since Putin assumed power.

Russia's dictator has also brought Russian media under his personal control. State media has become his mouthpiece, and independent journalists have been eliminated or cowed into submission.

In sum, Russia is an autocratic state. During Russia's experiments with greater openness in the 1990s, Russia was considered partly free. Now it rated as a "consolidated authoritarian regime."[12]

Russia's Autocratic Economics

Given the arguments presented earlier in this book, we should expect Russia's economy to be suffering under autocratic rule. And that is exactly what we find. Russia lacks a diversified economy and instead is heavily dependent on oil and gas exports from its state-controlled energy companies, such as Gazprom. Indeed, Russia is one of the world's top three largest oil producers.[13] When commodity prices are booming, as they were in the 2000s, the Russian economy grows. When they fall, however, as they did during the Great Recession and, again since 2014, Russia's economy swoons. Indeed, Russia has suffered several quarters of technical recessions since 2014. Its current annual growth rate at the time of writing was about 2 percent per year.

To improve growth rates, the requirements for reform are clear. Putin would need to liberalize markets, allow competition, and establish good economic institutions to protect property rights, encourage investment, innovation, and entrepreneurship. Such steps could help diversify the economy and wean Russia off of its dependence on oil and gas exports.

Instead, Putin has gone in the opposite direction, renationalizing key industries, including energy. Between 2005 and 2015, the state's share of the economy doubled from 35 percent to 70 percent.[14] Rather than awarding successful entrepreneurs, Putin sends them to jail, ensuring that no one amasses enough independent economic power to become a threat to him and his rule.[15]

Like many autocracies, Russia's economy operates according to a political logic, not an economic one. So long as the only way to amass wealth is through staying in the good graces of Mr. Putin, his position of power is secure. The system allows Putin to pay off elites and provide jobs to the working class in big state-owned industries, but prevents the rise of a middle class that could be a force for political change.[16] The system suits the purpose it is intended to serve, but it comes at the cost of Russia's economic competitiveness.

The Russian economy may best be described as a kleptocracy.[17] Russian leaders exploit the country's national resources and steal for their own personal gain. Corruption can be lucrative, especially for those at the very top. Putin's official government salary over the past two decades has been about US$130,000 per year, but that has not stopped him from amassing enormous wealth through crooked dealings. Indeed, he may be the world's richest man, with an estimated net worth as high as $200 billion.[18] Some clever sleuths calculated the price of wristwatches Putin has worn in photographs over the past several years alone to total more than $700,000.[19] Former Russian president Dmitry Medvedev appears to have acquired massive real estate holdings and luxury yachts while working as a public servant.[20] In addition, several of Putin's closest friends have become billionaires since he has been in power.[21] In Russia, it pays to have friends in high places. The massive corruption filters down to every level of society. According to some indices, Russia is among the world's most corrupt countries.[22] Officials will look the other way when crimes are committed if the price is right. Often state employees demand a bribe simply to do their job. Police, for example, often require payment in order to conduct a routine crime scene investigation.[23] Bribes also help to ensure that firms can win lucrative government contracts. According to official Russian government statistics, 15 percent of Russia's GDP occurs in the shadows, but many independent experts estimate that the black market makes up a much larger share of the Russian economy.

Talented people unwilling to play this shady game know they cannot get ahead in Putin's Russia, so those who can leave do. Consequently, Russia has suffered a massive "brain drain" in recent years, with educated professionals fleeing the country, further setting back Russia's economic potential.[24]

Russia's financial position is also weak due to both economic mismanagement and Western sanctions following Russia's invasion of Crimea in 2014. The Russian stock market lost over half its value in 2014 and has only partially recovered since then. The Russian currency, the ruble, was also devalued by more than 50 percent between 2014 and 2016. The Russian government took steps to prop it up but, in the process, spent down its foreign currency reserves. The yield on a Russian ten-year bond is currently 6.5% compared to 1.8% for a U.S. treasury bond. This means that the Russian government must pay investors more than three times as much to persuade them to buy Russian debt.

Russia's weak economic position can also be seen in "capital flight." Rich Russians do not feel comfortable keeping their money in the country and by some estimates, "wealth stashed outside the country by rich Russians is now around three times larger than official net foreign reserves."[25] From 2000 to 2007, Russia was the beneficiary of a $79 billion net inflow of capital. But, that has reversed in recent years, and the country has suffered a massive net outflow of $646 billion from 2008 to 2016.[26]

Russia's role as an energy superpower does provide it with some geopolitical leverage due to "pipeline politics." Many European nations depend on Russian oil and gas exports, and Russia threatens to turn off the flow or raise prices, especially in the winter, as a way to exert coercive pressure. In addition, Gazprom, the state-owned energy supplier, charges different rates based on the client states' support for Putin's policies. For example, Bulgaria pays more than Hungary.

This may be a wasting asset, however, as European nations seek to diversify their energy sources to reduce their vulnerability, including through purchasing American liquefied natural gas (LNG). In 2017, Gazprom provided about 40 percent of Europe's gas, but already the United States produces more natural gas than Russia (27 trillion cubic feet to 16.6 trillion cubic feet, respectively).[27] U.S. exports will only increase as the United States is expected to soon become the world's largest natural gas exporter.

Russia's economy may be able to sustain slightly higher growth rates if energy prices rise in the future. But, absent fundamental economic reforms that will not happen under Putinism, Russia will remain an economic basket case.

Russia's GDP is currently $1.7 trillion, smaller than Italy's ($2.1 trillion) and dwarfed by the United States ($20.5 trillion). Viewed in terms of net wealth, the Russian Federation's position is even worse. Its net wealth is lower than in Switzerland, Spain, and South Korea and only one-fiftieth that of the United States.[28]

Russia may have great power ambitions, but it lacks a great power economy.

Russia's Autocratic Diplomacy

We have seen above that Russia is adept at meddling in America's alliance system, but how skilled is it at building its own? Theory tells us that autocracies are unable to build effective alliances, they lack soft power, and their clumsy attempts to gain influence will provoke counterbalancing coalitions. This is exactly what we see in the Russian case.

Following the collapse of the Soviet Union, Moscow lost its large alliance system. When given the freedom to choose, the countries of Eastern Europe flocked to the West. They aspired to become free-market democracies aligned with the United States. Again, contrary to "realist" IR theory, states bandwagon with liberal hegemons. They no longer wanted to be under Russia's autocratic thumb. NATO gained thirteen new members, and the Warsaw Pact dissolved. The central front dividing East from West in Europe shifted 800 miles to the east from Berlin to Kyiv, greatly altering the balance of power between the United States and Russia (and freedom and tyranny) in Europe and eliminating Russia's sphere of influence.

Russia has attempted to resurrect an alliance system in the post–Cold War era, but the results have been less than impressive. When the Soviet Union collapsed, Moscow established the Commonwealth of Independent States

(CIS). The CIS is not a formal defense pact but has alliance-like elements, including a council of defense ministers and military cooperation. The CIS is made up of the now-independent countries that were once part of the Soviet Union during the Cold War. The three Baltic countries, Estonia, Latvia, and Lithuania, refused to join because they considered their time in the Soviet Union an illegal occupation. According to their CINC scores, Russia's remaining CIS allies together possess about 1 percent of world military power. It is not exactly the all-star team.

Like past autocracies, Russia has a hard time keeping its word. It invaded two of its CIS "allies," Georgia in 2008 and Ukraine in 2014. In addition, Russia violated the Budapest Memorandum of 1994, in which Moscow promised to protect Ukraine's sovereignty and territorial integrity in exchange for Kyiv returning Russian nuclear forces stationed on its territory. Countries invaded by Russia apparently prefer not to be joined in a formal alliance with it, and Georgia and Ukraine both subsequently withdrew from CIS.

Russia's new role in the Middle East is certainly a cause for concern, but it currently does not extend much beyond Syria. The regional security order still revolves primarily around the United States and its security partners in the region. The United States and its democratic allies and partners should stay attuned to, and actively counter, Russia's growing influence in Latin America and Africa. But influence in these regions is unlikely to be central to the coming competition. Unlike Berlin during the Cold War, Bangui is unlikely to be the pivotal city on which the great power rivalry of the 21st century turns.

Furthermore, not only has Moscow been unable to build its own effective alliance network, but it lacks soft power as well. In a recent survey, Russia ranked twenty-eighth out of thirty nations scored.[29]

Further, Russia's aggressive actions are prompting a counterbalancing coalition. The United States, the European Union, and other countries and organizations have passed sanctions against Russia in response to its invasion of Ukraine. In recent years, there are growing signs that Belarus is more resistant to Russian demands and at least open to improving relations with NATO. Further, Sweden and Finland are more seriously considering NATO membership than at any time in their history. Stalin was not scary enough to get them to join NATO, but Putin just might be. Putin's invasions have only further reinforced Georgian and Ukrainian desires to become part of NATO.

Importantly, for the first time since the end of the Cold War, NATO has once again officially identified Russia as a threat in its formal statements. The Alliance is taking concrete steps to deter and defend against possible Russian aggression. NATO nations are increasing defense spending, including on a rapid reaction force to respond to Russian attacks. NATO has deployed trip wire forces to the Baltic states. There is serious discussion of building a permanent NATO military base in Poland. The United States is developing two types of low-yield nuclear weapons and strengthening missile defenses to deter Russia's nuclear "escalate-to-de-escalate" strategy. In response to Russia's cheating on the Intermediate-Range Nuclear Forces (INF) Treaty, the United States has formally withdrawn from the agreement and is now building its own intermediate-range conventional missiles for possible deployment in Europe and Asia. Finally, Washington has provided lethal aid to the Ukrainian government in its fight against Russia.

In sum, Russia can meddle in the alliances of others, but it has not succeeded in building its own network of effective security partners. And its overly bellicose foreign policy has prompted reactions that have, on balance, arguably weakened its political-military position, especially in Europe.

Russia's Autocratic Military

Military matters are the one area where Russia seems to be punching above its weight, but there is reason to believe that this will not last. Putin is spending lavishly on military modernization despite his weak economic base. Following the United States, China, Saudi Arabia, and France, Russia is the world's sixth-largest military spender. At $61 billion per year, Russia's defense budget is only roughly one-tenth of America's.

Indeed, part of the reason that Russia is relying heavily on nuclear weapons in its military strategy is because it cannot afford more advanced conventional forces. Nuclear weapons, literally and figuratively, provide more bang for the buck.

In addition to lower overall spending levels, there are other reasons to be skeptical about the mightiness of the Russian military. Russia is facing demographic challenges with a low birth rate and a high death rate, leaving too few young men for military service. Moreover, many of them are ineligible due to endemic Russian health problems, including tuberculosis, heart disease, HIV/AIDS, and widespread alcoholism.[30] An estimated 1 percent of the Russian population is infected with HIV/AIDS, and the life expectancy of an average Russian male is only 67 years, less than in North Korea. This compares to 76 years in the United States. Of those who are eligible, too few are willing to volunteer for military service, and Russia is forced to rely on lower-quality conscription troops and hired mercenaries. Many of those eligible (up to one-half, according to one estimate) dodge the draft or pay bribes to avoid it.[31] Russia does have capable special forces, but it faces real shortages when it comes to rank-and-file soldiers.

Moreover, Russia's performance in recent conflicts raises questions about its battlefield effectiveness.[32] In the war against Georgia in 2008, the overmatched Georgians were still able to shoot down several Russian aircraft. Russia lacked the reconnaissance and precision-strike capabilities needed to find, fix, and finish Georgia's air defenses, leaving their aircraft vulnerable. In addition, Russian forces rode into Georgia on top of their armored personnel carriers. The poorly constructed vehicles are not well protected, and Russian soldiers felt safer on top, where at least they could escape quickly, rather than remain stuck in a death trap—that usage of course defeats the entire purpose of an armored vehicle. Russia's recent military modernization is in part a response to the recognized problems in the Georgia campaign, and there is reason to believe it could do better in the future. Still, the war in Georgia demonstrates the limitations of Russia's battlefield effectiveness against even a weak and overmatched enemy.

Theory tells us that autocrats often engage in heedless decision-making on matters of war and peace. Russia's decision to violate the INF Treaty may be a case in point. Russia will not be deploying intermediate-range missiles in the Americas anytime soon, but Russia's violations have prompted the United States to develop its own intermediate-range missiles, which, when operational, would likely be deployed in Europe and Asia within range of Russia. Russia has much more to lose from a runaway intermediate-range missile race in Eurasia than does the United States.

Experts debate whether the decisions to intervene in Ukraine and Syria were masterstrokes or a foolhardy plunge into quagmire. On one hand, Russia appears to have prevented Ukraine from joining the European Union and NATO and reclaimed a role in the Middle East, at least for the time being. On the other hand, Russian forces are facing tougher fights, especially in eastern Ukraine, than they likely expected.

Moreover, while the Russian people are proud of their nation's bigger role on the world stage, they are sensitive to casualties. Putin has gone to great lengths to limit the casualties of Russian soldiers in Ukraine and Syria and to hide them from the Russian public. To protect the lives of Russian forces, Putin has undermined military effectiveness by engaging in indiscriminate bombing of civilians and relying more heavily on private mercenaries.[33] As Machiavelli wrote half a millennium ago, "Mercenary armies offer only slow, laborious and feeble victories, but their losses are sudden and astonishing."[34] Indeed, in the only time U.S. and Russian forces engaged in direct combat in decades, it is reported that a single U.S. airstrike killed dozens of Russian mercenaries in Syria in 2018. No U.S. personnel were harmed.[35]

Like other autocracies, Russia continues to struggle with innovation and incorporating high technology into its military. Conventionally-armed, sea-launched, land-attack cruise missiles have been a mainstay of America's forces since the end of the Cold War, but Russia only succeeded in employing such a capability in 2015. Moreover, as we saw in Syria, they are not very accurate. America's precision-guided munitions can go through a window, whereas Russia's often missed their targets by miles. Indeed, one Russian missile intended for Syria actually ended up hitting Iran.[36] This is not even to mention higher-end technologies, like stealth, in which Russia has essentially given up due to budget constraints.[37]

Russia's technological limitations are also apparent in the crown jewels of the Russian military forces: nuclear weapons. Russia rarely sends its nuclear submarines to sea. During the Cold War, as discussed previously, Russia followed a "bastion strategy" of keeping its nuclear submarines in waters just off Russia's coast where they would be safer. Today, they mostly stay in port at Russian naval bases.[38]

Russia is so worried about the vulnerability of its nuclear forces that it is developing new nuclear capabilities, including a nuclear-powered nuclear-armed cruise missile, but Russia is struggling to get the technology to work.[39] And most U.S. defense experts are happy to see Russia spend on more nuclear weapons, where Russia already has a substantial stockpile, and not other technologies that might prove to be more of a game changer on the battlefield.

Russia will also struggle with next-generation, emerging technologies. Artificial intelligence (AI) will be important for the future of national security and will have many defense applications, including the possibility of creating lethal autonomous weapon systems, or "killer robots." Putin has recently declared that whichever country masters AI will rule the world. We can rest assured that it will not be Russia.

Perhaps Russia's greatest military weakness, however, is its precarious domestic political situation. Putin, like nearly all autocrats, must wake up every morning, and go to bed every night, fearing regime collapse. This means Russia must spend heavily on domestic security. While the United States spends twice as much on international security as on domestic security, in Russia those numbers are roughly equal.[40] Resources and attention devoted to repressing the Russian people are those that are not going toward strengthening Russia's military.

If Putin were to lose power, it is uncertain what would come next. Given his tight grip on the state apparatus, it is likely a crony would fill his shoes and reinforce some form of Putinism. Still, it is also quite possible that a less aggressive government would come into office, buying the free world another quarter-century respite from great power rivalry with Moscow.

Even with Putin in charge, however, Russia can only put up so much of a fight. Russia simply does not have the economic basis to sustain a superpower military. Russia, therefore, faces a choice between spending itself into exhaustion or scaling back its ambitions. During the Cold War, Moscow chose the former path only to fail spectacularly in the end. Russia is currently asserting itself on the world stage, but Putin may be astute enough to avoid repeating the Soviet Union's mistakes. Indeed, in 2016, Russia reduced its military spending for the first time since 1998, and Russian military spending continued to decline in both 2017 and 2018.[41]

Democracy versus Autocracy

The case of contemporary Russia further strengthens our confidence in the democratic advantage theory. The return of great power competition with Russia poses a serious threat to U.S. national security, and the United States and its allies should deal with the challenge accordingly. After all, war with Russia is once again possible and nuclear war with Russia is the only threat on the planet that could result in us all being dead within thirty minutes.

At the same time, we must put the threat in perspective. If Russia is a great power, it is barely one. Its autocratic system is undermining its economic, diplomatic, and military performance. Its economy is smaller than Italy's. Its financial system is under serious strain. Russia lacks effective alliances and soft power and its aggressive behavior has provoked rival alliances to take countervailing measures. Its military is overly focused on domestic threats and is ill-equipped for the strategic-technological competitions of the 21st century.

To be sure, Putin does benefit from some of the identified autocratic advantages. He has followed a fairly consistent course for elevating Russia's role on the global stage since taking office. He has taken decisive action, including in Ukraine and Syria, as the United States dithered. And Putin has certainly shown a knack for deception and ruthlessness when necessary. Still, as argued previously, these benefits come with costs as well. Putin's dissembling has weakened Russia's position diplomatically, for example, as few trust Russia anymore to comply with its international agreements. And it is precisely Russia's bold actions overseas that have worried its neighbors and led them to strengthen their defenses against the Russian threat. Most importantly, however, these autocratic advantages simply cannot compensate for the serious autocratic weaknesses that Putin's dictatorship brings in the economic, diplomatic, and military space. In sum, Russia is dangerous and it can certainly disrupt the U.S.-led order. But it will not be in a position to be a true peer competitor to the United States any time soon.

There is only one country that presents a serious challenge to U.S. global mastery. That country will be the subject of our next chapter.

| The People's Republic of China

T HE MOST SERIOUS challenge to U.S. global leadership since the end of the Cold War comes from China. China is home to the world's biggest population, and in the coming decade it could overtake the United States as the globe's largest economy. Beijing is increasingly putting its economic might behind its military and political initiatives. It is challenging U.S. primacy in East Asia and contesting U.S. leadership around the world. Some argue that we must begin to come to grips with what life will be like "when China rules the world."[1] Others maintain that the United States will not pass so easily into the night and, instead, we must gird ourselves for the coming World War III.[2]

Fortunately, from the perspective of the United States and the rest of the free world, these predictions are much too dire. China has a storied past, and it will likely always remain a great power, but it will not overtake the United States as the world's leading state any time soon. Its underlying institutions are simply not up to the task.

China's Thousands of Years of Civilization

The Chinese word for their country is *Zhong Guo*, or Central Kingdom, and through much of its history, China saw itself as the center of the universe.[3] In 221 BC, Qin Shi Huangdi conquered other warring states and enthroned himself as the first emperor of a unified China. From that time until the early

20th century, China was ruled by a succession of imperial dynasties: Qin, Han, Xin, Jin, Sui, Tang, Song, Liao, Jin, Yuan, Ming, and Qing. The emperor (also known as the Son of Heaven) was believed to be part divine and god's representative on Earth. In East Asia, China was the center of the international system with smaller, tributary states on its periphery. Leaders from smaller states in Asia would visit Beijing to kowtow to the Son of Heaven and pay tribute in the form of food, precious metals, art, and other valuable goods.

China was the leading power in Asia for centuries, and it may have possessed the globe's largest economy through much of this time. After all, in an era when economies were mostly subsistence agriculture, land and people were the two primary economic assets, and China had plenty of both. The Chinese are proud of this glorious past and often speak about their thousands of years of continuous civilization.

To be sure, China did well when competing against other autocrats. But its first encounter with democratic power led to the beginning of a bad century.

The Chinese refer to the years between 1839 and 1949 as the "Century of Humiliation." When European explorers first reached China in the 1500s, they wanted to establish trading and diplomatic relations. But the emperor viewed the Europeans merely as another group of potential tribute bearers. China was not especially interested in trade with Europe and certainly did not believe that European diplomats and the rulers they represented deserved an equal platform with the Son of Heaven. The emperor allowed some limited trade under tightly controlled conditions over the coming centuries, but the European powers were not satisfied with this arrangement.

To pry China open, the United Kingdom (as we will recall from Chapter 8, the world's leading democratic power at the time), launched the Opium Wars from 1839 to 1842. Britain had overtaken the Dutch as the world's largest opium trader and, in what was not the proudest moment in Western history, it was willing to wage war for the right to traffic narcotics in China. In the end, London was victorious. The Chinese military was simply no match for modern British warships and firepower.

The emperor conceded to British demands. He set up five new trading posts (including in Shanghai) and ceded in perpetuity to the United Kingdom the small island of Hong Kong to be used for commercial purposes.

Other European powers followed Britain's lead. In a series of what China considers "unequal treaties," major powers forced China to cede territory for trading ports and spheres of influence. The United States (1844) and France (1844) were granted the same trading rights as Great Britain. Russia reclaimed territory in Outer Manchuria in 1858. In 1887, the Qing dynasty signed Macau over to Portugal for "permanent occupation." Germany seized Tsingtao in 1898 and established the first European colony on the Chinese mainland. (Thanks to Germany's presence, Tsingtao produces some of China's best beer to this day; granted, this is not a very high bar.)

In what may have been the ultimate humiliation, however, China even lost territory to an Asian power. Unlike China, which had shunned Western ways, Japan whole-heartedly adopted the lessons of European modernization and industrialization and, by the late 1800s, Tokyo was a major regional power. It defeated Beijing in the First Sino-Japanese War of 1894–1895. China was forced to recognize Korean independence and to cede Taiwan and parts of Manchuria to Japan. In addition, Japan annexed the disputed Senkaku/Diayou islands—a source of contention to this day.

China's internal weaknesses, combined with these external pressures, contributed to a series of domestic rebellions. The Taiping Rebellion, from 1850 to 1864, was one of the bloodiest civil wars in history, resulting in tens of millions of fatalities. Hong Xiuquan, the leader of the rebel forces, believed he was the brother of Jesus Christ and aspired to overthrow the Chinese empire and establish a Christian nation. He succeeded in generating a large following and controlling much of Southern China before his eventual defeat in the decade-long struggle.

The Boxer Rebellion, from 1899 to 1901, was an uprising against the growing foreign encroachments into China and it won the backing of the Chinese imperial court. This official Chinese resistance, however, only further antagonized the European powers, who crushed the Rebellion, marched on Beijing, and sacked the city.

In the midst of these serious military challenges, and in a textbook example of poor autocratic decision-making, China's Empress Dowager Cixi decided to divert money from the Chinese navy in order to rebuild a sumptuous stone boat pavilion in the royal Summer Palace. Her empire may have been destroyed, but she had by the far the nicest pavilion in the neighborhood.

The powerlessness of the Chinese empire in the face of expansionist foreign powers, and the corruption of the Chinese imperial court, inspired young reformers with a desire to overthrow the traditional imperial system. Sun Yat-sen achieved this goal in 1912, establishing a Republic of China led by his Kuomintang Party (KMT) and terminating the over two-thousand-year period of rule by the Sons of Heaven.

Sun Yat-sen was never able to consolidate his power, however, leading to decades of internal conflict. The most powerful quarreling factions were the KMT, led by Chiang Kai-Shek after 1925, and supported by the United

States, and Mao Zedong's Chinese Communist Party (CCP). These parties combined forces to fight Japanese occupation during World War II. As soon as Japan was defeated, however, they turned back on each other.

Drawing on his strong popular support in the Chinese countryside and the credit he won for defeating the Japanese imperialists in World War II, Mao eventually emerged victorious. The KMT fled to the island of Taiwan, where they set up a rival government in exile that remains to this day. Mao established the communist People's Republic of China in Beijing in 1949. In announcing the new system, he declared that the century of humiliation was over and that, finally, the "Chinese people have stood up."

In reality, China's period of humiliation was far from over; but this time the wounds were self-inflicted. Mao was a charismatic leader who had succeeded in defeating the Japanese in World War II, winning the Chinese civil war, and unifying the country. But, he was an ineffective governor.

As autocrats are wont to do, he made one rash decision after another, lurching China from catastrophe to catastrophe. In his "Hundred Flowers Campaign" of 1956, he encouraged open debate and urged those who disagreed with his policies to freely express their views. Then he promptly arrested them and pressed them into forced labor. In his "Great Leap Forward" campaign from 1958 to 1962, he tried to rapidly industrialize China by ordering peasants to start "backyard furnaces" for producing iron. Millions of Chinese farmers collected metal from their homes and farms and melted it down. Instead of rapid development, the campaign led to the Great Chinese Famine, in which tens of millions of people starved to death. Undeterred by his unbroken string of failures, Mao launched a "Cultural Revolution" from 1966 to 1976 with the goal of restoring ideological purity and purging noncommunists. The campaign led to a decade of persecution of innocents, the destruction of precious cultural and historical artifacts, and massive economic losses. Later, the CCP would formally admit that the Cultural Revolution was "responsible for the most severe setback and the heaviest losses suffered by the Party, the country, and the people since the founding of the People's Republic."[4]

Mao's record in foreign policy was slightly better, but also saw major mistakes. On the positive side of the ledger, he successfully prevented his ally, North Korea, from being overrun in the Korean War in the early 1950s and helped China to become a nuclear-armed power in 1964. On the down side, he instigated two Taiwan Straits crises in the 1950s that nearly caused a nuclear war with the United States. Not bothered by the prospect of war with nuclear superpowers, he then attacked his former ally, the Soviet Union, in a border dispute in 1969. This conflict also saw Mao ultimately capitulate under Soviet nuclear threats.[5] To his credit, Mao, in a tight spot with

Moscow, switched sides and engineered an opening to the United States in the early 1970s.

The Rise of a Chinese Superpower

Mao died in 1976. While he had declared that China stood up in 1949, the country did not begin to recover fully until after his death. His successor, Deng Xiaoping, put in place much-needed economic reforms in 1978. Deng believed that China could adopt elements of the market-economy that had proven successful in the West, while maintaining strict Party control of politics. He opened up China to foreign investment and loosened restrictions on internal markets. When asked whether this economic policy was communist or capitalist, Deng famously replied that it does not matter whether a cat is black or white, so long as it catches mice.

The tacit quid pro quo the CCP made with its people was that the Party would provide economic growth and improved living standards, so long as people keep their nose out of politics. The CCP refers to this combination of market economics and strict party control as "socialism with Chinese characteristics."

When pro-democracy protestors arrived in Tiananmen Square in June 1989, holding a papier mâché "Goddess of Democracy," modeled after the Statue of Liberty, the CCP shot them and ran them over with tanks. When other communist systems, including in Moscow, came crashing down at the end of the Cold War, the CCP remained firmly in charge in Beijing.

Starting from a low baseline, Deng's economic reforms turbo-charged China's economy. It benefited from infusions of technology and capital from abroad. Masses of peasants moved from the countryside to cities to find higher-paying jobs in industry. Chinese entrepreneurs started their own enterprises and, benefiting from cheap labor, were able to produce inexpensive goods for export in the international market.

Deng also placed China on a sounder footing in foreign policy. He believed that China would eventually become a leading power, but it was still relatively weak. For the foreseeable future, he advised that China "hide its capabilities and bide its time." In other words, he believed China would be wise to maintain a low profile on the international stage as it continued to rise. Then, in the future, when it was sufficiently powerful, it could boldly announce its great power status.

Deng stepped back from his position atop China in 1992, but China's subsequent leaders Jiang Zemin (1993–2003) and Hu Jintao (2003–2013) followed his same basic approach to economic development and foreign policy.

China's rapid economic development since Deng's reforms are perhaps the most remarkable economic success story in world history. China maintained double-digit rates of economic growth for decades.[6] This economic expansion lifted 500 million people out of poverty. There is now a robust middle class in China. The average Chinese person's standard of living is much higher than her parents. Average GDP per capita has risen from $194 current U.S. dollars in 1980 to over $10,000 in 2019.[7] In 1980, China did not rank among the world's ten largest economies and it possessed less than 2 percent of world GDP. In 2010, China surpassed Japan as the world's second-largest economy and it currently possesses about 15 percent of world GDP. Indeed, by 2030, many economists predict that China could displace the United States as the world's largest overall economic power—a spot the United States has held since the late 19th century.

When the global financial crisis hit the West in 2008, China emerged relatively unscathed. The CCP intervened to prop up the Chinese economy with a massive stimulus package that included easy credit and infrastructure investments. The Chinese economy continued to grow. For years, people admired the U.S. economic model, but the financial crisis led many around the world to wonder whether China might in fact have the better system.

For years, economists argued that to become a leading economic power, China would need to go beyond the steps that lifted it from poverty. It would have to transition from export-led growth to a more consumer-driven economy. In addition, it would need to go beyond importing technology from abroad and become a true technology innovator itself. Some now believe it has successfully made that transition. Through its program formerly known as "Made in China 2025," the CCP has set out to dominate the most important technologies of the 21st century. And by some measures China may be ahead of the United States in key areas, such as 5G wireless technology, artificial intelligence, and quantum computing.

As it grew economically, Washington had hoped that China would become a "responsible stakeholder" in the U.S.-led, rules-based international order. The hope was that, like South Korea and Taiwan before it, China would integrate into the global economic system, transition to a democratic form of government, and cooperate internationally through formal institutions.

Unfortunately, these fond hopes were not borne out. China stubbornly resisted democratization even as its economy grew. Most importantly, China's newest leader has discarded many of Deng's dictums as he has launched China on a new, more confrontational path.

China's Third Revolution

In 2013, China experienced its third revolution.[8] There was the communist revolution of 1949, Deng's reforms of 1978, and the Xi Jinping revolution of 2013.

Mao ruled China as a dictator. Following his passing, there was the development of a more institutionalized decision-making process with a Politburo Standing Committee led by a general secretary. Since the mid-1990s, the general secretary of the CCP has also been the president of China. Over this period, China's governance structure was described by political scientists as a "bureaucratic authoritarian," or single-party state.

In recent years, however, dictatorship has returned to China.[9] Since coming to power in 2013, Xi Jinping has ruthlessly consolidated power. Xi systematically eliminated rivals in an "anticorruption" campaign. To be clear, there is massive corruption within the CCP with party officials becoming multimillionaires, but Xi was selective in how he cracked down, going after enemies and not friends. Moreover, in 2018, the Chinese National People's Congress lifted term limits on the presidency, paving the way for Xi to become president for life. He is the most powerful Chinese leader since Chairman Mao.

Xi has also discarded Deng's guidance about "hiding and biding" and launched China on a new, more assertive path in foreign and defense policy. In the last chapter we marked 2014 as the year in which great power rivalry returned. In Europe, this was the date in which Russia invaded Ukraine. In Asia, it was when China began its island building campaign in the South China Sea.

For years, China and a number of Southeast Asian claimants disputed ownership of islands in the South China Sea and the natural resource rights that come along them. In 2014, China began taking the islands—including from U.S. treaty ally the Philippines—through military coercion. China used land reclamation techniques to build contested reefs into larger islands and then occupied them. President Xi lied to President Obama's face in a Rose Garden ceremony in 2015, declaring that China would not militarize the islands. Within months, the CCP was outfitting the islands with landing strips, naval ports, and surface-to-air missiles. International tribunals have ruled against Chinese claims, but the CCP remains undaunted. The United States and the international community have no good options for forcing China out and the illegal seizures of these contested islands could become permanent.

Xi's signature foreign policy agenda, however, is the Belt and Road Initiative (BRI). Formally, BRI is a plan to use China's vast cash reserves to invest in roads, bridges, and ports in Central Asia and the Middle East in order to resurrect the old Silk Road trading routes between China and Europe. In practice, it is also a grand strategy designed to increase China's geopolitical clout by making countries around the world dependent on Chinese investments. Through BRI, China has increased its presence and influence in Asia, Africa, Latin America, and even Europe.

Beijing has promised to invest up to $150 billion over the next five years on top of the estimated $56 billion spent since 2014 on the prodigious effort. This would be 53 percent higher than what the United States spent on the Marshall Plan to rebuild Europe after World War II.[10]

China's BRI inroads have been most impressive in Asia, where it has gained a greater presence in Pakistan, Myanmar, Laos, Cambodia, Central Asia, Bangladesh, and Sri Lanka.

In Sri Lanka, China agreed to build a port in exchange for the Sri Lankan government repaying China over time from the proceeds derived from the port's operations. But, the agreement turned out to be a debt trap. The terms of the deal were structured in such a way as to make it impossible for Sri Lanka to ever really repay the loan. When Sri Lanka fell behind on its payments, China seized control of the port and the surrounding territory. Many suspect that the CCP will use the port as a military base as it seeks to expand its global footprint.

Indeed, some believe that China is attempting to construct a "string of pearls" of ports and naval bases from China, through South and Southeast Asia, to the Horn of Africa. This would enable China to protect its sea lines of communication and project commercial, diplomatic, and military power throughout the Indo-Pacific region.

The European portion of this BRI effort includes the "16+1" project. This is an attempt by China to curry favor with sixteen nations of Eastern Europe that had formerly been part of the communist bloc during the Cold War. Since the end of the Cold War, these European nations and members of NATO were America's home base, but they are increasingly becoming a battlefield of the new Cold War among the United States, Russia, and China.

In Western Europe, a Chinese state company now operates the port of Piraeus in Greece and Trieste in Italy. The former was used by the Athenians in the Peloponnesian wars, and the latter was formerly part of the Venetian Empire. The European colonization of Asia began with the acquisition of ports in Galle and elsewhere on the way to greater geopolitical influence. Piraeus and Trieste may be the first steps toward China's attempted colonization of Europe.

As China's economy continues to grow, many countries around the world have become increasingly dependent on Chinese trade and investment. Even though many are concerned about China's new, more aggressive stance, they are unwilling to confront Beijing because they feel they have no choice but to do business with this new economic superpower.

Xi has also attempted to cultivate better relations with America's other great rival, Russia. In recent years, Russia and China have conducted joint military exercises and the U.S. Director of National Intelligence has stated that Sino-Russian relations are closer today than at any time since the 1950s.[11]

China has also made a dedicated effort to increase its "soft power" overseas. Here, China was blessed with much raw material, as it possesses a deep history and rich culture that is awe-inspiring to many. To leverage this strength, China has founded Confucius Institutes all over the world to promote Chinese language and culture. These Institutes are funded by the CCP's propaganda arm with the unstated purpose of promoting a pro-China viewpoint and blunting criticism of Chinese policies in the West.

In addition, the CCP has been engaged in more malign and systematic "sharp power" efforts, seeking to use the openness of democratic societies to its advantage.[12] China's "United Front" operates in democratic states, including the United States, to influence government, business, media, and the academy.[13] In the most egregious example, the CCP delivered sacks of cash to an Australian member of parliament in exchange for his advocacy of pro-China policies.[14]

As many have perceived the United States pulling back from the world in recent years, President Xi has attempted to step in and fill the void. He has given speeches in high-profile venues, such as the World Economic Forum in Davos, attempting to portray China as the new global champion for free trade and combating climate change.

The new China challenge also includes an important military dimension. The Chinese People's Liberation Army (PLA) has made military modernization a major priority over the past several decades. Chinese strategists have gone to school on the United States and developed a sophisticated Anti-Access Area Denial (A2/AD) strategy designed to defeat the projection of American military power into East Asia and, over time, to push American forces out of Asia altogether.

The PLA is also investing heavily in the military capabilities needed to support this strategy. In many areas, such as land-based anti-ship missiles and counterspace, China has an edge over the United States.[15] Moreover, while the United States must defend a far-flung system of alliances, Beijing can focus its energies on an East Asia contingency. A decade ago, U.S. military planners joked that China's only option for invading Taiwan would be a million-man swim. Today, they doubt whether the Pentagon could still defend the island from a Chinese attack.

Moreover, China is already lifting its sights beyond East Asia. It is establishing an overseas military presence with a naval base in Djibouti and a listening station in Argentina.[16] Like with civilian technology, some suspect that China may also have an edge when it comes to the military technology of the 21st century, including with militarized AI, directed energy, and hypersonic missiles.

As noted in the introduction, the 2018 U.S. National Defense Strategy states clearly that the return of great power competition with Russia and China is the greatest threat to U.S. national security. Offline, many U.S. defense officials will say that China is the bigger concern. Then-acting U.S. Secretary of Defense Patrick Shanahan set out three priorities in 2019: China, China, and China.[17] Washington can throw money at the Russia problem, but China may be the first true peer-competitor the United States has ever faced. Many in the U.S. defense establishment fear that World War III is possible and, if so, the United States might very well lose.

In sum, over the past several years, China's economic, political, and military power has grown rapidly. Many believe that these trends will continue and the United States, like great powers of the past, will eventually be passed by a rising China.

From our current vantage point, we cannot know, of course, how exactly this rivalry will play out. But we can assess the strength of China's domestic political institutions and this exercise demonstrates that Xi is launching this new challenge from a fragile base.

CHINA'S AUTOCRATIC POLITICS

China is an autocracy. As stated earlier, the CCP maintains complete political control in China and President Xi is the most dictatorial Chinese leader since Mao Zedong. As in other autocracies, the Chinese people lack basic political and civil liberties. They are not allowed a voice in the selection of their government. The CCP uses censorship and repression against those who dare to speak out against it. In one comical example, the party banned online images of the children's cartoon character Winnie the Pooh when commentators noted the unflattering likeness between the rotund and pale bear and President Xi.

Turning to more serious matters, China keeps over one million Muslim Uighurs locked up against their will in "re-education" camps in China's western Xinjiang province. There they are tortured, instructed to recite communist propaganda, and force-fed pork and alcohol in contravention of Muslim beliefs. The purpose is nothing short of the ethnic cleansing of this minority group in order to force them to be part of a unified Chinese nation.

Chinese dissidents, including world-renowned artist Ai Weiwei, are routinely jailed and subjected to inhuman treatment for no more serious offense than criticizing government policy.

The CCP uses facial-recognition technology to follow citizens and monitor their behavior. Each Chinese citizen is given a "social credit" score that can be marked down for infractions as minor as jaywalking. People with poor social credit lose basic freedoms and cannot, for example, purchase train tickets or engage in other quotidian affairs.

Many are rightly concerned about the growing authoritarianism in China, and these trends are certainly worrisome for the Chinese people. From the perspective of great power rivalry, however, creeping authoritarianism in China has another implication: it renders China less fit to compete on the global stage.

CHINA'S AUTOCRATIC ECONOMICS

Many analysts believe that the "China Model" of "state-led capitalism" is the way of the future.[18] Unlike in the United States, when the CCP decides something is necessary for development, like new infrastructure investment, it cracks some skulls and gets it done. No messy political debates get in the way. This model is certainly attractive to many autocrats around the world who seek legitimation for their selfish desire to rule with an iron fist.

Theory and history suggest, however, that state-planned economies cannot generate high rates of return over the long term. Their poor economic institutions do not incentivize growth-enhancing activity. They do not build deep and liquid capital markets. And they are less innovative. Indeed, a closer look at these areas reveal that China's future economic prospects are much bleaker than many appreciate.[19]

Many Western analysts focus on the modernizing capitalist forces in China's economy and overlook the vast segments that are still mismanaged by the CCP. Autocratic leaders choose political control over economic efficiency, and China has been no different. While the "reform and opening" period offered gradual adjustments away from communism in some areas, the Chinese state maintained tight control in other ways. Indeed, the entire purpose of the reforms was to develop the Chinese economy in order to strengthen the CCP and the state.

Small- and medium-sized firms were privatized but large state-owned enterprises (SOEs) remain in the hands of the government. They serve the CCP by, for example, offering employment to large numbers of people. But these large public firms are inefficient and many are unprofitable, but they continue to play an outsized role in the Chinese economy.

Moreover, CCP control has meant that all of China's major factors of production are mismanaged.[20] Functioning capital markets channel money to its most efficient uses, but the CCP directs money to the politically most-expedient applications. The Party requires state banks to provide financing to SOE "zombie firms" to keep them alive, but the banks will likely never recover these bad debts. These and other unprofitable loans are causing a major debt problem in China. America's debt-to-GPD ratio is much too high at about 100 percent, but unofficial estimates put China's debt at three times that amount.[21] This is a financial ticking time bomb embedded in the Chinese financial system.

Land use decisions are also made to advance political goals at the cost of economic performance. The CCP, for example, gives tracts of land to local party officials for pet development projects that make little economic sense. Furthermore in a bid to get rich quick, the CCP neglected environmental safeguards during China's industrialization. The result has been pollution of water, air, and soil.[22] This has major implications for quality of life in China. Chinese colleagues have warned me, for example, against bringing my daughter to China because the pollution would be too harmful on her developing lungs. When I ask about the respiratory health of their children, they reply that it is a major problem, but that, unlike me, they do not have a choice. Indeed, environmental degradation is taking a direct toll on Chinese economic performance by negatively impacting the health of its workforce and contributing to substandard agricultural output.

The CCP has also kneecapped its own labor force. China restricts the movement of people for reasons of political control (such as by limiting the number of people who can live in Beijing), but this undermines labor market mobility. Moreover, decades of China's "one child policy" means that China will have a declining population. Economic productivity depends on maintaining a large portion of one's population in the labor force, but China will soon have large numbers of people ageing out of the workforce and too few working-age people to support them. China will get old before it gets rich.

China could supplement its working-age population with immigration, but China, like most autocracies, is a closed society. Indeed, China suffers from a flow of human capital going the other way, with many talented Chinese studying in the United States and Europe and never returning home. Increasing numbers of Chinese students have been returning in recent years, but the net brain drain is still working against China, not for it.

In a bid to stimulate China's slowing economy, the CCP has made massive infrastructure investments, but much of this investment has been wasted. Basic infrastructure, like roads, bridges, real estate, and airports, were needed in the early days of China's reform period, and investments in these areas contributed to China's rapid growth. But the government has continued to make infrastructure investments even though there is much less need today. I have traveled into China's interior, where I have passed entire ghost towns with entire blocks of empty buildings and no people. This infrastructure spending goosed China's declining growth numbers (because by definition, any government spending increases the size of a country's GDP) but ghost cities in the middle of nowhere do not provide a good return on investment.

In addition, even China's once successful export-led model of growth is coming under new pressures. Autocracies do not mind cheating on international agreements, and for decades Beijing systematically violated the rules of the global trading system. China stole technology from Western firms through industrial espionage and forced technology transfer. Its malicious and widespread theft of intellectual property may have been the largest transfer of wealth in human history. The CCP gives its firms an unfair advantage on global markets by providing them with government subsidies and manipulating China's currency. It forced foreign firms to find a Chinese partner in order to access China's large market. And the list goes on.

For decades, the rest of the world was willing to turn a blind eye to these egregious violations because it hoped that as China grew richer, it would become more cooperative on the international stage. Instead, a richer China only became more combative under President Xi. The rest of the world is no longer willing to be taken advantage of by the CCP and a backlash is forming. Japan, the European Union, and the United States have all decried China's unfair trade practices and they are taking concrete steps to fight back. The United States, for example, launched a trade war against China in 2018 and China's trade and growth numbers are suffering as a result.

The eventual slowing of China's economy was to be expected. Acemoglu and Robinson have argued that autocracies can generate high rates of growth over the short term by directing unproductive resources toward more efficient uses. The CCP's early growth model relied on moving unproductive rural labor in agriculture to urban manufacturing jobs to support export-led growth. It also relied on catching up with the advanced world by importing foreign technology. And it was boosted by government infrastructure spending. They argue that the easy gains from this model have been fully exploited, however, and absent the adoption of more inclusive economic policies, China's growth model will run out of steam.

Many countries in the past found themselves in a similar "middle income trap." They were able to move from low to middle-income status through industrialization, but they eventually stalled out.[23] As China has become richer, it has undermined its own model of export-led growth because its wealthier workers demand higher salaries and make Chinese exports less competitive on international markets. China has been attempting to move up the value chain of production and transition to a more consumer-driven economy, but the results have not yet met expectations.

To continue to grow, therefore, China needs a next act. One obvious step would be to continue its liberalizing reforms and open up more of its economy to a market-based approach. As Acemoglu and Robinson point out, however, closed governments do not like opening their economies.[24] Indeed, today President Xi is moving in the exact opposite direction, reasserting CCP control over the economy and undermining the liberalization of the economy. According to a study conducted by the Asia Society, for example, in ten key areas in which the CCP has promised economic reforms, Xi has stalled or reversed course in eight of them.[25]

China's growth rates have been slowing in recent years as a result. For decades, the Chinese economy regularly grew at over 10 percent a year. It is not possible to keep such high growth rates indefinitely and many economists suspected that Chinese growth would slow as it began to catch up with the industrialized world. Indeed, in 2019, the CCP set its growth target at a mere 6 percent, the lowest since 1990. In the words of President Xi, slower growth rates in China have become the "new normal."[26] Signs of China's slowing economy abound. In 2018, for example, the number of automobile purchases in China declined for the first time in nearly three decades.

Furthermore, even the reported growth numbers may be too high. There is growing evidence that the CCP has for years been cooking the books and exaggerating its official growth numbers. We know that autocracies tend to dissemble, so it is surprising that we accepted the CCP's growth numbers at face value for so long. Indeed, the CCP may have even been lying to itself. When a totalitarian government instructs a provincial official that his target growth rate will be 10%, is it any wonder that he reports that he effectively met his target?

No one really knows China's true economic growth rate, but it is almost certainly less than what the CCP is reporting. Some Chinese academics have estimated that the current growth rate is 1.5 percent, lower than in the United States.[27] Other market analysts believe it might even be "closer to zero and declining."[28]

A decade ago, economists predicted that China would overtake the United States as the world's largest economy by 2020. Now, they are saying it will happen by 2030. By 2030, the projections might be pushed back to 2040. Indeed, China may never surpass the United States as the world's largest economy.

China's financial outlook is even dimmer still. When it comes to global finance, we still live in a unipolar world dominated by the U.S. dollar and financial system. When investors want a safe investment, they buy U.S. Treasury bills; they certainly do not look to Chinese bonds. The yield on a 10-year Chinese bond is currently just over 3%, roughly double that in the United States. Investors demand a premium to hold Chinese debt. Officials in Beijing have called for the dollar to be replaced as the global reserve currency, but short of the creation of an open, deep, and liquid financial market and a more sustainable and transparent economy, the Chinese Renminbi will not dethrone the dollar anytime soon.

Here, too, the CCP has been reluctant to undertake the market reforms necessary to become a true financial powerhouse The Shanghai Free Trade Zone was set up in 2013 to give financial reforms a trial run, but the experiment has been a disappointment. Again, the prioritization of regime survival is stunting the implementation of reforms. The free flow of capital, currency convertibility, establishment of foreign financial institutions, competition in the banking sector, and ease of investment and doing business all remain problems in China. In short, Beijing lacks the kind of financial institutions that have propelled and sustained other great powers in the past. Financial markets simply do not flourish in autocratic states.

Indeed, the biggest testament to the lack of faith in the Chinese economic system is that wealthy Chinese do not keep their assets in China. Fearful that their gains may disappear if left in the Central Kingdom, they instead offshore their wealth, investing heavily in foreign real estate.[29] According to laws in some countries, a large real estate purchase is enough to guarantee citizenship, providing an escape hatch in case the CCP cracks down, or if the system collapses altogether. As such, the most precious investments of the CCP leadership, their children, are often sent to study in Europe and the United States for the same reason. With property, a degree, and a good job after graduation, they can remain in the West if China turns pear shaped. This is not exactly a vote of confidence by Chinese elites in China's economic future.

Can China Innovate?

With market-based reforms out of the question for now, then the future of China's growth depends in large part on the success of future state-led planning, and the CCP is ready to place its next big bet. The program formerly known as "Made in China 2025" is a CCP-led program to help China become the world leader in the next round of technological breakthroughs, including AI, quantum computing, 3D printing, robotics, 5G wireless technology, genetic engineering, and more.

Many believe that China is leading or will win this new tech arms race over the United States. China currently seems to have an advantage in quantum computing and certain applications of AI, for example, including driverless cars and facial recognition technology. As an autocracy, China has certain advantages. It can mass resources toward a specific goal, and it has spent billions on AI. The CCP can also coerce its citizens to adopt new technologies. If the CCP wants to put a billion people in driverless cars, for example, it can force that to happen in a way that the United States simply cannot.[30]

In addition, China has the advantage of scale. The success of a social media firm, for example, is directly related to the size of the network. The more people, the more eyeballs, the more clicks, the more advertisements, the more revenue. There are more people in China than the United States, so social media firms can build bigger networks. Scale advantages help other industries as well.

China also has the advantage of being ruthless. It has less concern about the welfare of its citizens. The United States could have more driverless cars on the road or more facial recognition tracking of its citizens, but for federal highway safety standards and privacy laws.

One widely read article, "Why Technology Favors Tyranny," went so far as to argue that new technology, like AI, gives dictators a systematic advantage over democracies.[31] In the past, it argued democracies excelled in growth and innovation because they were better at processing data, but, since autocracies like the CCP will have access to more data in an AI-centric world, the tables will soon be turned.

To be sure, China has some advantages in this new tech arms race. On the other hand, we have hundreds of years of theory and history to suggest that innovation does not tend to happen in autocratic states.

Indeed, on closer inspection, we see that China's innovation model suffers from the same dysfunctions as its regular economy. Instead of relying on bottom-up innovation, China's strategy rests heavily on placing big bets on mammoth, state-supported, national-champion firms, such as Alibaba, Baidu, Tencent, and Huawei. These firms are doing well for now, but large national champions are not good at sustaining innovation over the long term. Big firms have an incentive to maintain the status quo and lock in large market shares with their existing products. They see new, disruptive technologies as a threat, not an opportunity.

Moreover, by betting on a few big firms, China is distorting the market and picking winners and losers. In so doing, it makes the winners less efficient and kills off other potential sources of innovation. Since the tech giants are backed by the Party, there are real risks for small startups looking to challenge the major players in China. Market systems tend to be better at hedging their bets across a broad range of possible growth trajectories. The CCP can throw substantial resources behind a technology, but it does not know whether it is picking the right winners. After all, China's big bets may be wrong.

Furthermore, China's innovation model is highly parasitic on the global innovation ecosystem and as China becomes more assertive internationally, it risks losing access and undermining its own model. To the degree China has had some success in tech innovation, it is because this has been an area in which the Party has allowed a greater degree of openness to foreign talent, investment, and international collaboration. China is producing vast numbers of scientists and others with technology-related degrees, but Chinese schools still cannot match America's leading universities. Indeed, China's most talented technologists today are still educated in the United States. After all, it is hard to produce world-class research when China's closed society prevents its scholars from accessing the World Wide Web or Google Scholar. Many swoon over China's supposed lead in AI, but AI requires microchips, and China's semiconductor industry lags behind. China is almost completely dependent on foreign-produced microchips. When the United States imposed a trade ban on Chinese tech giant ZTE in April 2018, for example, the firm announced that it would have to shut down. It simply could not operate without access to U.S. microchips. The United States subsequently reversed the decision, but it revealed the vulnerability of China's innovation model to access to global markets. With increased economic nationalism, ongoing trade wars, and the de-coupling of the U.S. and Chinese economies, China's innovation model will likely suffer.

Moreover, China cannot become a worldwide technological leader if there is not worldwide demand for its technology. China is good at building AI algorithms to spy on its citizens, for example. It is currently exporting this capability to other autocratic states. But this will not be a marketable product in democratic nations, which include most of the world's major economies.

More fundamentally, however, CCP meddling undermines the consumer trust that is necessary for technology firms to succeed. China requires the establishment of a CCP organization inside all firms in China, including foreign companies and technology firms. Its policy of "civil-military" fusion requires firms to share technology and data with the CCP whether they like it or not. The Chinese firm Huawei produces high-quality and affordable 5G wireless technology, but many Western nations do not want it. They rightly fear that the CCP will use the control of these networks for espionage, cyberattacks and more. Countries from Australia, to Poland, to the United States have banned Huawei products because they will not allow a potentially hostile CCP to control the digital infrastructure of the 21st century. China cannot become a global technology leader if the rest of the world does not trust its technology.

Finally, the idea that new technology systematically favors tyranny reflects a fundamental misunderstanding about the sources of democratic advantage. Democracies have not made better decisions historically because they possess and process more data. They excelled because they used the data they had to consider multiple points of view, weigh pros and cons, and make sound decisions. Dictators make poor decisions because they dismiss, or are not even exposed to, contrary arguments. Even if China and other autocracies could control all the data in the world, it will not help them fix their poor, politically-driven decision making process. In sum, China's autocratic system will continue to hold back China's economic power.

CHINA'S AUTOCRATIC DIPLOMACY

How does China fare in the diplomatic sphere? Many see China on the march, growing its influence in every major world region. The analysis throughout this book, however, suggests that autocracies like China will lack soft power, and will be likely to provoke counterbalancing coalitions.

Consistent with this expectation, Beijing is a poor alliance builder. Depending on how one counts, China has either zero or one formal ally. In 1961, China and North Korea signed the Sino–North Korean Mutual Aid and Cooperation Friendship Treaty. The treaty contains a mutual defense clause and has been continually renewed and is currently valid until 2021. North Korea is not among the world's most effective alliance partners, however, and on my frequent trips to Beijing, Chinese officials and scholars have increasingly complained that Pyongyang is more of a liability than an asset. North Korea's repeated nuclear and missile tests over the past fourteen years have provoked an international crisis that could escalate into conflict on China's doorstep.[32] China desires geopolitical stability that will provide it the time and space to continue its rise, but that objective is placed at risk by North Korea's illegal nuclear and missile program.

Beijing would prefer that North Korea tone down its provocative behavior, but it is unwilling and unable to stop it. With friends like that, who needs enemies?

Beyond North Korea, China possesses no other formal allies. Beijing has long insisted that it does not need formal alliance partners. In fact, Chinese interlocutors spin this as an advantage. They see the U.S. alliance system as imposing a major burden on the United States, and Beijing, therefore, has made a strategic decision to eschew entangling alliances. This may be a sincerely held view, but to be a true regional and then global power, China will need partners and allies around the world.

Some worry that China and Russia may band together to form a grand autocratic anti-American counterbalancing coalition, but this is unlikely. While these autocratic powers will continue to cooperate in some areas, they are unlikely to ever form a deep and trusting security partnership. There are many conflicts of interest pushing these two autocratic powers apart. Russia is fearful of China's rising power. Given the vast natural resources and declining population in Russia's Far East, some have speculated that China, with its need for resources and growing population, may attempt to make a land grab there. Indeed, Russian experts tell me that their country must maintain a large stockpile of tactical nuclear weapons, not because of the United States, but to deter China. For a Moscow-Beijing axis to form, the roles would need to reverse from the Cold War pattern and President Putin would need to be content to play the role of junior partner to President Xi. That seems unlikely.

The most fundamental obstacle to the formation of a Sino-Russian alliance, however, is their domestic political systems. As we have seen throughout this book, autocracies do not make effective alliance partners. Neither leader fully trusts the other, and autocratic allies fight with each other more than with the enemy. The last time Moscow and Beijing tried to form an alliance, they nearly fought a nuclear war. Even if Putin and Xi sign a formal defense pact tomorrow, it will not mean much because autocracies do not keep their commitments. Autocratic allies often stab each other in the back. These alliances only hold together when they are sustained by coercion (like the Warsaw Pact during the Cold War), and China is not yet, and likely will never be, powerful enough to mold Russia into a puppet state.

Not only has China not forged alliances but its heedless decision-making and aggressive behavior in recent years has begun to provoke counterbalancing behavior. Lacking other sources of legitimacy, the CCP often generates support for its rule by ginning up nationalist sentiment. Provoking a crisis with Japan or harping on other threats to China's "core interests" are a good way to gain public approval, but it comes at a cost internationally. Moreover, with a Marxist-Leninist system of government at home, Beijing habitually exports this model of politics into its international relations. It strikes backroom deals with foreign leaders with or without the support of their populations and clumsily seeks to exert outright control over the policies of smaller states. Increasingly, these and other behaviors are turning countries against China.

This is certainly true for the largest Pacific power: the United States. For decades, the reigning strategy toward China was dual-tracked: hope for cooperation, especially in the economic sphere; but prepare for the worst, including hedging against the Chinese military threat. The U.S. business community was the most sympathetic to China because it saw opportunities to get rich in China's vast internal market. But, now even the American Chamber of Commerce in Beijing has soured on China. Defense and national security experts are even more united on the need to get tough with China. After decades of attempting to cultivate China as a partner, there is now a bipartisan consensus in the U.S. national security community that China is the number one security threat facing the country.[33]

Other major powers in Asia are also concerned by China's recent behavior, especially the democracies. The United States, Japan, India, and Australia have formed "The Quad." This diamond of leading democracies in Asia has set up a mechanism to allow for joint military training and exercises. Although not explicitly directed at China, the true purpose is not lost on anyone.

Many smaller powers in Asia face a dilemma. On one hand, they are dependent on China economically, they are forced to live in China's neighborhood, and they would like to maintain good relations with Beijing. On the other hand, they are afraid of the CCP and hope that the United States will help to guarantee their security against possible Chinese aggression. They do not want to choose, and as long as the United States provides them an option, they will not side with China.

There are many examples of China playing hardball with the very neighbors it is trying to court. In 2014, for example, China built a billion-dollar rig in disputed waters off of Vietnam's coast. The rig may have completed its mission, but at high cost to the Sino-Vietnamese relationship. Ties between Washington and Hanoi have since flourished, with the State Department announcing soon after that the United States would lift its ban on the sale of lethal weapons to Vietnam.

Similarly, when South Korea deployed U.S. THAAD missile defense systems over Chinese objections in 2016, Beijing tightened the screws. The CCP banned Chinese tourists from visiting South Korea and shut down a successful South Korean supermarket chain on the mainland.[34] The gambit worked in showing Seoul that there would be costs to crossing the CCP, but it was also somewhat self-defeating to Beijing's long-run strategy of trying to peel off America's allies in Asia. Increasingly, South Korean officials are willing to speak openly about the threat they face from China.

The BRI is a major effort that the United States must take seriously, but as a Chinese grand strategy (which is how some in the West describe it), it leaves something to be desired. The CCP is almost certainly inflating the numbers.

China has not and likely will not spend anywhere near the advertised amounts on the initiative. Moreover, BRI is an economic loser for China. The best way to understand it is not as an economic strategy, but rather as a means for China to use its vast economic resources for strategic purposes to win over countries along the old Silk Road. Furthermore, BRI is in part a sign of Chinese weakness, not strength. Boxed in from expanding in the East by America and its allies, the expansionist CCP had no choice but to look west to Central Asia.[35] It is betting big on countries that were not central in the U.S.-led international system. But the idea that China is going to win great power competition by forging closer relationships in Central Asia seems a bit implausible.

Further, China's heavy-handed autocratic approach to BRI is already turning away potential partners. The investments have not provided the hoped-for economic development for many host nations because China brings in Chinese firms and guest workers instead of relying on local contractors and laborers. These practices and others are fueling a backlash in some BRI countries. There were major anti-China protests, for example, in Kazakhstan in 2016 and Kyrgyzstan in 2019.

In addition, after witnessing the Sri Lanka debt trap episode mentioned above, many nations have awoken to the fact that Chinese loans come with strings attached. To be sure, some are still attracted to the lure of brand-new ports and highways. And infrastructure in much of Asia is badly needed. But governments are now approaching the Chinese with eyes wide open. The Malaysian government, for example, has declined BRI investments, citing the Sri Lankan example. And a newly elected democratic government in Sri Lanka is attempting to renegotiate terms with China.

The growing backlash against China has also spread to Europe. Just a few years ago, European colleagues were pleased with the economic opportunities provided by Chinese trade and investment, but now they are coming to appreciate the dark side of Chinese money. The European Union has protested China's unfair trade practices. While some European countries have installed China's 5G infrastructure, others have already banned it. Militarily, France and Britain have joined the United States in conducting naval freedom of navigation operations in the South China Sea to challenge China's claims of sovereignty in the area. In March 2019, French President Emmanuel Macron declared that the "time of European naïveté" toward China is over. And in April 2019, an EU document declared for the first time that China should be treated as a "systemic rival."

China's efforts to cultivate soft power have not been very effective either. In a recent ranking of global soft power, China came in twenty-seventh of thirty nations.

The West is also catching on to, and combatting, China's "sharp power" efforts. While there was serious debate in Australia just a few years ago about how to deal with China, there is now a broad consensus that China is a problem and Australia needs a tougher approach. The U.S. Department of Defense has just announced that it will no longer provide Chinese language scholarships to universities with Confucius Institutes. From now on, U.S. universities will need to choose if they want their Chinese language programs funded by the USG or the CCP, but they cannot have both. This may be a prelude to even tougher measures to protect democratic societies from China's malign influence campaigns.

In short, China's efforts to win friends and influence people suffers from Beijing's autocratic politics. The National Bureau of Asian Research reports that "it will be increasingly difficult for the [Chinese] government to prevent its domestic record on political and civil freedoms from affecting China's international credibility."

The free nations of the world will be unlikely to trust an autocratic country to lead on the global stage.

CHINA'S AUTOCRATIC MILITARY

China's military expansion has eroded the U.S. military edge in Asia, but theory and history suggest that autocracies have disadvantages in defense and national security. Viewing the competition through the democracy-versus-autocracy lens sheds new insights on China's military liabilities.

Geographically, China is hemmed in by several island-chains made up mostly of U.S. allies. To project power much beyond its borders, therefore, China will need allies and partners, but, as reviewed earlier, Beijing is doing more to antagonize its neighbors than to win them over. It is surrounded by hostile, democratic neighbors, including Japan, India, and Australia. If it comes to World War III, the United States may be able to draw on up to thirty formal treaty allies that combined make up roughly 60 percent of world GDP. A World War III would be messy and hard to predict, but the pre-bout tale of the tape suggests the U.S. formal alliance system is more powerful than anything China could hope to put together.

Moreover, even though China is purchasing new military hardware, there are doubts about China's ability to employ its newly acquired military kit in battle. The United States military has been battle hardened from over a decade of war, but the PLA's last international conflict was with Vietnam in 1979. Experience matters, and it is simply unclear how the PLA will be able to function in combat.

Moreover, autocratic politics are also undermining PLA effectiveness. To ensure loyalty, the CCP maintains absolute party control of the military. The PLA devotes much of its soldiers' schedules to "political work," or Communist Party indoctrination.[36] President Xi calls this "political work," the "lifeline" of the army, but this is valuable time that is not being devoted to training and exercising. Furthermore, PLA military units are each assigned a minder from the Party, which potentially confuses lines of command and control. In addition, the PLA demands strict obedience to orders, and it is unlikely that lower-level PLA officers will be willing or able to improvise on the battle-field. It is much safer to wait for orders from above than risk being charged with insubordination. No plan survives contact with the enemy, and PLA soldiers will be paralyzed without a plan. The PLA may be fine in the early stages of a tightly controlled military engagement, but it is hard to imagine it doing well once the chaos of war descends.

This is a problem the Party understands. In 2015, the CCP promulgated the "five incapables," stating that some officers cannot: judge situations, understand higher authorities' intentions, make operational decisions, deploy troops, nor deal with unexpected situations.[37] This is a major problem for any military.

The PLA occasionally publishes a "Science of Military Strategy," which functions as a rough equivalent to the U.S. National Defense Strategy.[38] What is most striking about the latest Chinese document is the pervasive belief that warfare must be strictly controlled. Signals will be clearly sent to the enemy and interpreted. The PLA will exert control to carefully escalate or de-escalate the conflict. This unrealistic view of war stands in stark contrast to Western notions of "the fog of war." When one better understands the personnel limitations of the PLA, however, it is understandable why the Chinese would want to believe that war can be carefully controlled. If not, they cannot win.

Like Russia and other autocracies, China struggles with many high-end military technologies. At a major air show in China in November 2018, China showcased its new J-20 fighter aircraft. It would have been an impressive feat, except for the fact that the Chinese planes had to fly with Russian engines because the Chinese-built motors did not work.[39]

The United States deployed its first stealth bomber in the 1980s. The PLA has been working on its own stealth aircraft since that time, but only managed to take its first plane to Initial Operational Capability (IOC) in 2017.[40] Moreover, the plane has not been tested against sophisticated air defense systems and questions remain about whether China's plane truly possesses stealth capabilities or not.

China's struggles with military technology extend to a capability the United States mastered over a half century ago. To maintain a secure, second-strike capability, the United States deploys nuclear weapons on submarines at sea on continuous deterrent patrols. It also arms its intercontinental ballistic missiles (ICBMs) with nuclear warheads, so they are ready to be launched on a moment's notice (this is why U.S. ICBMs are referred to as the "minutemen"). But China has never felt comfortable deploying nuclear weapons on missiles or submarines. Rather, it places its nuclear warheads in central depots with the idea that it would upload its missiles in the event of a crisis or conflict.[41] There is a political logic to this decision. It is easier to ensure strict command and control over nuclear warheads if they are kept in a few central locations. But it also undermines their military utility, rendering China more vulnerable to an American or Russian disarming first strike. Indeed, China placed its first nuclear-capable submarine in the water in 1986, but still at the time of writing, over thirty years later, does not conduct regular deterrent patrols.[42] China simply does not trust its officers to go to sea with nuclear weapons. Moreover, Chinese submarines are noisy and the PLA fears they may be vulnerable to sophisticated U.S. anti-submarine warfare. Indeed, according to Chinese colleagues, part of the rationale for China's island-building strategy in the South China Sea is to provide a "bastion" where China's nuclear submarines can remain protected. But, as with Russia's bastion strategy during the Cold War, the United States will likely be able to hunt Chinese submarines if they are bottled up in a small bastion. Once again, this is an example of how the limitations imposed by China's autocratic system are undermining its military effectiveness.

China is paranoid that the United States possesses an effective nuclear first-strike capability, and they worry greatly about the survivability of their deterrent. China refuses to engage in nuclear arms control talks with Russia and the United States. Beijing's stated reason for this reticence is that their arsenal is much smaller than the superpowers' so there is nothing yet to discuss. I suspect that the real reason is that they fear that greater international transparency about the size and location of their nuclear forces (which is necessary for an effective arms control agreement) will make them even more vulnerable to an enemy attack.

Proponents of autocratic advantage theory state that autocracies can make long-term plans and stick to them. But, theory and history suggest that autocracies are erratic strategic decision-makers. What does the evidence say in China's case? China bounced all over the place under Mao. Things were pretty stable after Deng, but Xi threw away Deng's dictums and his new, aggressive foreign policy is generating a sizable backlash.

Perhaps the CCP will be able to course-correct, but autocracies are not great at self-reflection. Moreover, China's mistakes in recent years have been fairly modest, but, given Xi's centralization over the system, he may only be days away from big, bold, top-down decisions that have cratered autocratic powers in the past. Moreover, the plans often cited as evidence of China's farsighted vision, BRI and Made in China 2025, were only announced in 2013 and 2015, respectively. We should give them at least a few more months before we put them in the pantheon with deterrence and containment or the U.S.-led, liberal international order, as examples of successful long-term strategies.

The most fundamental weakness in China's military forces, however, is the one shared with autocracies as far back as ancient Sparta: the need to "omni balance."[43] Due to real risks of domestic political instability and insurrection, China spends more on domestic security than on foreign security.[44] And the imbalance has been increasing in recent years. It is a world leader in AI technology, but instead of developing killer robots, or other capabilities that would directly threaten U.S. allies and forces, Beijing is leveraging it for facial recognition technology to track potential troublemakers at home.

Moreover, China is devoting significant resources and generating an international backlash in order to lock up its Uighur population in "re-education camps."[45] And, as we discussed earlier, when the CCP worries about domestic instability, it seeks external accommodation.

Finally, there is the very real possibility that the CCP could collapse tomorrow. In 2019, widespread protests broke out in Hong Kong as citizens rejected the CCP's growing authoritarian influence after having enjoyed freedom under more than a century of British rule. Autocratic regimes are most vulnerable at times of leadership transition and by eliminating the CCP's institutionalized succession procedures, Xi has virtually guaranteed that the only way he leaves office will be in a coffin. Indeed, Xi's widespread crackdown on political opposition is not the behavior of a man secure in his rule or confident in the stability of his system. The end of the CCP could mean a new Chinese civil war and another major change in China's foreign policy orientation, contrary to the canard that autocratic systems are more stable or better at selecting and prosecuting long-term strategies. A CCP collapse, like the end of the Cold War, could mean the end of the contemporary China challenge and a renewed global respite from great power competition.

In sum, the CCP is more fearful of its own people than of the Pentagon, and this will limit its ability to become a global military superpower.

Democracy versus Autocracy

China has arguably been a major power for thousands of years and, if the country manages to hang together, it could be a major power thousands of years hence. Its economic growth over the past several decades has been nothing short of remarkable. And there is no doubt that the growing diplomatic and military challenge it presents to the United States and its allies must be addressed with the utmost seriousness.

At the same time, we should understand that a China led by the CCP is unlikely to become the world's leading state. Its Marxist-Leninist model is not well suited to building a world-beating, innovative economy, to winning friends and allies around the world, or to constructing a lethal military force with global power-projection capabilities. China's autocratic system has undermined its competitiveness before, including under the Qing dynasty and Mao's CCP. China did better when it followed Deng's liberalizing economic guidance, but it is reverting to its old form of dysfunctional authoritarianism under President Xi.

Provocatively, the analysis in this chapter suggests that Taiwan's island democracy may actually have an even brighter future than a mainland China controlled by the CCP. This might seem preposterous at first blush given the relative sizes of these countries today, but let us review the historical record. Few would have predicted that the Venetian Republic would sack the capital of its former autocratic imperial master, the Byzantine Empire. No one expected the Dutch Republic to defeat its authoritarian overlords in Madrid. And the United States was an underdog to become the most powerful country in the history of the world when it was a mere colony of the British Empire. Small democratic upstarts have a history of overawing their former imperial masters and becoming global powers in their own right. Perhaps the same future awaits Taipei and Beijing.

In the end, there are only three likely futures for the CCP that will be explored in greater detail in this book's conclusion: reform, stagnate, or collapse. But a world run by the CCP is not in the cards.

Rather, the country best positioned to be a true global leader for the next several decades is the same country that has led the way for the past seventy-five years. That country is the subject of our next chapter.

CHAPTER 13

The United States of America

THE UNITED STATES has been the world's leading liberal leviathan for seventy-five years. It rose from its origins as a grouping of small British colonies to an independent nation and then a global superpower. Its intervention in the world wars of the 20th century pushed the democracies over the edge and secured victory against autocratic rivals. Washington squared off against the Soviet Union in a Cold War for a half century and emerged victorious; its political and economic system proved superior to Russia's communist dictatorship. Then, for twenty-five years, the United States reigned as the world's undisputed superpower. It employed its power to deepen the rules-based international order. This U.S.-led order brought about unprecedented levels of global stability, prosperity, and freedom.

It has been a good ride, but many pundits argue that it is coming to a close. They maintain that we have reached the end of the American era and that other rising powers, such as Russia and China, will disrupt or displace the U.S.-led order. These experts are betting on the wrong horse.

Persistent Pessimism about America's Future

To be sure, the United States has its problems. At home, growing economic inequality, crumbling infrastructure, and rising levels of national debt threaten U.S. economic vitality. America's margin of economic primacy is shrinking, and it is possible it will be surpassed by China as the world's largest economy at some point. The U.S. government lacks an overarching plan for developing emerging technologies, possibly allowing China a first-mover advantage in the new tech arms race.

Diplomatically, relations with allies are strained. Populist movements in the United States and abroad are undermining support for traditional models of global engagement. To the dismay of many, Washington has been criticizing traditional allies and pulling out of long-standing global agreements. State-led capitalism is proving to be a more appealing model than open-market democracy to many autocratic leaders around the world. Russia and China are making diplomatic advances in every geographic region, including in America's traditional backyards of Europe and the Americas. Even some nations who find China's autocratic politics and aggressive foreign policy distasteful cannot resist the temptation of Chinese trade and infrastructure investment.

The United States' margin of military superiority has also been eroded. The United States squandered enormous blood and treasure in Iraq and Afghanistan, but failed to secure lasting victories. Adversaries like Russia and China undermine U.S. and allied security through gray-zone activities, like cyber attacks and election meddling, that fall below the threshold of full-scale war. Moreover, World War III is possible, and if it comes, the United States might very well lose.

The United States once served as a "shining city on a hill," but critics question the health of American democracy, citing increasing polarization across party lines, gridlock in Congress, and other flaws. Partisan divides have become so intense that many Americans now say they would be disappointed if a child married someone from the other side of the political aisle. Others warn that the current occupant of the Oval Office is a dictator in waiting, trampling democratic norms. Some even see the possibility that democracy itself could die in America.[1] I have heard serious people in Washington even claim that, at this point, they are not certain there remains any real moral difference between American democracy and the autocratic political systems in Russia and China.

Given these developments, does the United States still have what it takes to be the undisputed global leader?

This is not the first time that pundits predicted the end of America. Indeed, declinism is something of an American pastime. In the 1970s, many believed the United States was losing the Cold War and that Soviet-style communism was the wave of the future. In the 1980s, some thought that Japan and its coordinated-market economy were superior to America's liberal-market model and that Japan would soon become the world's largest economy. The unipolar era had barely started before scholars began predicting anti-American balancing coalitions and a return to a multipolar world.[2] It almost seems as if these U.S.-based analysts were rooting for the decline of their own country. Whatever their motivation, they got it wrong. Instead, the United States emerged from each of these past periods of predicted decline stronger than ever.

Decades from now, it is possible that we will, with the benefit of hindsight, look back on the current strain of pessimism with a similar bemusement. The United States certainly has its flaws, but where it really counts—in its institutions—it remains second to none.

American Democracy

The United States is the world's oldest constitutional democracy. Fleeing persecution by European monarchs, the American founding fathers set up a system to check and balance the chief executive. The authors of the U.S. constitution were also very much inspired by the mixed system of government that proved so successful for the ancient Roman Republic. Individuals are selected for political positions through competitive elections. Freedom of the press, assembly, and many other liberties help to ensure that citizens have the opportunity for meaningful political participation. According to Polity, the United States has been rated as a democracy for over two centuries.[3]

Contemporary warnings of a possible decline in American democracy should be taken seriously, but, on inspection, they are often overblown. To be sure, American democracy is imperfect, but democracy does not require perfection. It requires free and fair elections and the broad range of civil and political rights that allow for meaningful political participation. There is no doubt that the United States meets this standard.

Worries about a U.S. president's putative autocratic tendencies are not new; they are baked into the system. America's founders were revolting against overbearing British monarchs and they wanted to be sure to prevent an overwhelming concentration of power in the executive branch. George Washington was criticized for his presumed monarchic ambitions. More recently, commentators criticized George W. Bush for supposedly consolidating power and creating an "imperial presidency."[4] What is truly most notable about the U.S. system, however, is not executive overreach, but the degree to which Congress and the courts, and the executive branch itself, continually step in to check the chief executive.[5] This continues to remain true, even in the current era.

In sharp contrast to Russia, journalists do not have to worry that they will be shot in the back for criticizing the president. And, in distinction to China, the United States does not keep millions of Muslims locked up in re-education camps. It is perverse to draw a moral equivalence between democratic politicking in the United States and the gross evils perpetrated in Russia and China.

American democracy is strong enough to survive contemporary controversies and political scandals. There is little reason to believe that today's headlines will be more damaging than the Teapot Dome Scandal, Watergate, Iran-Contra, or the Monica Lewinsky affair.

Indeed, contrary to the prevailing narrative, intense domestic political fights and polarization are not evidence that American democracy has failed; rather, they are proof that the system is working. Yes, democracy can be messy, but that is what makes the system great. These disagreements are not even permitted in autocratic states. Serious political conflicts of interest in autocracies often result in dead bodies. Our democratic political system gives us the ability to work out our differences through a mutually accepted and peaceful, institutionalized process. Legislative gridlock is not necessarily a problem. If half of the country strongly disagrees with a proposal, then it is not obviously a good idea, and probably should not become national law. The purpose of the U.S. government is not to enact legislation for its own sake but to ensure "life, liberty, and the pursuit of happiness." By those measures the country is doing pretty well.

As Machiavelli argued five hundred years ago, discord within a republican system of government is not always pretty, but the results are more than worth it. Nations that desire expanded freedom at home and influence abroad should not rebuke domestic political struggles within a democracy, but celebrate them.

Indeed, the institutionalized tumult and discord in the United States will likely continue to be the primary engine for its continued international power and influence abroad.

America's Economic Position

Theory and history suggest that democracies are more likely to sustain high, long-run rates of economic growth, to innovate, and to be global financial centers. The United States exemplifies each of these rules.

America's democratic system continues to fuel the world's largest and most dynamic economy. It has possessed the world's largest GDP since the late 1890s. Today, roughly 24 percent of the world's economic output ($20 trillion) happens in the United States. China only possesses about 15 percent of world GDP ($12 trillion). For years, China was gaining ground, but that may no longer be the case. The U.S. annual growth rate at the time of writing was about 3 percent. The reported number in China is 6 percent, down from consistent 10 percent annual returns from just a few years ago. And, as we saw in the last chapter, many suspect the true rate of growth in China is lower, perhaps even zero.

As the American Enterprise Institute's Derek Scissors puts it, "The year 2030 turns out not to be a bad estimate for when China will pass the U.S. in economic size, but so is never."[6]

Moreover, even if Beijing does grab the top spot, it might not keep it. Given its aging workforce, some projections have China overtaking the United States only to fall back into second place shortly thereafter.

In short, the United States has possessed the world's largest economy for over a century and it is quite possible that it will retain the top spot for decades to come. Moreover, even if it falls to number two, it may still be well positioned to remain the world's global leader for some time. After all, Great Britain's economy was surpassed by the United States in the 1890s, but London was still the single-most influential state in the international system until 1945.

Furthermore, GDP is only one measure of economic heft. America's GDP per capita dwarfs China's ($59,000 to $8,000, respectively). The United States is a high-income country. China is a middle-income country with some wealthy areas, such as Shanghai, and impoverished, rural areas that have more in common with sub-Saharan Africa than with Ohio.

Perhaps the most important measure of a state's economic capacity for great power competition, however, is net wealth, and here the gap is large ($100 billion to $50 billion) and growing in America's favor. GDP is an annual measure of production. Net wealth measures the stocks of wealth a society has accumulated over time. America has been a wealthy country for over a century; China is just getting started. Stocks of net wealth are highly relevant because a state can draw on all available resources for major power competition, not just what is produced in a given year.

America has been the world's leading economy in part because it has been the world's most innovative economy. For centuries the most important economic innovations have taken place in the United States: lightbulbs, airplanes, the assembly line, nuclear weapons, the silicon microchip, the Internet, Global Positioning System, the iPhone, and Facebook, among many others.

For years, U.S. leaders worried about their dependence on imports of oil and gas from the Middle East. In the 1970s, an OPEC oil embargo brought an economic recession to American shores. Many analysts argued that a desire for energy security was leading the United States to become overly engaged in the Middle East. Instead of fretting over the problem, America fixed it. The shale gas revolution unlocked trapped energy resources in North America and almost overnight transformed the United States into a global energy superpower.[7]

Who knows what lies just around the corner? At present, the world stands on the cusp of what could be the biggest technological revolution since the coming of the digital age. The Fourth Industrial Revolution includes artificial intelligence, robotics, advanced manufacturing, biotechnology, and many other emerging technologies that have the potential to fundamentally reshape modern economies and societies. Some fear that China may have the lead in these new domains because they have a unified government plan and because they are throwing a lot of money at the problem. But there are centuries of theory and history that tell us that the biggest technological breakthroughs happen in open societies. The First and Second Industrial Revolutions occurred in Great Britain. The Third Industrial Revolution took place in the United States. And there is good reason to believe that the fourth installment will also be made in the USA.

As we saw in the last chapter, China's economy is dominated by large, state-owned enterprises. These companies are so important politically that China will not allow them to go out of business. They cannot fail.

In the United States, we succeed because we fail. Many different ideas and products are brought to market. Almost all fail. The ones that do not can change the world.

U.S. government investments in basic science have been critical in past technological breakthroughs, including nuclear power and the Internet. And the United States could do more to invest in the technologies of the future. Democracies are often slow to build consensus for a problem, and that helps them to avoid big mistakes. But when a national consensus is achieved, they can mass resources toward a problem just as well as any autocracy. And Washington is beginning to awake to this new Sputnik moment. When it does, it will be well positioned to compete.

According to the World Economic Forum (WEF), the United States is the world's overall number one most competitive economy, while China lags far behind at number 28. Looking at subcomponents of the survey, WEF ranks the United States number one for its labor market, financial system, and business dynamism. It is in the top three for product markets, skills, market size, and innovator capability. China on the other hand ranks in the top five for only a single subcategory: market size. The United States still spends more than China on R&D and has higher levels of venture capital investments. The United States is ahead of China on venture capitalism spending in eight out of nine measured emerging technologies, including autonomous driving, robotics and drones, AI and machine learning, big data, 3D printing, and education technology.

The United States' most commanding economic advantage, however, may be its financial system. Since the time of the Venetian Republic, capital markets have only flourished in open societies. The United States has been at the center of global finance since 1945. The New York Stock Exchange is the largest stock market on Earth. This helps to ensure that U.S. businesses have the capital they need to make investments and help grow the American economy.

U.S. Treasury Bonds remain the world's safest investment. This allows the U.S. government to borrow at low rates of interest and to run deficits to finance spending, including for national defense.

The dollar remains the most important global reserve currency. Foreigners' desire to hold the U.S. dollar as a store of wealth provides the United States with the "exorbitant privilege" of "seigniorage."[8] The United States is the only country in the world that can create wealth simply by printing money. It costs the U.S. government a few cents to print a $100 bill, but foreigners must give up $100 worth of goods or services to obtain one.

America's central financial position also contributes to its ability to conduct economic statecraft. Every other economic actor on Earth requires access to the U.S. economic and financial system in order to function. They must be able to access the dollar to conduct international transactions. They would like to have access to the U.S. stock exchange to raise capital and to the U.S. domestic consumer market, the world's largest, in order to sell their goods. Washington can, therefore, promise to grant, or threaten to cut off, access as a tool of influence.

In recent years, the United States developed an innovative new means of economic statecraft: secondary sanctions. To address the Iran and North Korea nuclear crises in the 2010s, Washington did not sanction Iran or North Korea, because direct U.S. trade and financial ties to both countries had long been cut off. Instead, it sanctioned the rest of the world. The U.S. Treasury threatened to designate for sanctions any government, firm, or bank around the world that transacted with Iran or North Korea. This forced the rest of the world to choose between doing business with either the United States, or Iran and North Korea. That is really no choice at all. The rest of the world cut off economic ties with both countries, helping to build unprecedented levels of economic pressure against them. That is a kind of economic hegemony that Russia and China, with their dysfunctional financial systems, simply cannot match.

Some, including in China, have called for a new reserve currency to replace the dollar, but there is no alternative in sight. Capital controls in China guarantee that the Renminbi (RMB) will not become a widely held reserve currency absent fundamental reforms. Russia is an economic basket case. And the political divisions within Europe make it less than ideal as a global financial center, as the European debt crisis demonstrated. Indeed, in recent years, as great power competition has grown more intense, the U.S. dollar has continued to grow stronger relative to other major currencies, including the Chinese RMB.

To be sure, the United States has economic problems. Growing inequality in the United States is a major issue.[9] The United States needs to figure out a way to compensate the losers from globalization and automation. The United States could use more infrastructure investment. A more coordinated approach to developing emerging technology could be helpful. And it must seek to reform entitlement spending to ensure fiscal solvency into the future.

Given that democracies are pretty good at course correction, especially in times of genuine crisis, the United States is well positioned to address these issues. While the challenges are serious, they are not nearly as severe as the problems plaguing the Russian or Chinese economies. Elites in Russia and China agree, and that is why they are investing their resources in the United States.[10] In 2018, 10,000 more millionaires immigrated to the United States than departed, while Russia and China experienced a net outflow (7,000 and 15,000, respectively) of high-net worth individuals. Of all the countries on the planet, none has a brighter economic future than the United States.

American Diplomatic Strength

It is often argued that America's greatest strength is its network of global allies and partners. Like democracies from time immemorial, Washington has tended to excel at winning friends and influencing people. Washington maintains over fifty formal allies in Europe, Asia, and Latin America. These allies are among the best-governed and wealthiest countries on the planet. Combined they make up roughly one-quarter of all states in the international system and almost two-thirds of world GDP. Moreover, Washington works with many more informal security partners, such as Taiwan in Asia and Israel, Jordan, and the Gulf States in the Middle East.

U.S. allies are partners for economic exchange and mutual wealth creation in the global economy. They amplify the power of U.S. sanctions. Allies supply Washington with diplomatic support in international fora to take difficult actions or tackle intractable problems. America's security partners provide the U.S. military with a global military presence, including basing and overflight rights. Their soldiers fight shoulder-to-shoulder with American men and women, enhancing battlefield effectiveness. Revisionist autocratic powers considering aggression should be deterred by the prospect of fighting the entire free world at the same time.

Some argue that U.S. alliances are fraying. They cite harsh criticism of old friends coming out of the current U.S. administration; policy differences over the Iran nuclear deal and climate change; increasing independence of formal treaty allies, like Turkey; and inroads made by Russia and China into America's traditional spheres of influence. These are real concerns, but they must also be put in perspective.

The current U.S. administration is not unique in asking America's allies to contribute more to their mutual defense. This has been a source of frustration since the dawn of history. Burden sharing caused tensions for democratic alliance leaders from the Delian League's tribute to Athens to Roman provinces contributing soldiers to the Roman legions. America encountered the same problems as soon as it emerged as the democratic leader in 1945. Every U.S. presidential administration since Eisenhower has asked the Europeans to do more for the common defense. President Obama's secretary of defense, Robert Gates, even used his final speech in office to travel to Brussels and lambast Europe over its meager defense spending. These tensions will continue, but they will also be manageable.

Moreover, lest we forget, Washington and its allies have made it through tough times in the past. They had serious disagreements about the Suez Crisis in 1956, the Vietnam War in the 1960s and 1970s, and the U.S. invasion of Iraq in 2003. Yet, the American-led league of democracies weathered the storm.

Further, things are better behind the scenes than one may suspect from reading the headlines. Even though White House messaging is inconsistent, the rest of the U.S. government has taken concrete steps to strengthen U.S. alliances on the ground. In stark contrast to the diplomatic problems face by Russia and China, when U.S. allies do complain it is generally because they demand more, not less, American involvement in their countries and regions. Moreover, societal support for America's traditional global leadership role remains strong. When NATO Secretary General Jens Stoltenberg addressed a joint session of the U.S. Congress in April 2019, he received an enthusiastic standing ovation. And in recent public opinion polling, record numbers of Americans expressed support for U.S. security alliances.

In addition to its formal network of allies, the United States also possesses significant reservoirs of "soft power."[11] American people, values, and culture are widely admired. Until recently, the United States ranked number one in a worldwide ranking of national soft power.[12] Under President Trump, the United States dropped to fourth place, but its position will likely rebound with a more conventional president in the future. Moreover, the top twenty countries are all democracies and all but a few are formal U.S. allies. China and Russia come in at numbers 27 and 28, respectively. While the U.S. brand may have been tarnished in recent years, it is still much more popular than that offered by Russia or China.

Russian and Chinese growing assertiveness is stressing U.S. alliances in some instances, but, on balance, it is helping to reinvigorate them. For twenty-five years after the end of the Cold War, NATO searched for a new mission. Now that mission is clear: collective defense of Europe against possible Russian aggression. And as we saw in the last chapter, China is provoking a significant counterbalancing coalition that is pushing other countries in Asia and around the world into Uncle Sam's embrace.

State-led capitalism appeals to some would-be autocrats, but the U.S. model of free politics and economics remains more attractive to our democratic friends in Europe and Asia. At the end of the day, it is likely that the free nations of the world will continue to prefer the United States, despite its flaws, over its corrupt, autocratic competitors.

America's Military Strength

America's final advantage is its military strength. The United States remains the world's only military superpower. It has global power-projection capabilities. As it demonstrated as far back as World War II, it can bring military forces to any spot on the globe and wage a sustained, major-theater war. It currently deploys forces on every major continent except Antarctica. Russia and China lack these capabilities.

When analysts worry about World War III, they are talking about a possible fight in Russia or China's backyard. Some international relations theorists argue that we are moving to a more multipolar world. But in the classic European balance of power system, Prussia's ability to threaten France was roughly equivalent to France's capacity to do harm to Prussia. Until

Russia and China have the ability to fight a full-scale war in North America, talk of genuine multipolarity is premature.

In addition, as the United States demonstrated in Iraq, Afghanistan, Serbia, and Libya, hostile dictators in small and medium-sized countries remain in power only at the mercy of the U.S. Department of Defense. While rebuilding governments has proved to be an insurmountable challenge, the Pentagon has shown that it can topple them with relative ease.

The United States uses its large economy to continue to invest in military strength. Its annual defense spending towers over that of its competitors at $718 billion per year, compared to $146 billion in China and $68 billion in Russia. Indeed, the United States spends more on defense than the next nine countries combined, and most of these countries are U.S. allies and partners.

China is certainly expanding its military capabilities, but it takes time (often a decade or more) to build major military platforms. Even if Xi Jinping makes the decision to do so today, it would take China until 2050 at the earliest to become a global military superpower.

Washington also has trust in its officer corps and strong civil-military relations. The United States is comfortable delegating tactical decisions to commanders on the ground. This provides a significant advantage over more sclerotic autocratic competitors, especially in a messy, high-intensity fight.

The United States also retains a healthy lead in military applications of high technology and strategic forces. Washington first deployed stealth technology in the late 1980s, for example. China has been working on stealth technology since that time, and it is still not clear whether it has mastered it. Washington is still the only great power that conducts regular nuclear deterrence patrols with its submarine force; this is a strategic advantage that is sixty years old and counting.

Washington is also exploring new military technologies: hypersonic glide vehicles, directed-energy lasers for missile defense, and other sci-fi-like capabilities. The United States is already incorporating 3D printing into its defense acquisition process, with the potential to produce better products while drastically lowering the defense budget.[13] China and Russia are also working in these areas, but history and theory, from the Greek phalanx to thermonuclear weapons, suggest that an open society will likely be the first to develop novel military technologies and the operational concepts to put them to good use.

Perhaps America's greatest military strength, however, is the simple fact that it can focus its defense strategy against foreign threats. Unlike its autocratic foes, U.S. leaders do not worry that the American system of government might fall tomorrow. As a result, they do not need to spend exorbitant amounts on domestic security. To be sure, the United States has effective law enforcement and provides adequate resources to the FBI and state and local police. But among the new great power competitors, the United States is unique in spending less on domestic security than on international security. If you follow the money, Russia and China believe that the greatest threat to their security comes from their own people. In the United States, domestic tranquility provides for our common defense.

U.S. domestic political stability will allow Washington to continue to execute its consistent grand strategy from the past seventy-five years and counting: expanding and defending the U.S.-led, rules-based international order. Pessimists have argued that this order is dead, but they are incorrect. It can and should be revitalized, adapted, and defended for a new era.[14]

The United States has certainly made some costly errors in foreign and defense policy. Most believe the Iraq war was a mistake and the execution of the conflicts in both Iraq and Afghanistan left something to be desired. Yet, consistent with democracies in the past, America's mistakes have been fewer and easier to rectify. Occupying Iraq and Afghanistan is not invading Russia in the winter. Despite fighting for nearly two decades in what may be considered losing wars, the United States remains the world's preeminent military power.

Most analysts worried about war with Russia and China agree that the American military is stronger in the aggregate. Rather, what frightens them is the prospect that Russia and China could conduct a limited land grab of an American ally or partner in their near-abroad, presenting the United States with a fait accompli. Russia may invade Estonia, or China could attempt to take Taiwan, for example. In this scenario, Russia and China would be on the defensive in their own backyard and it would fall on the United States to fight a costly war of liberation against their formidable opponents. Russian and Chinese forces include so-called Anti-Access Area Denial (A2/AD) capabilities, such as submarines and anti-ship missiles, that would make it hard for the United States to project power near Russian and Chinese territory. Moreover, they argue the balance of resolve would favor China and Russia in these contingencies because, after all, they would care deeply about a war on their border, whereas for Washington the stake is merely protecting a small ally on the other side of the world.

Russia and China's ability to contest the United States and its allies in Russia and China's near abroad is growing, and this is a cause for concern. But this challenge must be put in perspective. U.S. military strategy is difficult today precisely because America is so powerful. The new military flashpoints have been pushed all the way to our adversary's sovereign borders, so it is no surprise that they may have an edge. We are playing an away game and they have home field advantage.

But, these scenarios also provide a number of advantages for Washington. Since the United States would be fighting on their doorstep, these conflicts would begin to directly threaten the homelands and possibly even the regimes of our autocratic allies even at relatively low levels of escalation, The United States, protected by two oceans, may very well be able to wage a full-scale war in these distant regions while the U.S. homeland remains untouched. Moreover, the reason Russia and China can invade U.S. allies in these scenarios is because they are surrounded by U.S. allies who would likely rally to fight alongside the United States. It is Russia and China, not the United States, that are surrounded by hostile Eurasian nations. Finally, the balance of resolve may actually favor the United States in this new era of great power rivalry. The U.S. stake in the conflict would be nothing less than defending the U.S.-led international system. If it lost a war to Russia or China, then one could kiss that system goodbye. While Russia and China would be fighting to carve out a sphere of influence over a small state on their borders, Washington would be fighting for everything it has built over the past seventy-five years.

After all, Germany's arguably greater stake and home field advantage in World War II–era Europe proved no match for American military might and its league of powerful allies. Defense planners in Beijing must be highly cognizant of the fact that the United States has arguably never lost a regular, state-on-state war. If, God forbid, China's rise does result in World War III, both theory and history suggest that it will turn out disastrously for Beijing.

Democracy versus Autocracy

In sum, America's vibrant economy, its strong alliance relationships, and its unmatched military, all reflections of the U.S. domestic political system, will continue to provide a significant source of strategic advantage for the United States over its autocratic competitors in the years to come. The international security environment is becoming more competitive, and the United States does not enjoy the unchallenged primacy it enjoyed in the 1990s. We have returned to an era of great power rivalry. But, there is no doubt that among these great powers, the United States remains far and away the *Primus Inter Pares*, or first among equals.

After all, ask yourself: if you had the option of playing the position of either Washington, Beijing, or Moscow in this new era of great power competition, which side would you choose? As an American, I, for one, would not switch places.

Social scientists might ask if the argument of this book is "falsifiable." In other words, how would we know if it is wrong? The answer is simple. The argument of this book will be proven wrong if the United States is surpassed as the clear global leader by an autocratic country, such as China. To accomplish this feat, China would need to come to possess more global economic and military power than the United States, be in a position to set the rules that govern the international system, and sustain this position for an enduring period of time. As the above analysis shows, however, this seems unlikely. We will not see the day when the United States is second among nations of the world any time soon.

So, what should Washington do with this unrivaled power?

PART IV | The Democratic Advantage in the Future

CHAPTER 14

Implications
for American Leadership

G REAT POWER RIVALRY has returned to international politics. After a quarter century of virtually uncontested American leadership, the United States faces serious geopolitical challenges from autocratic competitors, Russia and China. Will the United States retain its position as the world's leading state, or will the U.S.-led global order be disrupted or displaced by Russia and China?

This book argued that democracies have built-in advantages in long-run geopolitical competitions and that the United States will likely remain the world's leading state for the foreseeable future. It came to this conclusion by building on the political philosophy canon and contemporary social science research to develop a new way of thinking about power in international politics, tracing the origins of global power to domestic political institutions. It argued that to succeed in international political competition, a state must possess economic, diplomatic, and military strength. It further maintained that democracies perform better in key economic, diplomatic, and military functions. For this reason, democracies tend to amass more wealth and power than their autocratic competitors and to excel in great power rivalries.

This argument was then demonstrated through some simple statistics and a series of seven historical studies, comparing democratic and autocratic rivals from the ancient world to the present, including Athens against Persia and Sparta, the Roman Republic versus Carthage and Macedon, the Venetian

Republic against the Byzantine Empire and the Duchy of Milan, the Dutch Republic and the Spanish Empire, Great Britain and France, the United Kingdom and Germany, and the United States and the Soviet Union. These studies did not show that democracies maintain permanent global hegemony, but they did reveal that open states have consistent, structural advantages in great power competitions. It also demonstrated that democracies have a knack for landing at or near the top of the global pecking order and that they have, on balance, fared better in enduring rivalries than their autocratic rivals. More open polities have played an outsized role in great power competition for over two thousand years and have ruled the international system for the past half a millennium. Autocrats, such as Xerxes, Phillip II, Louis XIV, Napoleon, Hitler, and Stalin, have repeatedly made bids for global mastery, but they failed in the end, with their democratic competitors standing triumphantly over them.

The same fate likely awaits Messrs. Xi and Putin. Indeed, this book examined the current competition between the democratic United States and its autocratic rivals, Russia and China. The exercise demonstrated that Washington possesses significant power advantages over Moscow and Beijing. In many important areas, the gap in America's favor even seems to be growing. A careful examination into the domestic political institutions of all three states showed that, for all of its problems, America's fundamentals still look much better than Russia's and China's.

Taken together, therefore, the book found significant support for the idea that democracies enjoy a systematic advantage in great power politics. The United States will likely remain the world's leading power and Russia and China may be in trouble.

The competing autocratic advantage argument was considered, but it did not hold up under investigation. To be sure, autocracies can perform certain tasks, like taking bold action, more easily than democracies, but this so-called advantage often leads to big mistakes. Moreover, other supposed advantages of autocracies are not really inherent to autocracies. Some argue that autocracies are better at steady, long-run planning or at acting without scruples, but throughout history we have seen many fragile and fickle autocrats and stable and stony democrats. Indeed, contrary to conventional wisdom, we saw that democracies tend to maintain a more stable long-term strategic direction. Further, the alleged weaknesses of democracies put forward by autocratic advantage advocates, such as checks and balances resulting in stalemate and discord, are actually among their greatest strengths. There is just not that much evidence for the idea that autocratic systems are better suited for great power rivalry.

Currently, many in the West are concerned that President Xi in China and Russia's President Putin are tightening their grips on power. They see these steps as indications of firm leadership, just as Western democracies appear to be more fractious and harder to govern than ever. But this is the wrong lesson to draw. The increasingly autocratic systems in Russia and China are a major problem, not for the United States, but for Russia and China. As Xi and Putin systematically eliminate any domestic political obstacles to their unchecked power, they also exacerbate the weaknesses inherent in their autocratic political models.

This book, therefore, made the "hard-power" case for democracy. Generally, democracy is admired because it is the best political system for advancing freedom, human rights, the rule of law, and human dignity. Those are important attributes, and democracy is rightly celebrated for these normative reasons. But by focusing too much on these softer assets, we overlook other important and practical benefits of democracy: Democracy is the best machine ever invented for generating enormous state wealth, influence, power, and prestige on the international stage. Indeed, it is difficult if not impossible to achieve lasting global mastery without it.

The United States and its democratic allies and partners should be proud of their domestic political systems not just because they are morally superior but also because they are more effective. Autocrats have some explaining to do, not just because their political systems are immoral, but also because they are corrupt, inefficient, and ultimately make their countries weaker.

International relations (IR) scholars have thoroughly studied the role of power in international politics, but they have largely overlooked some of the most interesting and important issues. They have asked: What kind of international distribution of power is more stable? Are bipolar worlds with two major powers more or less peaceful than multipolar worlds with three or more great powers? What are the conditions under which power transitions lead to war? Do international systems with one dominant power tend to have greater levels of economic openness? And the list goes on.

In all of these studies, however, IR scholars have been obsessed with the effects of power, not its causes. Rather, they take power as a given, or "exogenous" variable, and do not examine what generates power in the first place.

But questions about the fundamental causes of power may be the most critical to understanding international politics. Why are some countries more powerful than others? Why do some countries rise to enter the circle of the great powers while others do not? Why do some great powers achieve global ascendancy while others burn out? Why do power transitions occur? After millennia of the world's leading thinkers pondering the role of power in world statecraft, we have barely begun to scratch the surface on this set of important questions.

This book advances IR theory, therefore, by providing a clear and novel theoretical explanation that traces the origins of power in world politics to domestic political institutions. The argument of this book is that democracies dominate.

There are other implications for international relations theory as well. IR scholars argue that states form coalitions to balance against dominant states, but this study showed that balancing behavior often depends on the regime type of the potential hegemon. States balance against autocracies, consistent with past theory, but they often bandwagon with powerful democracies. In addition, foreign-imposed regime change is often seen as an aberration, especially following the U.S. invasion of Iraq, but the historical review in this book revealed that it is actually a recurring feature of international politics. Democratic and autocratic states alike regularly attempt to overthrow the enemy's form of government and install a new one in their own image. Moreover, democratic peace theory may hold in more modern times, but open states often engaged in direct warfare in the past, from the ancient world to the Italian Renaissance.

Turning to real-world implications, while many predict an end to the American era, this book gives us good reason to believe that the United States will continue to be the world's leading country indefinitely. We are no longer living in the "unipolar moment" of overwhelming American primacy that we witnessed for the twenty-five years from 1989 to 2014.[1] But the United States is and likely will continue to be the leading state among multiple, competing great powers.

By my calculation, the average reign for a dominant democracy atop the international system is 130 years, with a range of 95 years for Athens at the low end and 221 years for Great Britain at the high end. The United States clocks in at 75 years and counting. If history is any guide, therefore, it still has a couple of good decades and maybe another century to go.

The laws of social science, however, are probabilistic and not deterministic. In other words, unlike the laws of gravity in physics, none of our theories are certain in international relations. As Machiavelli cautions, success in international politics is the result of both *virtu* and *fortuna*. The literal translations of these words are virtue and fortune, but his intended meaning was somewhat closer to what we would today call skill and circumstances. Machiavelli argued that even the most skilled leaders sometimes fail due to other overriding forces and that when circumstances are propitious, skilled leaders must still be prepared to seize the moment.

In other words, the U.S. system is competitive, but Washington still must compete. So, what should the United States do at this moment to maximize its chances of success?

To design a sound strategy, one must first accurately survey the strategic environment. Russia and China are unlikely to replace the United States as global leader, but they do pose a serious threat to U.S. and allied security and economic well-being.

Moscow and Beijing rightly believe that the U.S.-led, liberal international order poses an existential threat. They do not like to see the United States projecting military power across the globe. They are bothered by the spread of America's alliance network right up to their sovereign borders. They do not have to play by the rules at home, so they chafe under an expectation that they follow a rules-based order abroad. They cannot outcompete market economies and they are frustrated that the democratic core is pushing back on their attempts to prey on the international economic system. They rightly fear that the spread of democracy could led to the very collapse of their regimes. In sum, they are threatened by the U.S.-led, rules-based order and they are doing their best to either revise it or tear it down; as President Putin has said, "new rules or no rules."

Make no mistake, the threat these states pose to the U.S.=led order is ideological in nature. The renewed great power competition with Russia and China is not purely a realist game of great powers pragmatically jockeying for power and influence. Rather, like many of the autocracy versus democracy battles we have seen throughout history, it is a clash of political models. It is a fundamental dispute about the best way to govern societies both at home and abroad. For some, the autocratic system of domestic repression, state-led economies, and an illiberal foreign policy will be appealing. But nearly all of America's traditional friends and allies will be much more attracted to the U.S. model of open markets and free politics. We must make it clear to these partners that their day-to-day engagements with Russia and China are not, therefore, isolated decisions about whether to, for example, buy cheap Russian gas or allow Chinese infrastructure investment, but rather a more fundamental choice between democracy and autocracy. They must decide what type of political system they want for themselves and others and what kind of world system they want to inhabit.

Some have argued that Russia and China do not pose an ideological challenge because, unlike the Soviet Union, they are not intentionally looking to export their model. China is, however, helping autocrats around the world deploy technology that will help governments repress their citizens. Moreover, Moscow and Beijing are contributing to an international environment characterized by democratic backsliding globally as other strongmen eagerly emulate their models. Furthermore, and perhaps most importantly, this is an ideological competition because Moscow and Beijing are threatened by democratic ideology. They want to create an international system in which their regimes can continue to survive and thrive; they want to make the world safe for autocracy.

These are not objectives that the United States and its allies should accommodate. While the U.S.-led order may not serve the interests of autocrats in Russia and China, it has made the world a more peaceful, prosperous and well-governed place over the past seventy-five years. Giving in to Russia and Chinese demands would mean a return to international conflict, decreased worldwide living standards, and the retreat of global democracy and good governance.

How then can the United States best maintain its international leadership position? To stave off decline, it can begin by learning from the fates of the liberal hegemons that have preceded it. We have seen in this book that democratic great powers have done quite well historically, but they have fallen for three reasons. Athens was defeated primarily due to a rash decision permitted by its system of direct democracy. Rome and Venice lost their vitality when they closed the open political systems that had sustained their rise. Finally, the Dutch Republic and Great Britain were surpassed by other, even more competitive, democratic rivals; England overtook the Dutch Republic and Great Britain passed the baton of democratic global leadership to the United States.

Domestically, therefore, Washington must continue to nurture its greatest source of strength: its institutions. Some argue that America's greatest advantage is its innovative economy, its global network of alliances, or its military dominance, but this book explained how all of these positive attributes are, in fact, byproducts of America's underlying domestic political system. Democracy is the master variable that explains U.S. success.

In recent years, some have worried about an erosion of the quality of American democracy. This book has shown that many of these fears are exaggerated, but we must remember that we are only as strong as our institutions. The United States must be vigilant about protecting its constitution from all threats, foreign and domestic. It should maintain its republican form of government and resist the temptations offered by new technology to move toward direct democracy through national referendums. Congress, the courts, and the press must continue to draw attention to, and check abuses of executive power. The government should defend the country against foreign interference into its democratic politics. It must also ensure that it continues to protect political and civil freedoms as the country strives to form a more perfect union.

As explained in this book, however, democracy is both an end and a means and Washington must also seek to strengthen the economic, diplomatic, and military advantages democracy provides. Open government spurs economic growth by providing access to economic opportunity to a broad cross-section of the population and by creating conditions that facilitate radical innovation. Growing inequality threatens to exclude certain segments of American society from contributing to growth-enhancing activity, and U.S. leaders must prioritize equal access of opportunity for all U.S. citizens. In addition, policymakers should continue to foster the conditions that facilitate radical innovation. The United States should let the brain drain work in its favor and continue to attract the best and the brightest immigrants from around the world. The federal government should also make adequate investments in basic science and R&D to stimulate our world-beating university system and private sectors to get to work on the next round of technological breakthroughs.

Democratic systems are prerequisites for successful financial systems. The sanctity of the U.S. government's word and its commitment to repay U.S. sovereign debt underwrite U.S. global hegemony. Washington must enhance its creditworthiness, including by reducing the national deficit and debt. This can only be done by reforming America's entitlement programs. It is simply not possible to balance the national budget on the back of a military that must be ready and able to defend the entire free world.

Democracies build larger and more reliable alliance systems. This is a significant source of advantage that must not be taken for granted. The U.S. and Chinese shares of global GDP currently stand at roughly 24% and 15%, respectively. That is too close for comfort. If one adds formal treaty allies and other democracies to the U.S. side of the ledger, however, then the balance tilts to 75% to 15%. That looks much better. The United States is much stronger when it is working with its allies and partners. To be sure, Washington and its allies will continue to have disagreements on important issues. Moreover, allies often freeride on American military power and, with some exceptions, do not pay their fair share of their mutual defense burdens. These are real problems and diplomats should have frank conservations about these disagreements behind closed doors. But the overriding U.S. priority should be to cultivate existing allies, pull them closer, and continue to attract new countries into the coalition of free nations. As Winston Churchill put it, "There is only one thing worse than fighting with allies, and that is fighting without them."

Washington must also foster its military strength and maintain a favorable balance of power over Russia and China. Taking the steps called for above will help a great deal in this regard. Sustaining the world's largest and most innovative economy and sitting at the center of the global financial system will allow the United States to invent and afford the next generation of military capabilities. Maintaining a military alliance system made up of the world's most effective democratic states does not hurt either. In addition, the United States should incorporate emerging technology into its forces and develop new, innovative operational concepts for deterring, and if necessary defeating, its autocratic rivals. Finally, Washington must ensure the free flow of ideas and debate on important foreign policy issues both inside and outside of government to ensure that U.S. leaders have access to the best information when making important foreign policy decisions, especially on issues of war and peace.

Once Washington has secured this base of hard power at home, what should guide its approach overseas? The answer is simple: It should follow a version of the same grand strategy it has successfully pursued for the past seventy-five years.

Contrary to the myth that democracies cannot pursue long-term grand strategies, the United States has been following the same basic grand strategy for three-quarters of a century. In fact, it is a variant of the same grand strategy that liberal leviathans have been pursuing for over two thousand years from Athens to Rome, from Venice to Amsterdam, and from London to Washington, DC. Step one, build a liberal international system. Step two, invite other nations to join. Step three, defend the system from challengers.

To build the system, the United States and its allies should continue to provide stability and security in important geostrategic regions. They should proceed with past designs to advance cooperation through international institutions. They should continue to champion an open economic system internationally. And they should sustain efforts to promote democracy, human rights, and good governance.

Some have argued that international conditions have changed drastically over the years and that the liberal international order is all but dead.[2] They are only half right.

International conditions always change, but the U.S.-led order has been too successful to abandon. At the same time, it would not make sense to cling to an outdated system. What Washington must do, therefore, is revitalize, adapt, and defend the system for a new era. Key aspects of the system continue to work, and the United States and its allies must breathe new life into these elements. This would include, for example, rallying the democracies at the core of the system and reaffirming their shared values.[3]

Other elements must be adapted for a new era. For example, America's alliance systems are regionally focused with NATO in Europe and a series of bilateral alliances in Asia. This made sense during the Cold War, but the world is increasingly globalized. America's democratic allies are facing similar global challenges, especially from revisionist autocratic states, like Russia and China. Moreover, the free nations of the world have often united to forget common policies for problems, from economic sanctions to joint military operations. Rather than resurrect global democratic coalitions on an *ad hoc* basis every time they need to deal with a new issue, however, it would be much better to have a standing organization. The United States should lead its democratic allies and partners in forming a new Alliance of Free Nations. This political alliance could serve as a forum for leading democratic nations to come together to assess threats and opportunities and coordinated common strategies. It would unite America's existing democratic allies from around the world into a single organization and bring in other rising democracies, including India.

The most difficult part of the strategy, however, may be in defending the international order from those who wish to tear it down. The list of adversaries includes rogue states and terrorist networks, but the biggest threats come from the autocratic great powers, Russia and China. The United States should offer autocrats in Beijing and Moscow a simple choice. If they want to become "responsible stakeholders" in the liberal international order and play by the rules, the door will always remain open. So long as they are intent on spoiling it for everyone else, however, the United States and its allies and partners will defend themselves and compete with Russia and China in a great power rivalry from a position of strength. They will show Moscow and Beijing that attempts to challenge the U.S.-led order will be futile and they will be better off to join or acquiesce to it.

When thinking about foreign threats, many analysts focus on the enemy's strengths and their own weaknesses. But, the best strategies often come about by identifying one's own strengths and the enemy's weaknesses. Where are the autocratic rivals vulnerable and how can the democracies stick it to them there?

The democracy versus autocracy framework adopted in this book reveals autocracies' greatest vulnerabilities. They cannot sustain high, long-run rates of economic growth and their financial markets are fragile. They are poor alliance builders and their aggressive actions often provoke counterbalancing coalitions. They struggle to develop high-end strategic military technologies.

They make big blunders in foreign and defense policy. And their biggest security threat comes from their own people, making their regimes unstable.

These are the raw ingredients for the democrats' competitive strategy over the autocrats.

Washington should combine forces with its democratic allies to counter China economically and combat its unfair trading practices. They should exploit their centrality in global financial markets to levy painful financial sanctions and impose penalties for bad behavior. They should also look to protect their technological innovations from theft by Russia and China.

Diplomatically, the United States and its allies should ensure that every country on Earth has an alternative to subjugation by Beijing or Moscow. They should not make the mistake of forcing nations to choose between Washington or their autocratic rivals. They should, however, draw attention to Russian and Chinese aggression and their atrocious human rights records and use their repulsive actions as an opportunity to expand their own alliance coalition. Every nation should understand it at least has the option of being part of the free world if it so chooses.

To make that promise credible, Washington and its security partners must maintain a defense strategy and posture capable of protecting vulnerable allies on the new geopolitical fault lines running through Eastern Europe and East Asia. Some might argue that great power war is a thing of the past, but they would be mistaken. Analysts had similar delusions in 1911, and World War I broke out only a few years later.[4] World War III is very much possible and the risks are growing.

To deter it, the United States and its allies should work to maintain a favorable balance of power in Europe and Asia. Consistent with the "competitive strategies" framework described previously, this can be achieved by forcing Russia and China to compete where they are weakest.

If you want to know where Moscow and Beijing are most insecure, you can simply ask them. Russia and China complain loudest about the United States supposedly seeking a strategic first-strike capability with advanced technologies, including by deploying missile defenses and conventional prompt global strike capabilities, like hypersonic missiles. They also charge that Washington is orchestrating "color revolutions" designed to bring down their regimes. Both charges are false, but it reveals much about Putin and Xi's greatest fears.

The United States and its allies should invest in advanced military technologies and operational concepts to once again gain an enduring strategic military advantage over Russia and China at the highest end of military competition. They could also encourage democracy and human rights inside

Russian and Chinese societies, especially during times of leadership transition when these systems are most fragile. Washington could, for example, provide assistance to civil society and pro-democracy groups and use cyber tools to thwart autocrats' attempts to tightly control information. At a minimum, democracy promotion measures could be held in reserve as a deterrent. If Moscow and Beijing continue to meddle in the domestic politics of democracies, then the democracies can do the same to them. This could serve as a potent deterrent because the autocrats' systems are much more brittle.

Ultimately, history suggests that this new era of great power rivalry could very well end in war, or regime change, or both. Indeed, with the exception of the Cold War, all the cases of rivalry reviewed in this book resulted in war. And six of the seven cases ended with the regime change of a principal competitor; in five of these six cases, it was the autocracy that crumbled.

Indeed, it is possible that President Putin has a heart attack or that the CCP falls tonight. The collapsing of regimes in Russia and China would mostly likely only lead to the rise of a new autocracy in their place; neither country has any experience with democratic governance. This could still, however, be a welcome outcome for the free world. Just as the collapse of the Soviet Union led to the post-Cold War world, the end of revisionist autocratic regimes in Russia and China could result in another period of extended great power peace.

There is the chance at some point, however, that Russia and China might undergo a thoroughgoing transition to more democratic forms of government. This would certainly be beneficial for the Russian and Chinese people, who would discover newfound freedoms and rights. Much less appreciated, however, is what this would do for these countries' power and influence.

Unlike under the CCP, a democratically ruled China would have less to fear from extensive economic reforms, which would increase the likelihood that Beijing eventually adopts the economic institutions necessary to become the world's leading economic power. With fewer capital controls in place and more political protections against arbitrary financial decisions, Shanghai would be much more likely to replace New York as the new hub of global finance and the RMB to take over as a new reserve currency. A liberal-democratic China would also have more soft power in diplomatic relations. Its neighbors would have less to fear, and a free China could establish webs of institutions and meaningful political alliances. Finally, a reformed decision-making process on national-security issues and a less corrupt People's Liberation Army would allow Beijing to better calibrate its diplomacy and to prevail in combat should diplomacy fail. It would also have less to fear from its own people and could focus its defense spending on international adversaries. In short, a liberal-democratic China would be much better positioned to seize global preeminence from the United States, while the autocratic CCP is much more likely to bungle China's rise.

Indeed, if or when the United States declines, it will most likely be overcome only by another democracy. Over the past four centuries, democratic hegemons have lost their positions exclusively to other democratic challengers. Autocrats have all tried and failed in their attempts. At present, a truly unified European Union, or possibly India, are the only democratic entities with enough power resources to plausibly rival the United States for global ascendance over the coming century. But a democratic transition in China would suddenly transform Beijing into a much more serious competitor.

U.S. leaders, therefore, may face an important and difficult dilemma when it comes to thinking about a long-term strategy for China. On the one hand, Washington can hope for, or even actively promote, democratization in China in an effort to liberalize China and make it more cooperative internationally, but only by increasing the risk that the United States eventually hands over the keys of global mastery to Beijing. Some may be quite comfortable with this outcome. After all, the United States will not be the leading state forever, and it would have less to fear from a truly liberal-democratic China. On the other hand, some may prefer that Washington seek to prolong the American era indefinitely, but this might come at the cost of continuing to coexist with a dysfunctional, autocratic, and belligerent CCP.

Perhaps the most difficult dilemma, therefore, rests with readers in Moscow and Beijing. Putin and Xi can continue to reign, but they will be consigned to rule over dysfunctional states destined for second-tier status. Or their nations can emerge as true world leaders, but only if they relinquish power and create the kind of open political system that has proven over the centuries to be a prerequisite for lasting international leadership.

Until that time, the United States will continue to enjoy a democratic advantage in this new era of great power rivalry.

NOTES

Preface

1. Matthew Kroenig. "Why Democracies Dominate: America's Edge over China." *The National Interest*, July/August 2015.

Introduction

1. "Freedom in the World 2019: Freedom in Retreat," *Freedom House*, Washington, DC, 2019.
2. Joseph S. Nye Jr., *Soft Power: The Means to Success in World Politics*, new edition (New York, NY: PublicAffairs, 2005).
3. David Shlapak and Michael Johnson, *Reinforcing Deterrence on NATO's Eastern Flank: Wargaming the Defense of the Baltics* (Santa Monica, CA: RAND Corporation, 2016).
4. "Putin Deplores Collapse of USSR," *BBC News*, April 25, 2005; Vladimir Socor, "Putin's Crimea Speech: A Manifesto of Greater-Russia Irredentism," Eurasia Daily Monitor, vol. 11, no. 56, 2018.
5. "China to Become World's Largest Economy in 2024 Reports IHS Economics," IHS Online Newsroom, September 7, 2014.
6. Magnus Nordenman, "China and Russia Joint Sea 2017 Baltic Naval Exercise Highlight New Normal in European Maritime," *USNI News* (blog), July 5, 2017.
7. Graham Allison, "What Xi Jinping Wants," *The Atlantic*, May 31, 2017.
8. Fareed Zakaria, *The Post-American World: Release 2.0*, Updated and expanded (New York, NY: W.W. Norton & Co, 2011).
9. Charles Kupchan, *No One's World: The West, the Rising Rest, and the Coming Global Turn* (New York, NY: Oxford University Press, 2012).

10. Martin Jacques, *When China Rules the World: The End of the Western World and the Birth of a New Global Order*, 2nd edition (New York, NY: Penguin Books, 2012).

11. Graham Allison, *Destined for War: Can America and China Escape Thucydides' Trap?* (Boston: Houghton Mifflin Harcourt, 2017).

12. United States, *National Security Strategy of the United States of America* (The White House, 2017), 27.

13. Daron Acemoglu and James Robinson, *Why Nations Fail: The Origins of Power, Prosperity, and Poverty*, reprint edition (New York, NY: Currency, 2013).

14. Kenneth A. Schultz and Barry R. Weingast, "The Democratic Advantage: Institutional Foundations of Financial Power in International Competition," *International Organization* 57, no. 1 (2003): 3–42.

15. Brett Ashley Leeds, "Alliance Reliability in Times of War: Explaining State Decisions to Violate Treaties," *International Organization* 57, no. 4 (2003): 813.

16. Beth Simmons, "Treaty Compliance and Violation," *Annual Review of Political Science* 13, no. 1 (2010): 273–96.

17. Bruce Russett et al., *Grasping the Democratic Peace: Principles for a Post–Cold War World* (Princeton: Princeton University Press, 1993).

18. Dan Reiter and Allan C. Stam, *Democracies at War* (Princeton: Princeton University Press, 2002).

19. Karen A. Rasler and William R. Thompson, "Global Wars, Public Debts, and the Long Cycle," *World Politics* 35, no. 4 (1983): 489–516.

20. Alexis de Tocqueville, *Democracy in America*, trans. Harvey C. Mansfield and Delba Winthrop, 1st edition (Chicago, IL: University of Chicago Press, 2002).

21. Thomas L. Friedman, *Hot, Flat, and Crowded: Why We Need a Green Revolution—and How It Can Renew America, Release 2.0*, 2nd revised and enlarged edition (New York, NY: Picador, 2009), Chapter 18.

22. Niccolò Machiavelli and Albert Russell Ascoli, *The Essential Writings of Machiavelli*, trans. Peter Constantine (New York, NY: Modern Library, 2007), 118.

23. Ibid, 240.

24. Abramo Fino Kenneth Organski and Jacek Kugler, "The War Ledger," *Bibliovault OAI Repository* (University of Chicago Press, June 1, 1981), 61–2.

25. Christian Gauss, *The German Emperor as Shown in His Public Utterances* (New York, NY: Scribner, 1915), 181–3.

26. Allison, *Destined for War*.

27. Ernest Barker, *The Politics of Aristotle*, 1st edition (London, UK: Oxford University Press, 1962); Machiavelli and Ascoli, *The Essential Writings of Machiavelli*.

28. See, for example, Stephen G. Brooks and William C. Wohlforth. *World Out of Balance: International Relations and the Challenge of American Primacy*

(Princeton: Princeton University Press, 2008); Stephen G. Brooks and William C. Wohlforth, *America Abroad: Why the Sole Superpower Should Not Pull Back from the World* (Oxford; New York, NY: Oxford University Press, 2016); Michael Beckley, *Unrivaled: Why America Will Remain the World's Sole Superpower* (Ithaca, NY: Cornell University Press, 2018); Charles Kupchan, *The End of the American Era: U.S. Foreign Policy and the Geopolitics of the Twenty-First Century*, 1st edition (New York, NY: Knopf, 2002); Kupchan, *No One's World*; Robert J. Lieber, *Power and Willpower in the American Future: Why the United States Is Not Destined to Decline* (Cambridge; New York, NY: Cambridge University Press, 2012); Robert J. Lieber, *Retreat and Its Consequences: American Foreign Policy and the Problem of World Order* (Cambridge; New York, NY: Cambridge University Press, 2016).

29. Zakaria, *The Post-American World*; Joseph S. Nye, *Is the American Century Over?* 1st edition (Malden, MA: Polity, 2015).

30. See, for example, Andrew Nathan and Andrew Scobell, *China's Search for Security*, 1st printing edition (New York, NY: Columbia University Press, 2012); Osnos, *Age of Ambition: Chasing Fortune, Truth, and Faith in the New China* (New York, NY: Farrar, Straus and Giroux, 2014); David Shambaugh, *China Goes Global: The Partial Power*, 1st edition (New York, NY: Oxford University Press, 2013); Warren I. Cohen, *America's Response to China: A History of Sino-American Relations*, 3rd edition (New York, NY: Columbia University Press, 1990); Edward S. Steinfeld, *Playing Our Game: Why China's Rise Doesn't Threaten the West*, 1st edition (New York, NY: Oxford University Press, 2010); Carl Minzner, *End of an Era: How China's Authoritarian Revival Is Undermining Its Rise*, 1st edition (New York, NY: Oxford University Press, 2018); Elizabeth Economy, *The Third Revolution: Xi Jinping and the New Chinese State* (New York, NY: Oxford University Press, 2018).

31. Henry Kissinger, *On China* (New York, NY: Penguin Books, 2012).

32. Michael McFaul, *From Cold War to Hot Peace: An American Ambassador in Putin's Russia* (New York, NY: Houghton Mifflin Harcourt, 2018); M. Steven Fish, *Democracy from Scratch*, 1st edition (Princeton: Princeton University Press, 1994); M. Steven Fish, *Democracy Derailed in Russia: The Failure of Open Politics* (Cambridge; New York, NY: Cambridge University Press, 2005); Angela Stent, *Putin's World: Russia against the West and with the Rest* (New York, NY: Twelve, 2019); Angela E. Stent, *The Limits of Partnership: U.S.-Russian Relations in the Twenty-First Century* (Princeton: Princeton University Press, 2014).

33. Allison, *Destined for War*; A. F. K. Organski, *The War Ledger* (Chicago, IL: University of Chicago Press, 1980); Ronald Tammen, Jacek Kugler, Douglas Lemke, Alan C. Stam III, Mark Abdollahian, Carole Alsharabati, Brian Efird, and A. F. K. Organski, *Power Transitions: Strategies for the 21st Century*, 1st edition (New York, NY: Seven Bridges Press/Chatham House, 2000); David M. Edelstein, *Over the Horizon: Time, Uncertainty, and the Rise of*

Great Powers, 1st edition (Ithaca, NY: Cornell University Press, 2017); Joshua
R. Itzkowitz Shifrinson, *Rising Titans, Falling Giants: How Great Powers
Exploit Power Shifts* (Ithaca, NY: Cornell University Press, 2018); Jack S. Levy
and William Mulligan, "Shifting Power, Preventive Logic, and the Response
of the Target: Germany, Russia, and the First World War," *Journal of Strategic
Studies* 40, no. 5 (July 29, 2017): 731–69.

34. Paul Kennedy, *The Rise and Fall of the Great Powers*, 1st edition (New York,
NY: Vintage, 1989); see also Robert Gilpin, *War and Change in World Politics*,
1st edition (Cambridge; New York, NY: Cambridge University Press, 1981).

35. For an example of how democracy promotes development, see Morton
Halperin, Joe Siegle, and Michael Weinstein, *The Democracy Advantage: How
Democracies Promote Prosperity and Peace* (New York, NY: Routledge, 2004).

36. Acemoglu and Robinson, *Why Nations Fail*; Reiter and Stam, *Democracies
at War*.

Chapter 1

1. On Machiavelli's life, see Christopher S. Celenza, *Machiavelli: A Portrait*
(Cambridge, MA: Harvard University Press, 2015).

2. Machiavelli and Ascoli, *The Essential Writings of Machiavelli*.

3. Ibid.

4. Ibid., 146.

5. Ibid., 129.

6. Ibid.

7. John Monfasani, "Machiavelli, Polybius, and Janus Lascaris: The Hexter
Thesis Revisited," *Italian Studies* 71, no. 1 (January 2, 2016): 39–48.

8. Polybius, *The Complete Histories of Polybius*, trans. W. R. Paton (Digireads.
com, 2009), 311.

9. Ibid., 372.

10. Ibid., 407.

11. Montesquieu, 169.

12. Herodotus, *The Histories* Further Revised Edition, Trans. Aubrey de
Sélincourt (New York, NY: Penguin Books, 2003): 5.78.

13. Hippocrates, *Airs, Waters, Places* 23.33–40.

14. Marcus Tullius Cicero, *Cicero: Selected Works* (New York, NY: Penguin
Books, 1960).

15. Kennedy, *The Rise and Fall of the Great Powers*, xvi.

16. Schultz and Weingast, "The Democratic Advantage."

17. Karen A. Rasler and William R. Thompson, *War and State Making: The
Shaping of the Global Powers* (Crows Nest, Australia: Unwin Hyman,
1989): 490.

18. John J. Mearsheimer, *The Tragedy of Great Power Politics* (New York,
NY: Norton, 2001).

19. J. David Singer, Stuart Bremer, and John Stuckey, "Capability Distribution, Uncertainty, and Major Power War, 1820–1965," *Peace, War and Numbers* (1972): 19–48.

20. Kennedy, *The Rise and Fall of the Great Powers*, xv.

21. Michael Coppedge, John Gerring, David Altman, Michael Bernhard, Steven Fish, Allen Hicken, Matthew Kroenig, et al., "Conceptualizing and Measuring Democracy: A New Approach," *Perspectives on Politics* 9, no. 2 (June 2011): 247–67.

22. Monty G. Marshall, and Keith Jaggers, "Polity IV Project: Political Regime Characteristics and Transitions, 1800–2017," Center for Systemic Peace, 2017.

23. Weber, Max. *The Protestant Ethic and the "Spirit" of Capitalism and Other Writings*. Trans. Peter Baehr and Gordon C. Wells (New York, NY: Penguin Books, 2002); Jeffrey Sachs, "Government, Geography, and Growth: The True Drivers of Economic Development," *Foreign Affairs* 91, no. 5 (August 2012), 142; Michael L. Ross, "What Have We Learned about the Resource Curse?" *Annual Review of Political Science* 18 (May 2015): 239–59.

24. Douglass Cecil North, *Institutions, Institutional Change, and Economic Performance* (Cambridge; New York, NY: Cambridge University Press, 1990), 3.

25. Joseph A. Schumpeter, *Capitalism, Socialism, and Democracy*, 3rd edition (New York, NY: Harper & Brothers, 1950).

26. Jeffrey Sachs and A. M. Warner, "Economic Reform and the Process of Global Integration," *Brookings Papers on Economic Activity* vol. 1 (1995): 1–118.

27. See, for example, Helen V. Milner and Keiko Kubota, "Why the Move to Free Trade? Democracy and Trade Policy in the Developing Countries," *International Organization* 59, no. 1 (2005): 107–43.

28. Ian Goldin, Andrew Pitt, and Benjamin Nabarro, *Migration and the Economy: Economic Realities, Social Impacts and Political Choices* (Citi GPS: Global Perspectives & Solutions, September 2018).

29. Ibid.

30. Schultz and Weingast, "The Democratic Advantage"; Douglass C. North and Barry R. Weingast, "Constitutions and Commitment: The Evolution of Institutions Governing Public Choice in Seventeenth-Century England," *Journal of Economic History* 49, no. 4 (1989): 803–32.

31. Youssef Cassis, *Capitals of Capital: The Rise and Fall of International Financial Centres 1780–2009*, trans. Jacqueline Collier, 2nd edition (Cambridge; New York, NY: Cambridge University Press, 2010).

32. Schultz and Weingast, "The Democratic Advantage"; North and Weingast, "Constitutions and Commitment."

33. David Stasavage, "Transparency, Democratic Accountability, and the Economic Consequences of Monetary Institutions," *American Journal of*

Political Science 47, no. 3 (2003): 389–402; Sebastian M. Saiegh, "Coalition Governments and Sovereign Debt Crises," *Economics and Politics* 21, no. 2 (2009): 232–54.

34. North and Weingast, "Constitutions and Commitment"; Schultz and Weingast, "The Democratic Advantage;" William R. Summerhill, *Inglorious Revolution: Political Institutions, Sovereign Debt, and Financial Underdevelopment in Imperial Brazil* (New Haven: Yale University Press, 2015); David Stasavage, "Polarization and Publicity: Rethinking the Benefits of Deliberative Democracy," *Journal of Politics* 69, no. 1 (2007): 59–72; Mark Dincecco, "The Political Economy of Fiscal Prudence in Historical Perspective," *Economics and Politics* 22, no. 1 (2010): 1–36.

35. See, for example, Barry Eichengreen, and David A. Leblang, "Democracy and Globalization," *Economics and Politics* 20 (2008): 289–334.

36. See, for example, Ross Levine and Sara Zervos, "Capital Control Liberalization and Stock Market Development," *World Development* 26, no. 7 (July 1, 1998): 1169–83.

37. Ross Levine, "Stock Markets, Economic Development, and Capital Control Liberalization," *Investment Company Institute Perspective* 3, no. 5 (December 1997): 1169–83.

38. Stephen M. Walt, *The Origins of Alliances*, Cornell Studies in Security Affairs (Ithaca, NY: Cornell University Press, 1987).

39. James D. Morrow, "Alliances: Why Write Them Down?" *Annual Review of Political Science* 3, no. 1 (2000): 63–83.

40. Douglass C. North, "Institutions and Credible Commitment," *Journal of Institutional and Theoretical Economics (JITE) / Zeitschrift Für Die Gesamte Staatswissenschaft* 149, no. 1 (1993): 11–23.

41. Brett Ashley Leeds. "Alliance Reliability in Times of War: Explaining State Decisions to Violate Treaties," *International Organization* 57, no. 4 (ed 2003): 801–27; Brett Ashley Leeds, "Do Alliances Deter Aggression? The Influence of Military Alliances on the Initiation of Militarized Interstate Disputes," *American Journal of Political Science* 47, no. 3 (2003); Ajin Choi, "Democratic Synergy and Victory in War, 1816–1992," *International Studies Quarterly* 48, no. 3 (September 1, 2004): 663–82.

42. D. Scott Bennett, "Testing Alternative Models of Alliance Duration, 1816–1984," *American Journal of Political Science* 41, no. 3 (1997): 846–78; Kurt Taylor Gaubatz, "Democratic States and Commitment in International Relations," *International Organization* 50, no. 1 (1996): 109–39; William Reed, "Alliance Duration and Democracy: An Extension and Cross-Validation of 'Democratic States and Commitment in International Relations,'" *American Journal of Political Science* 41, no. 3 (1997).

43. Brett Ashley Leeds, Michaela Mattes, and Jeremy S. Vogel, "Interests, Institutions, and the Reliability of International Commitments," *American Journal of Political Science* 53, no. 2 (2009): 461–76.

44. Randolph M. Siverson and Juliann Emmons, "Birds of a Feather: Democratic Political Systems and Alliance Choices in the Twentieth Century," *Journal of Conflict Resolution* 35, no. 2 (June 1, 1991); Brian Lai and Dan Reiter, "Democracy, Political Similarity, and International Alliances, 1816–1992," *Journal of Conflict Resolution* 44, no. 2 (April 1, 2000): 203–27.

45. Matthew Fuhrmann and Jeffrey D. Berejikian, "Disaggregating Noncompliance: Abstention versus Predation in the Nuclear Nonproliferation Treaty," *Journal of Conflict Resolution* 56, no. 3 (June 1, 2012): 355–81.

46. Simmons, "Treaty Compliance and Violation."

47. Nye, *Soft Power*.

48. "The Soft Power 30," USC Center for Public Diplomacy, available at https://softpower30.com/.

49. Stephen G. Brooks and William C. Wohlforth, *World Out of Balance: International Relations and the Challenge of American Primacy* (Princeton: Princeton University Press, 2008).

50. Reiter and Stam, *Democracies at War*.

51. Jack I. Snyder, *Myths of Empire: Domestic Politics and International Ambitions* (Ithaca, NY: Cornell University Press: 1991(.

52. Reiter and Stam, *Democracies at War;* David A. Lake, "Powerful Pacifists: Democratic States and War," *American Political Science Review* 86, no. 1 (March 1992): 24–37.

53. Victor Davis Hanson, *Why the West Has Won: Carnage and Culture from Salamis to Vietnam* (London, UK: Faber & Faber, 2001).

54. Martin L. Van Creveld, *Technology and War: From 2000 B.C. to the Present* (New York, NY; London, UK: Free Press, 1989).

55. Stephen D. Biddle, *Military Power: Explaining Victory and Defeat in Modern Battle* (New Delhi, India: Manas Publications, 2005).

56. Steven R. David, "Explaining Third World Alignment" *World Politics* 43, no. 2 (1991): 233–56.

57. M. Taylor Fravel, *Strong Borders, Secure Nation: Cooperation and Conflict in China's Territorial Disputes* (Princeton: Princeton University Press, 2008).

58. Caitlin Talmadge, *The Dictator's Army: Battlefield Effectiveness in Authoritarian Regimes* (Ithaca, NY: Cornell University Press, 2015).

59. For the arguments that democracies do not make better allies or are not more effective militarily, see, for example, Erik Gartzke, and Kristian Skrede Gleditsch, "Why Democracies May Actually Be Less Reliable Allies," *American Journal of Political Science* 48, no. 4 (October 1, 2004): 775–95; Alexander B. Downes, "How Smart and Tough Are Democracies? Reassessing Theories of Democratic Victory in War," *International Security* 33, no. 4 (April 1, 2009): 9–51.

60. Robert A. Dahl, "The Concept of Power," *Behavioral Science* 2, no. 3 (1957): 201–15.

61. Leviathan is a sea monster in ancient Jewish thought. The English philosopher Thomas Hobbes used the term to describe an all-powerful state capable of overpowering other actors and enforcing peace. Thomas Hobbes, *Leviathan*, Wordsworth Classics of World Literature (Ware, United Kingdom: Wordsworth Editions, 2014).

Chapter 2

1. Tocqueville, *Democracy in America*.
2. Tocqueville, *Democracy in America*.
3. Plato and Tom Butler-Bowdon, *The Republic: The Influential Classic*, 1st edition (Chichester, West Sussex, UK: Capstone, 2012).
4. Hobbes, *Leviathan*.
5. Adolf Hitler and Bob Carruthers, *Mein Kampf: The Official 1939 Edition*, trans. James Murphy (Slough, United Kingdom: Archive Media Publishing, 2011).
6. Vladimir Ilyich Lenin, *Essential Works of Lenin: "What Is to Be Done?" and Other Writings*, 1st edition (New York, NY: Dover Publications, 1987).
7. Henry Kissinger, *Diplomacy*, reprint edition (New York, NY: Simon & Schuster, 1995).
8. Francis Fukuyama, *The End of History and the Last Man* (New York, NY; Toronto, CA: Free Press, 1992).
9. Michael Pillsbury, *The Hundred-Year Marathon: China's Secret Strategy to Replace America as the Global Superpower* (New York, NY: Henry Holt and Co., 2015).
10. Thomas Friedman, *The Colbert Report, Comedy Central*, November 21, 2008.
11. David French, "How Our Overly Restrictive Rules of Engagement Keep Us from Winning Wars," *National Review*, December 21, 2015.
12. Richard Fontaine, "The Shutdown Is Great News for Russia," *The Atlantic*, January 19, 2019.
13. John J. Mearsheimer, *The Great Delusion: Liberal Dreams and International Realities* (New Haven, CT: Yale University Press, 2018).
14. Walter Russel Mead, *Power, Terror, Peace, and War: America's Grand Strategy in a World at Risk* (New York, NY: Vintage, 2005).
15. Machiavelli and Ascoli, *The Essential Writings of Machiavelli*, 219.
16. Alexander B. Downes, *Targeting Civilians in War*, Cornell Studies in Security Affairs (Ithaca, NY: Cornell University Press, 2008).
17. Downes, *Targeting Civilians in War*.
18. Machiavelli and Ascoli, *The Essential Writings of Machiavelli*, 121.
19. Ibid.
20. Kenneth N. Waltz, *Theory of International Politics*, 1st edition (Long Grove, IL: Waveland Press, 2010).
21. Jessica L. P. Weeks, *Dictators at War and Peace*, 1st edition (Ithaca, NY; London, UK: Cornell University Press, 2014).

22. Jessica Chen Weiss, *Powerful Patriots: Nationalist Protest in China's Foreign Relations*, 1st edition (New York, NY: Oxford University Press, 2014).

23. Elizabeth N. Saunders, "War and the Inner Circle: Democratic Elites and the Politics of Using Force," *Security Studies* 24, no. 3 (July 3, 2015): 466–501.

24. Alfred Mahan, *Influence of Sea Power upon History, 1660–1783* (Gretna: Pelican Publishing, 2003); William H. McNeill, *The Pursuit of Power: Technology, Armed Force, and Society since A.D. 1000* (New York, NY: ACLS Humanities E-Book Project, 2009).

25. Alfred Mahan. *Influence of Sea Power Upon History, 1660–1783.*

26. Adam Przeworski and Fernando Limongi, "Modernization: Theories and Facts," *World Politics* 49, no. 2 (1997): 155–83.

Chapter 3

1. William R. Thompson, "Uneven Economic Growth, Systemic Challenges, and Global Wars," *International Studies Quarterly* 27, no. 3 (September 1, 1983): 341–55.

2. J. David Singer, Stuart Bremer, and John Stuckey, "Capability Distribution, Uncertainty, and Major Power War, 1820–1965," *Peace, War and Numbers* (1972) 19–48; D. Scott Bennett and Allan C. Stam, "Eugene: A Conceptual Manual," *International Interactions* 26, no. 2 (January 1, 2000): 179–204.

3. Singer, Bremer, and Stuckey, "Capability Distribution."

4. Keith Jaggers and Ted Robert Gurr, "Tracking Democracy's Third Wave with the Polity III Data," *Journal of Peace Research* 32, no. 4 (July 1, 2016): 469–82.

5. To be precise, the number is 0.0870.

6. To be precise, the exact number is 0.0188.

7. Pearson Chi Squared = 381.654, Pr = 0.000.

8. Observations are country-years. Think man-hours.

9. Pearson Chi Squared = 14.8365, Pr = 0.000.

10. This relationship is also statistically significant. Pearson Chi Squared = 27.0629, Pr = 0.000.

11. According to the CINC scores, China was the most powerful state in the system in the most recent year it was measured, 2007. The CINC score heavily weights population size and, therefore, overstates China's hard power, in my view. As I wrote, this is a poor measure, but it provides a rough proxy to begin the analysis. The more nuanced analysis later in the book demonstrates that the United States remains the system leader.

12. I employ a logit estimator with robust standard errors clustered by country. The dichotomous dependent variable measures whether a state has the highest CINC score in a given year. The independent variable is Polity2 scores, ranging from −10 to +10. I control for the number of states in the international system and a country's population size.

13. Gary King, Robert O. Keohane, and Sidney Verba, *Designing Social Inquiry: Scientific Inference in Qualitative Research* (Princeton: Princeton University Press, 1994).

14. The Polish-Lithuanian Commonwealth was established the next year.

Chapter 4

1. On the Persian Wars, see, for example, Peter Green, *The Greco-Persian Wars* (Berkeley: University of California Press, 1996).

2. Because of the elected bodies and its egalitarianism among citizens, some have argued that Sparta possessed a republican form of government. See Mark D. Fisher, "Heroic Democracy: Thucydides, Pericles, and the Tragic Science of Athenian Greatness," PhD dissertation, University of California, Berkeley, 2017 (ProQuest ID: Fisher_berkeley_0028E_17222. Merritt ID: ark:/13030/m57x183w).

3. Victor Davis Hanson, *Why the West Has Won: Carnage and Culture from Salamis to Vietnam* (London, UK: Faber & Faber, 2001).

4. Sun Tzu, *The Art of War*, 1st edition (Las Vegas, NV: Filiquarian, 2007).

5. For a classic statement on the Western way of war, see Carl von Clausewitz, *On War* (Scotts Valley, CA: CreateSpace Independent Publishing Platform, 2012).

6. Aristotle, *Politics* 1269a37–39.

7. McGregor, *The Athenians and Their Empire* (Vancouver: UBC Press, 1987): 33.

8. Ibid.

9. Thucydides, *The Peloponnesian Wars*, V.84–116.

10. It bears noting that Syracuse and Athens were both democracies and they fought a major war with each other. The democratic peace theory, the idea that democracies do not go to war with other democracies, is among the strongest laws in contemporary political science, but, as we will see in this book, there are many exceptions to this rule before the 19th century.

Chapter 5

1. For classic works on the history of the Roman Republic, see Polybius, *The Complete Histories*; and Titus Livius, *The History of Rome: The Only Complete and Unabridged Edition in One Volume*, ed. Jake E. Stief, trans. D. Spillan, Cyrus Edmonds, and William A. M'Devitte (Santa Fe, NM: Stief Books, 2018).

2. For the classic study of the rise of Rome, see Livius, *The History of Rome*.

3. Plutarch, *Lives of the Noble Grecians and Romans*, ed. Arthur Hugh Clough (Oxford, United Kingdom: Benediction Classics, 2010).

4. Aristotle, *Politics* 1272b24–1273b25.

5. Livius, *The History of Rome*, Book XLIX.

Chapter 6

1. On the history of Venice, see, for example, John Julius Norwich, *A History of Venice*, 1st Vintage Books edition (New York, NY: Vintage, 1989).

2. Machiavelli, *Discourses on Livy* I.34.

3. On the history of Venice, see, for example, William Carew Hazlitt, *The History of the Venetian Republic* (New Delhi, India: Sagwan Press, 2018).

4. Michele Fratianni and Franco Spinelli, "Italian City-States and Financial Evolution," *European Review of Economic History* 10, no. 3 (December 1, 2006): 257–78.

5. David Stasavage, "Cities, Constitutions, and Sovereign Borrowing in Europe, 1274–1785," *International Organization* 61, no. 3 (2007): 522.

6. John F. Padgett and Paul D. McLean, "Economic Credit in Renaissance Florence," *Journal of Modern History* 83, no. 1 (2011): 1–2.

7. See, for example, "Capitals of Capital," *The Economist*, May 13, 2014.

8. Pierre Moukarzel, "Venetian Merchants in Thirteenth-Century Alexandria and the Sultans of Egypt: An Analysis of Treaties, Privileges and Intercultural Relations," *Al-Masāq* 28, no. 2 (May 3, 2016): 187–205.

9. John Francis Guilmartin. "The Earliest Shipboard Gunpowder Ordnance: An Analysis of Its Technical Parameters and Tactical Capabilities." *The Journal of Military History* 71, no. 3 (July 26, 2007): 649–69. https://doi.org/10.1353/jmh.2007.0204.

10. John Julius Norwich, *A History of Venice*, 1st Vintage Books edition (New York, NY: Vintage, 1989), 494.

11. Machiavelli, *The Prince* XIV.

12. Daniel H. Nexon, *The Struggle for Power in Early Modern Europe: Religious Conflict, Dynastic Empires, and International Change* (Princeton: Princeton University Press, 2009).

13. Acemoglu and Robinson, *Why Nations Fail*, 219.

14. Jakub J. Grygiel, *Great Powers and Geopolitical Change*, 1st edition (Baltimore, MD: Johns Hopkins University Press, 2007).

15. Jo N. Hays, *Epidemics and Pandemics: Their Impacts on Human History*, 1st edition (Santa Barbara, CA: ABC-CLIO, 2005).

16. Acemoglu and Robinson, *Why Nations Fail*, 152–199.

Chapter 7

1. For an authoritative history of the Dutch Republic, see Jonathan Israel, *The Dutch Republic: Its Rise, Greatness, and Fall 1477–1806*, reprint edition (Oxford: Clarendon Press, 1998).

2. Acemoglu and Robinson, *Why Nations Fail*, 219; Kennedy, *The Rise and Fall of the Great Powers*.

3. Pepijn Brandon, *War, Capital, and the Dutch State*, reprint edition (Chicago, IL: Haymarket Books, 2017), 21.

4. Friso Wielenga, *A History of the Netherlands: From the Sixteenth Century to the Present Day*, trans. Lynne Richards (London, UK: Bloomsbury Academic, 2015).

5. Geoffrey Parker, "The 'Military Revolution,' 1560–1660—a Myth?" *Journal of Modern History* 48, no. 2 (1976): 196–214.

6. Wielenga, *A History of the Netherlands*.

7. Angus Maddison, *The World Economy*, Development Centre Studies (Paris, France: Development Centre of the Organisation for Economic Co-operation and Development, 2006), 77.

8. Kennedy, *The Rise and Fall of the Great Powers*, 69.

9. Jan de Vries and Ad van der Woude, *The First Modern Economy: Success, Failure, and Perseverance of the Dutch Economy, 1500–1815* (Cambridge; New York, NY: Cambridge University Press, 1997), 114–5.

10. Vries and Woude, *The First Modern Economy*, 11.

11. Vries and Woude, *The First Modern Economy*, 97.

12. Acemoglu and Robinson, *Why Nations Fail*, 219.

13. Maddison, *The World Economy*, 90.

14. Maddison, *The World Economy*, 81.

15. Hugo Grotius, *The Freedom of the Seas*, trans. Ralph Van Deman Magoffin (Scotts Valley, CA: CreateSpace Independent Publishing Platform, 2018).

Chapter 8

1. Guy Rowlands. *The Financial Decline of a Great Power: War, Influence, and Money in Louis XIV's France*. 1 edition. Oxford: Oxford University Press, 2012).

2. Ibid.

3. Kennedy, *The Rise and Fall of the Great Powers*, 105.

4. Ann Carlos, Larry Neal, Kirsten Wandschneider, "The Origins of National Debt: The Financing and Re-financing of the War of the Spanish Succession." International Economic History Annual Meeting, Helsinki, Finland, 2006.

5. On the causes of the French Revolution, see Theda Skocpol, *States and Social Revolutions: A Comparative Analysis of France, Russia, and China* (Cambridge; New York, NY: Cambridge University Press, 2015).

6. Nicholas Crafts, "Forging Ahead and Falling Behind: The Rise and Relative Decline of the First Industrial Nation," *Journal of Economic Perspectives* 12, no. 2 (1998): 193–210.

Chapter 9

1. Barbara W. Tuchman, *The Guns of August*, reprint edition (New York, NY: Random House Trade Paperbacks, 1994).

2. On the Britain-Germany competition, see also David M. Edelstein, *Over the Horizon: Time, Uncertainty, and the Rise of Great Powers*, 1st edition (Ithaca, NY; London, UK: Cornell University Press, 2017).

3. On Germany's imitation of the British warships, see Andrea Gilli and Mauro Gilli, "Why China Has Not Caught Up Yet: Military-Technological Superiority and the Limits of Imitation, Reverse Engineering, and Cyber Espionage," *International Security* 43, no. 3 (February 1, 2019): 141–89.

4. Stephen Van Evera, *Causes of War: Power and the Roots of Conflict*, 1st edition (Ithaca, NY: Cornell University Press, 2001).

5. Keir A. Lieber, "The New History of World War I and What It Means for International Relations Theory," *International Security* 32, no. 2 (2007): 155–91.

6. Stephen Van Evera, "The Cult of the Offensive and the Origins of the First World War," *International Security* 9, no. 1 (1984): 58–107.

7. Biddle, *Military Power*.

8. Margaret MacMillan, *Paris 1919: Six Months That Changed the World*, 1st edition (New York, NY: Random House, 2002).

9. Rein Taagepera, "Expansion and Contraction Patterns of Large Polities: Context for Russia," *International Studies Quarterly* 41, no. 3 (1997): 475–504.

10. E. H. Carr, *The Twenty Years' Crisis, 1919–1939: Reissued with New Introduction*, ed. M. Cox (Houndmills, Basingstoke, Hampshire, United Kingdom; New York, NY: Palgrave Macmillan, 2001).

11. Gerhard L. Weinberg, *A World at Arms: A Global History of World War II* (Cambridge; New York, NY: Cambridge University Press, 1993).

12. Gilpin, *War and Change in World Politics*.

13. Roberta Wohlstetter, *Pearl Harbor: Warning and Decision*, 1st edition (Stanford, CA: Stanford University Press, 1962).

14. Stam and Reiter, *Democracies at War*.

15. Data from UK Public Spending, available at https://ourworldindata.org/uploads/2013/08/ourworldindata_uk-defence-spending-as-a-percentage-of-gdp.png.

Chapter 10

1. On the rise of the United States, see Robert Kagan, *Dangerous Nation: America's Foreign Policy from Its Earliest Days to the Dawn of the Twentieth Century*, reprint edition (New York, NY: Vintage, 2007).

2. Maddison, *The World Economy*, 90.

3. Fareed Zakaria, *From Wealth to Power* (Princeton: Princeton University Press, 1998).

4. On the history of the Cold War, see, for example, John Lewis Gaddis, *The Cold War: A New History* (New York, NY: Penguin Press, 2005).

5. George F. Kennan, "The Sources of Soviet Conduct," *Foreign Affairs* 25, no. 4 (1947): 566–582.

6. John Ikenberry, *After Victory: Institutions, Strategic Restraint, and the Rebuilding of Order after Major Wars* (Princeton: Princeton University Press, 2000).

7. Matthew Kroenig, *The Logic of American Nuclear Strategy: Why Strategic Superiority Matters* (New York, NY: Oxford University Press, 2018).

8. Hal Brands, *Making the Unipolar Moment: U.S. Foreign Policy and the Rise of the Post–Cold War Order* (Ithaca, NY: Cornell University Press, 2016).

9. Mark Harrison, "Soviet Economic Growth since 1928: The Alternative Statistics of G. I. Khanin," *Europe-Asia Studies* 45, no. 1 (1993): 141–67.

10. Acemoglu and Robinson, *Why Nations Fail*, 131.

11. Clifford G. Gaddy, *The Price of the Past: Russia's Struggle with the Legacy of a Militarized Economy* (Washington, DC: Brookings Institution Press, 1997).

12. The World Bank, "Military Expenditure (% of GDP)" *Stockholm International Peace Research Institute (SIPRI), Yearbook: Armaments, Disarmament and International Security*.

13. Austin Long and Brendan Rittenhouse Green, "Stalking the Secure Second Strike: Intelligence, Counterforce, and Nuclear Strategy," *Journal of Strategic Studies* 38, no. 1–2 (January 2, 2015): 38–73.

14. All points in this paragraph are from Long and Green, "Stalking the Secure Second Strike."

15. Mary Elise Sarotte, "How an Accident Caused the Berlin Wall to Come Down," *Washington Post*, November 1, 2009.

16. John J. Mearsheimer, "Back to the Future: Instability in Europe after the Cold War" *International Security* 15, no. 1 (Summer 1990), 5–56.

17. Paul Kennedy, "The Greatest Superpower Ever," *New Perspectives Quarterly* 19, no. 2 (2008): 12, cited in Beckley *Unrivaled*, 1.

18. This is not the first time a similar argument has been applied to this case. In a landmark book, Princeton professor Aaron Friedberg argued that America's political system prevented the United States from becoming a "garrison state" during the Cold War and its weak government institutions were actually its greatest strength against its centralized and statist opponent. Aaron Friedberg, *In the Shadow of the Garrison State* (Princeton: Princeton University Press, 2000).

19. Fiona Hill and Clifford G. Gaddy, *Mr. Putin: Operative in the Kremlin* (Washington, DC: Brookings Institution Press, 2013).

Chapter 11

1. Nicholas V. Riasanovsky and Mark Steinberg, *A History of Russia: Combined Volume*, 7th edition (New York, NY: Oxford University Press, 2004).

2. M. Steven Fish, *Democracy Derailed in Russia: The Failure of Open Politics* (Cambridge; New York, NY: Cambridge University Press, 2005), 40.

3. Stent, *Putin's World*.

4. Katie Rogers, "Trump Warns Russia to 'Get Out' of Venezuela," *New York Times*, March 28, 2019.

5. Eric Schmitt, "Russia's Military Mission Creep Advances to a New Front: Africa," *New York Times*, April 1, 2019.

6. Dustin Volz and Warren P. Strobel, "China and Russia, Aligned More Closely, Seen as Chief Security Threat to U.S.," *Wall Street Journal*, January 29, 2019.

7. Matthew Kroenig, "Facing Reality: Getting NATO Ready for a New Cold War," *Survival* 57, no. 1 (January 2, 2015): 49–70.

8. Shlapak and Johnson, *Reinforcing Deterrence on NATO's Eastern Flank*.

9. Dima Adamsky, "Cross-Domain Coercion: The Current Russian Art of Strategy," *Proliferation Papers* 54 (November 2015).

10. Kroenig, "Facing Reality."

11. Fish, *Democracy Derailed in Russia*, 40.

12. Nate Schenkkan, *Nations in Transit 2017: The False Promise of Populism*, (Freedom House, Washington DC, 2017).

13. "World's Top Oil Producers," *CNN Money*, July 22, 2016.

14. "Milk without the Cow," *The Economist*, October 22, 2016.

15. Miles Parks, "Businessman Paints Terrifying and Complex Picture of Putin's Russia," *NPR.org*, July 28, 2017.

16. M. Steven Fish, "What Is Putinism?" *Journal of Democracy* 28, no. 4 (October 2017): 61–75.

17. Anders Aslund, *Russia's Crony Capitalism: The Path from Market Economy to Kleptocracy* (New Haven, CT: Yale University Press, 2019).

18. Adam Taylor, "Ahead of Russian Elections, Putin Releases Official Details of Wealth and Income," *Washington Post*, February 7, 2018.

19. Kirit Radia, "Putin's Extravagant $700,000 Watch Collection," *ABC News*, June 8, 2012.

20. Ivan Nechepurenko, "Kremlin Critic Says Russian Premier, Dmitri Medvedev, Built Property Empire on Graft," *New York Times*, December 22, 2017,

21. Dan Alexander, "Russian Billionaires, Including Several Tied to Putin, Are up $104 Billion in the Last Year," *Forbes*, March 29, 2017.

22. "Corruption Perceptions Index 2017," *Transparency International*, February 21, 2018.

23. "Cops for Hire," *The Economist*, March 18, 2010.

24. John Herbst and Sergei Erofeev, "The Putin Exodus: The New Russian Brain Drain," *Atlantic Council* (February 21, 2019).

25. Mike Eckel, "Report: Russian Offshore Wealth Likely Equal to Country's Entire Household Wealth," *RadioFreeEurope/RadioLiberty*, August 24, 2017.

26. Stanislav Secrieru, "The Real and Hidden Costs of Russia's Foreign Policy," *European Union Institute for Security Studies*, February 2018.

27. Chuck DeVore, "U.S. Liquefied Natural Gas Exports Just Quadrupled—It's Good for the Economy and National Security," *Forbes*, May 14, 2018.

28. Michael O'Sullivan, "Global Wealth Databook 2017," *Credit Suisse*, 2017, 165.

29. "The Soft Power 30," https://softpower30.com/.

30. Elisabeth Braw, "Russia's Conscription Conundrum," *Foreign Affairs*, August 25, 2015.

31. Ibid.

32. Christian Lowe, "Georgia War Shows Russian Army Strong but Flawed," *Reuters*, August 21, 2008.

33. Lionel Beehner, "Russia Is Trying to Limit Its Casualties in Syria. Here's Why That Is Bad for Syrian Civilians." *Washington Post*, March 28, 2018,

34. Machiavelli, *The Prince* XII.

35. Thomas Gibbons-Neff, "How a 4-Hour Battle between Russian Mercenaries and U.S. Commandos Unfolded in Syria," *New York Times*, July 13, 2018.

36. Kashmira Gander, "Russia Just Accidentally Bombed Iran Instead of Syria," *The Independent*, October 8, 2015.

37. David Axe, "Russia's Su-57 Stealth Fighter Is No Game Changer." *The National Interest*, November 30, 2018.

38. Keir A. Lieber and Daryl G. Press, "The End of MAD? The Nuclear Dimension of U.S. Primacy," *International Security* 30, no. 4 (April 1, 2006): 7–44,

39. Geoff Brumfiel, "Russia's Nuclear Cruise Missile Is Struggling to Take Off, Imagery Suggests," *Morning Edition, NPR*, September 25, 2018.

40. Jennifer Bronson, "Justice Expenditure and Employment Extracts, 2015," *Bureau of Justice Statistics*, June 29, 2018; Leonid Bershidsky, "Russia's Military Is Leaner, But Meaner," *Bloomberg*, December 14, 2017.

41. Rick Noack, "Even as Fear of Russia Is Rising, Its Military Spending Is Actually Decreasing," *Washington Post*, May 2, 2018.

Chapter 12

1. Jacques, *When China Rules the World*.

2. Allison, *Destined for War*.

3. This section draws on Pamela Kyle Crossley, *The Wobbling Pivot, China since 1800: An Interpretive History* (Chichester, West Sussex, UK; Malden, MA: Wiley-Blackwell, 2010); and Morris Rossabi, *History of China* (Hoboken, UK: John Wiley & Sons, 2013).

4. Charles River Editors, *The Cultural Revolution: The Controversial History of Mao Zedong's Political Mass Movement after the Great Leap Forward* (Scotts Valley, CA: CreateSpace Independent Publishing Platform, 2016).

5. Kroenig, *The Logic of American Nuclear Strategy*, chapter 4.

6. The World Bank "GDP Growth (annual %): China," The World Bank National Accounts Data and OECD National Accounts, 2017.

7. Ibid.

8. Elizabeth Economy, *The Third Revolution: Xi Jinping and the New Chinese State* (New York, NY: Oxford University Press, 2018).

9. Economy, *The Third Revolution*.

10. "Will China's Belt and Road Initiative Outdo the Marshall Plan?" *The Economist*, March 8, 2018.

11. Dustin Volz and Warren P. Strobel. "China and Russia, Aligned More Closely, Seen as Chief Security Threat to U.S." *Wall Street Journal*, January 29, 2019, sec. Politics. https://www.wsj.com/articles/allies-seeking-more-independence-from-u-s-intelligence-leaders-warn-11548773031.

12. Joseph S. Nye Jr., "How Sharp Power Threatens Soft Power," *Foreign Affairs*, January 24, 2018.

13. Larry Diamond and Orville Schell, "China's Influence and American Interests: Promoting Constructive Vigilance," Hoover Institution, November 2018.

14. "How China's 'Sharp Power' Is Muting Criticism Abroad." *The Economist*, December 14, 2017. https://www.economist.com/briefing/2017/12/14/how-chinas-sharp-power-is-muting-criticism-abroad.

15. Eric Heginbotham. "The U.S.-China Military Scorecard: Forces, Geography, and the Evolving Balance of Power, 1996–2017," *RAND Corporation*, 2015.

16. John Fei, "China's Overseas Military Base in Djibouti: Features, Motivations, and Policy Implications," *The Jamestown Foundation*, China Brief 17, December 22, 2017.

17. Paul McLeary, "Acting SecDef Shanahan's First Message: 'China, China, China,'" *Breaking Defense* (blog), Accessed May 6, 2019, https://breakingdefense.com/2019/01/acting-secdef-shanahans-first-message-china-china-china/.

18. Stefan Halper, *The Beijing Consensus: How China's Authoritarian Model Will Dominate the Twenty-First Century* (New York, NY: Basic Books, 2010).

19. Acemoglu and Robinson, *Why Nations Fail*.

20. "Emerging Economies See Debt Rise $1 Trillion in Second Quarter," *Reuters*, November 14, 2018.

21. Derek M. Scissors, "Is China's Economic Power a Paper Tiger?" *The National Interest*, November 27, 2017.

22. Elizabeth Economy, *The River Runs Black: The Environmental Challenge to China's Future*, 2nd edition (Ithaca, NY: Cornell University Press, 2010).

23. Jesus Felipe, Arnelyn Abdon, and Utsav Kumar, "Tracking the Middle-Income Trap: What Is It, Who Is in It, and Why?" Working Paper, *Levy Economics Institute*, no. 715 (2012).

24. Acemoglu and Robinson, *Why Nations Fail*.

25. "The China Dashboard: Tracking China's Economic Reform Program," Asia Society Policy Institute and the Rhodium Group.

26. Damien Ma, "The Year the Training Wheels Came off China," *Foreign Policy*, December 31, 2014.

27. "Just How Badly Is China's Economy Doing?" *South China Morning Post*, January 3, 2019.

28. Jeremy Blum, "China's Real GDP Isn't 7%: Its Closer to Zero and Declining," *Seeking Alpha*, September 4, 2015.

29. Damien Ma and William Adams, *In Line behind a Billion People: How Scarcity Will Define China's Ascent in the Next Decade*, 1st edition (Upper Saddle River, NJ: Pearson FT Press, 2013), 154.

30. Economy, *The Third Revolution*.

31. "Yuval Noah Harari, "Why Technology Favors Tyranny." *The Atlantic*, October 2018. https://www.theatlantic.com/magazine/archive/2018/10/yuval-noah-harari-technology-tyranny/568330/.

32. Karen DeYoung and John Wagner, "Trump Threatens 'Fire and Fury' in Response to North Korean Threats," *Washington Post*, August 8, 2017.

33. United States, *National Security Strategy of the United States of America*, The White House, 2017.

34. Cynthia Kim and Adam Jourdan, "Ghost Stores, Lost Billions as Korea Inc.'s China Woes Grow," *Reuters*, September 21, 2017.

35. Nadège Rolland, *China's Eurasian Century? Political and Strategic Implications of the Belt and Road Initiative* (Seattle, WA: The National Bureau of Asian Research, 2017).

36. Timothy Heath, "Towards Strategic Leadership: Chinese Communist Party People's Liberation Army Relations in the Hu Era," in *Assessing the People's Liberation Army in the Hu Jintao Era*, ed. Roy Kamphausen, David Lai, and Travis Tanner (Carlisle, PA: U.S. Army War College Strategic Studies Institute, 2014), 399–439.

37. Dennis J. Blasko, "The Chinese Military Speaks to Itself, Revealing Doubts," *War on the Rocks*. February 18, 2019. https://warontherocks.com/2019/02/the-chinese-military-speaks-to-itself-revealing-doubts/.

38. Joe McReynolds, "China's Evolving Perspectives on Network Warfare: Lessons from the Science of Military Strategy," *Jamestown Foundation*, China Brief 15, no. 8 (April 17, 2015).

39. "China's Cutting-Edge Fighter Engine a No-Show after Failing Tests," *South China Morning Post*, November 7, 2018.

40. Dave Majumdar, "China's New J-20 Stealth Fighter Has Officially Entered Service," *The National Interest*, September 28, 2017.

41. Hans M. Kristensen and Robert S. Norris, "Nuclear Notebook: Chinese Nuclear Forces, 2018," *Bulletin of the Atomic Scientists* 74, no. 4 (July 4, 2018): 289–95.

42. US Department of Defense, "China Military Power Report, 2018."

43. David, "Explaining Third World Alignment."

44. Sheena Chestnut Greitens. "Rethinking China's Coercive Capacity: An Examination of PRC Domestic Security Spending, 1992–2012." *The China Quarterly* 232 (December 2017): 1002–25. https://doi.org/10.1017/S0305741017001023.

45. James A. Millward, "Opinion: What It's Like to Live in a Surveillance State," *New York Times*, February 5, 2018.

Chapter 13

1. Steven Levitsky and Daniel Ziblatt, *How Democracies Die*, reprint edition (New York, NY: Broadway Books, 2019).

2. Mearsheimer, "Back to the Future."

3. Marshall, Gurr, and Jaggers, "Polity IV Project.

4. The Editors, "The Imperial Presidency," *The Nation*, August 29, 2002.

5. Matthew Kroenig and Jay Stowsky, "War Makes the State, but Not as It Pleases: Homeland Security and American Anti-Statism," *Security Studies* 15, no. 2 (July 2006): 225–70.

6. Scissors, "Is China's Economic Power a Paper Tiger?"

7. Meghan L. O'Sullivan, *Windfall: How the New Energy Abundance Upends Global Politics and Strengthens America's Power*, 1st edition (New York, NY: Simon & Schuster, 2017).

8. Barry Eichengreen. *Exorbitant Privilege: The Rise and Fall of the Dollar and the Future of the International Monetary System*. 1 edition. Oxford ; New York, NY: Oxford University Press, 2011).

9. Thomas Piketty, *Capital in the Twenty-First Century*, trans. Arthur Goldhammer, reprint edition (Cambridge, MA: Belknap Press: An Imprint of Harvard University Press, 2017).

10. Dina Gusovsky, "Why Chinese Money Is Flooding American Markets," *CNBC*, September 17, 2014.

11. Nye, *Soft Power*.

12. "The Soft Power 30." USC Center for Public Diplomacy.

13. Matthew Kroenig and Tristan Volpe, "3-D Printing the Bomb? The Nuclear Nonproliferation Challenge," *Washington Quarterly* 38, no. 3 (July 3, 2015): 7–19.

14. Ash Jain and Matthew Kroenig, "Present at the Re-Creation: A Global Strategy for Revitalizing, Adpating, and Defending a Rules-Based International System," *Atlantic Council Strategy Paper* (Washington DC: Atlantic Council), October 2019.

Chapter 14

1. Charles Krauthammer, "The Unipolar Moment," *Foreign Affairs*, January/February 1990.

2. Daniel W. Drezner, "This Time Is Different," *Foreign Affairs*, May/June 2019.

3. Madeleine Albright, Stephen Hadley, Carl Bildt, Yoriko Kawaguchi, "Declaration of Principles for Freedom, Prosperity, and Peace," *Atlantic Council*, Washington, DC, 2019.

4. Norman Angell, *The Great Illusion: A Study of the Relation of Military Power in Nations to Their Economic and Social Advantage* (New York, NY; London, UK: G. P. Putnam's Sons, 1911).

BIBLIOGRAPHY

Acemoglu, Daron, and James Robinson. *Why Nations Fail: The Origins of Power, Prosperity, and Poverty*. New York, NY: Crown Publishing Group, 2012.

Adamsky, Dima. "Cross-Domain Coercion: The Current Russian Art of Strategy." *Proliferation Papers* 54 (2015).

Albright, Madeleine, Stephen Hadley, Carl Bildt, and Yoriko Kawaguchi. "Declaration of Principles for Freedom, Prosperity, and Peace." *Atlantic Council*, Washington, DC, 2019.

Alexander, Dan. "Russian Billionaires, Including Several Tied to Putin, Are up $104 Billion in the Last Year." *Forbes*, March 29, 2017. https://www.forbes.com/sites/danalexander/2017/03/29/putin-vladimir-donald-trump-russia-billionaires-oligarchs/.

Allison, Graham. *Destined for War: Can America and China Escape Thucydides's Trap?* Boston: Houghton Mifflin Harcourt, 2017a.

Allison, Graham. "What Xi Jinping Wants." *The Atlantic*, May 31, 2017b. https://www.theatlantic.com/international/archive/2017/05/what-china-wants/528561.

Angell, Norman. *The Great Illusion: A Study of the Relation of Military Power in Nations to Their Economic and Social Advantage*. New York, NY; London, UK: G. P. Putnam's Sons, 1911.

Axe, David. "Russia's Su-57 Stealth Fighter Is No Game Changer." *The National Interest*, November 30, 2018.

Barker, Ernest. *The Politics of Aristotle*. 1st edition. London, UK: Oxford University Press, 1962.

Beckley, Michael. *Unrivaled: Why America Will Remain the World's Sole Superpower*. Cornell Studies in Security Affairs. Ithaca, NY: Cornell University Press, 2018.

Beehner, Lionel. "Russia Is Trying to Limit Its Casualties in Syria: Here's Why That Is Bad for Syrian Civilians." *Washington Post*, March 28, 2018. https://

www.washingtonpost.com/news/monkey-cage/wp/2018/03/28/russia-wants-to-protect-its-troops-heres-why-that-is-bad-for-syrian-civilians/?utm_term=.d903a40a0cfa

Bennett, D. Scott. "Testing Alternative Models of Alliance Duration, 1816–1984." *American Journal of Political Science* 41, no. 3 (1997): 846–78.

Bennett, D. Scott, and Allan C. Stam. "Eugene: A Conceptual Manual." *International Interactions* 26, no. 2 (2000): 179–204.

Bershidsky, Leonid. "Russia's Military Is Leaner, But Meaner." *Bloomberg*, December 14, 2017. https://www.bloomberg.com/view/articles/2017-12-14/russia-s-military-is-leaner-but-meaner.

Biddle, Stephen D. *Military Power: Explaining Victory and Defeat in Modern Battle*. New Delhi, India: Manas Publications, 2005.

Blasko, Dennis J. "The Chinese Military Speaks to Itself, Revealing Doubts," *War on the Rocks*. February 18, 2019. https://warontherocks.com/2019/02/the-chinese-military-speaks-to-itself-revealing-doubts/.

Blum, Jeremy. "China's Real GDP Isn't 7%: It's Closer to Zero and Declining." *Seeking Alpha*, September 4, 2015.

Brandon, Pepijn. *War, Capital, and the Dutch State*. Reprint edition. Chicago, IL: Haymarket Books, 2017.

Brands, Hal. *Making the Unipolar Moment: U.S. Foreign Policy and the Rise of the Post-Cold War Order*. Ithaca, NY: Cornell University Press, 2016.

Braw, Elisabeth. "Russia's Conscription Conundrum." *Foreign Affairs*, August 25, 2015. https://www.foreignaffairs.com/articles/russia-fsu/2015-08-25/russias-conscription-conundrum.

Bronson, Jennifer. "Justice Expenditure and Employment Extracts, 2015." Bureau of Justice Statistics. June 29, 2018. http://www.bjs.gov/index.cfm?ty=pbdetail&iid=6310.

Brooks, Stephen G., and William C. Wohlforth. *World Out of Balance: International Relations and the Challenge of American Primacy*. Princeton, NJ: Princeton University Press, 2008.

Brooks, Stephen G., and William C. Wohlforth. *America Abroad: Why the Sole Superpower Should Not Pull Back from the World*. Oxford, New York: Oxford University Press, 2016.

Brumfiel, Geoff. "Russia's Nuclear Cruise Missile Is Struggling to Take Off, Imagery Suggests." *Morning Edition, NPR*, September 25, 2018.

Cassis, Youssef. *Capitals of Capital: The Rise and Fall of International Financial Centres 1780–2009*. Translated by Jacqueline Collier. 2nd edition. Cambridge; New York, NY: Cambridge University Press, 2010.

Carr, E. H. *The Twenty Years' Crisis, 1919–1939: Reissued with New Introduction*, Edited by M. Cox. Houndmills, Basingstoke, Hampshire; New York, NY: Palgrave Macmillan, 2001.

Cartwright, Mark. "Carthaginian Trade." *Ancient History Encyclopedia*. 2016. http://www.ancient.eu/article/911/carthaginian-trade/.

Celenza, Christopher S. *Machiavelli: A Portrait*. Cambridge, MA: Harvard University Press, 2015.

Cheung, Tai Ming. Fortifying China: The Struggle to Build a Modern Defense Economy. 1st edition. Ithaca: Cornell University Press, 2008.

"China to Become World's Largest Economy in 2024 Reports IHS Economics." *IHS Markit*, September 7, 2014. http://news.ihsmarkit.com/press-release/economics-country-risk/china-become-worlds-largest-economy-2024-reports-ihs-economics.

"China's Cutting-Edge Fighter Engine a No-Show after Failing Tests." *South China Morning*, November 7, 2018.

Choi, Ajin. "Democratic Synergy and Victory in War, 1816–1992." *International Studies Quarterly* 48, no. 3 (2004): 663–82.

Cicero, Marcus Tullius. *Cicero: Selected Works.* Translated by Michael Grant. New York: Penguin Books, 1960.

Cohen, Warren I. *America's Response to China: A History of Sino-American Relations.* New York, NY: Columbia University Press, 1990.

Colaresi, Michael P., Karen Rasler, and William R. Thompson. *Strategic Rivalries in World Politics: Position, Space and Conflict Escalation.* Cambridge University Press, 2008.

Coppedge, Michael, John Gerring, David Altman, Michael Bernhard, Steven Fish, Allen Hicken, Matthew Kroenig, et al. "Conceptualizing and Measuring Democracy: A New Approach." *Perspectives on Politics* 9, no. 2 (June 2011): 247–67.

"Corruption Perceptions Index 2017." *Transparency International*, February 21, 2018. https://www.transparency.org/news/feature/corruption_perceptions_index_2017.

Crafts, Nicholas. "Forging Ahead and Falling Behind: The Rise and Relative Decline of the First Industrial Nation." *Journal of Economic Perspectives* 12, no. 2 (1998): 193–210.

Crossley, Pamela Kyle. *The Wobbling Pivot, China since 1800: An Interpretive History.* 1st edition. Malden, MA: Wiley-Blackwell, 2010.

Dahl, Robert A. "The Concept of Power." *Behavioral Science* 2, no. 3 (1957): 201–15.

David, Steven R. "Explaining Third World Alignment." *World Politics* 43, no 2 (1991): 233–56.

DeVore, Chuck. "U.S. Liquefied Natural Gas Exports Just Quadrupled: It's Good for the Economy and National Security." *Forbes*, May 14, 2018.

DeYoung, Karen, and John Wagner. "Trump Threatens 'Fire and Fury' in Response to North Korean Threats." *Washington Post*, August 8, 2017.

Dickson, Bruce J. *The Dictator's Dilemma: The Chinese Communist Party's Strategy for Survival.* 1st edition. New York, NY: Oxford University Press, 2016.

Dincecco, Mark. "The Political Economy of Fiscal Prudence in Historical Perspective." *Economics and Politics* 22, no. 1 (2010): 1–36.

Downes, Alexander B. "How Smart and Tough Are Democracies? Reassessing
Theories of Democratic Victory in War." *International Security* 33 no. 4
(2009): 9–51.

Doyle, Michael W. *Ways of War and Peace: Realism, Liberalism, and Socialism.*
New York, NY: W. W. Norton & Company, 1997.

Drezner, Daniel W. "This Time Is Different." *Foreign Affairs*, May/June 2019.

Eckel, Mike. "Report: Russian Offshore Wealth Likely Equal to Country's Entire
Household Wealth." RadioFreeEurope/RadioLiberty. August 24, 2017. https://
www.rferl.org/a/russia-offshore-wealth-capital-flight-income-inequality-report/
28695293.html.

Economy, Elizabeth. *The River Runs Black: The Environmental Challenge to China's
Future.* 2nd edition. Ithaca, NY: Cornell University Press, 2010.

Economy, Elizabeth. *The Third Revolution: Xi Jinping and the New Chinese State.*
New York, NY: Oxford University Press, 2018.

Edelstein, David M. *Over the Horizon: Time, Uncertainty, and the Rise of Great Powers.*
Ithaca, NY: Cornell University Press, 2017.

Eichengreen, Barry. *Exorbitant Privilege: The Rise and Fall of the Dollar and the Future
of the International Monetary System.* 1st edition. Oxford; New York, NY: Oxford
University Press, 2011.

Eichengreen, Barry, and David A. Leblang. "Democracy and Globalization."
Economics and Politics 20 (2008): 289–334.

Fearon, James D. "Domestic Political Audiences and the Escalation of International
Disputes." *American Political Science Review* 88, no. 3 (1994): 577–92.

Fei, John. "China's Overseas Military Base in Djibouti: Features, Motivations,
and Policy Implications." *The Jamestown Foundation* China Brief 17 (December
22, 2017).

Felipe, Jesus, Arnelyn Abdon, and Utsav Kumar. "Tracking the Middle-Income
Trap: What Is It, Who Is in It, and Why?" *Levy Economics Institute*, Working
Paper no. 715 (2012).

Fish, M. Steven. *Democracy Derailed in Russia: The Failure of Open Politics.*
Cambridge; New York, NY: Cambridge University Press, 2005.

Fish, M. Steven. "What Is Putinism?" *Journal of Democracy* 28 no. 4 (2017):
61–75.

Fontaine, Richard. "The Shutdown Is Great News for Russia." *The Atlantic*, January
19, 2019.

Fratianni, Michele, and Franco Spinelli. "Italian City-States and Financial
Evolution." *European Review of Economic History* 10, no. 3 (December 1,
2006): 257–78.

Fravel, M. Taylor. *Strong Borders, Secure Nation: Cooperation and Conflict in China's
Territorial Disputes.* Princeton, NJ: Princeton University Press, 2008.

"Freedom in the World 2019." Freedom House. https://freedomhouse.org/report/
freedom-world/freedom-world-2019/democracy-in-retreat.

French, David. "How Our Overly Restrictive Rules of Engagement Keep Us from Winning Wars." *National Review*, December 21, 2015. https://www.nationalreview.com/2015/12/rules-engagement-need-reform/.

Friedberg, Aaron. 2000. *In the Shadow of the Garrison State*. Princeton, NJ: Princeton University Press.

Friedman, Thomas L. *Hot, Flat, and Crowded: Why We Need a Green Revolution—and How It Can Renew America, Release 2.0*. New York, NY: Picador, 2009.

Fuhrmann, Matthew, and Jeffrey D. Berejikian. "Disaggregating Noncompliance: Abstention versus Predation in the Nuclear Nonproliferation Treaty." *Journal of Conflict Resolution* 56, no. 3 (June 1, 2012): 355–81.

Fukuyama, Francis. *The End of History and the Last Man*. New York, NY; Toronto, CA: Free Press, 1992.

Gaddis, John Lewis. *The Cold War: A New History*. New York, NY: Penguin Press, 2005.

Gaddy, Clifford G. *The Price of the Past: Russia's Struggle with the Legacy of a Militarized Economy*. Washington, DC: Brookings Institution Press, 1997.

Gander, Kashmira. "Russia Just Accidentally Bombed Iran Instead of Syria." *The Independent*, October 8, 2015. http://www.independent.co.uk/news/world/middle-east/syria-conflict-russian-cruise-missiles-crash-in-iran-a6686856.html.

Gartzke, Erik, and Kristian Skrede Gleditsch. "Why Democracies May Actually Be Less Reliable Allies." *American Journal of Political Science* 48, no. 4 (October 1, 2004): 775–95.

Gaubatz, Kurt Taylor. "Democratic States and Commitment in International Relations." *International Organization* 50, no. 1 (1996): 109–39.

Gauss, Christian. *The German Emperor as Shown in His Public Utterances*. New York, NY: Scribner, 1915.

Gibbons-Neff, Thomas. "How a 4-Hour Battle between Russian Mercenaries and U.S. Commandos Unfolded in Syria." *New York Times*, July 13, 2018.

Gilli, Andrea, and Mauro Gilli. "Why China Has Not Caught Up Yet: Military-Technological Superiority and the Limits of Imitation, Reverse Engineering, and Cyber Espionage." *International Security* 43, no. 3 (February 1, 2019): 141–89.

Gilpin, Robert. *War and Change in World Politics*. 1st edition. Cambridge; New York, NY: Cambridge University Press, 1981.

Grotius, Hugo. *The Freedom of the Seas*. Translated by Ralph Van Deman Magoffin. Scotts Valley, CA: CreateSpace Independent Publishing Platform, 2018.

Grygiel, Jakub J. *Great Powers and Geopolitical Change*. 1st edition. Baltimore, MD: Johns Hopkins University Press, 2007.

Golden, John M., and Hannah J. Wiseman. 2015. "The Fracking Revolution: Shale Gas as a Case Study in Innovation Policy." *Emory Law Journal* 4, no. 4 (2015): 955–1040.

Goldin, Ian, Andrew Pitt, and Benjamin Nabarro. *Migration and the Economy: Economic Realities, Social Impacts and Political Choices*. Citi GPS: Global Perspectives & Solutions, September 2018.

Greitens, Sheena Chestnut. "Rethinking China's Coercive Capacity: An Examination of PRC Domestic Security Spending, 1992–2012." *The China Quarterly* 232 (December 2017): 1002–25.

Gusovsky, Dina. "Why Chinese Money Is Flooding American Markets." *CNBC*, September 17, 2014.

Haas, Mark L. *The Ideological Origins of Great Power Politics*, 1789–1989. Cornell University Press, 2007.

Halper, Stefan. *The Beijing Consensus: How China's Authoritarian Model Will Dominate the Twenty-First Century*. New York: Basic Books, 2010.

Halperin, Morton, Joe Siegle, and Michael Weinstein, *The Democracy Advantage: How Democracies Promote Prosperity and Peace*. New York. NY: Routledge, 2004.

Hanson, Victor Davis. *Why the West Has Won: Carnage and Culture from Salamis to Vietnam*. London, UK: Faber & Faber, 2001.

Harari, Yuval Noah, "Why Technology Favors Tyranny." *The Atlantic*, October 2018.

Harrison, Mark. "Soviet Economic Growth since 1928: The Alternative Statistics of G. I. Khanin." *Europe-Asia Studies* 45, no. 1 (1993): 141–67.

Hays, Jo N. *Epidemics and Pandemics: Their Impacts on Human History*. 1st edition. Santa Barbara, CA: ABC-CLIO, 2005.

Hazlitt, William Carew. *The History of the Venetian Republic*. New Delhi, India: Sagwan Press, 2018.

Heath, Timothy. "Towards Strategic Leadership: Chinese Communist Party People's Liberation Army Relations in the Hu Era." In *Assessing the People's Liberation Army in the Hu Jintao Era*, edited by Roy Kamphausen, David Lai, and Travis Tanner, 399–439. Carlisle, PA: U.S. Army War College Strategic Studies Institute, 2014.

Heginbotham, Eric. "The U.S.-China Military Scorecard: Forces, Geography, and the Evolving Balance of Power, 1996–2017." *RAND Corporation*, 2015.

Herbst, John, and Sergei Erofeev. "The Putin Exodus: The New Russian Brain Drain." *Atlantic Council*, February 21, 2019.

Hill, Fiona, and Clifford G. Gaddy. *Mr. Putin: Operative in the Kremlin*. Washington, DC: Brookings Institution Press, 2013.

Hitler, Adolf, and Bob Carruthers. *Mein Kampf—The Official 1939 Edition*. Translated by James Murphy. Slough, United Kingdom: Archive Media Publishing, 2011.

Hobbes, Thomas. *Leviathan*. Wordsworth Classics of World Literature. Ware, United Kingdom: Wordsworth Editions, 2014.

Ikenberry, John. *After Victory: Institutions, Strategic Restraint, and the Rebuilding of Order after Major Wars*. Princeton, NJ: Princeton University Press, 2000.

Ikenberry, G. John. *Liberal Leviathan: The Origins, Crisis, and Transformation of the American World Order*. First Edition edition. Princeton, N.J: Princeton University Press, 2011.

Israel, Jonathan. *The Dutch Republic: Its Rise, Greatness, and Fall 1477–1806*. Reprint edition. Oxford: Clarendon Press, 1998.

Itzkowitz Shifrinson, Joshua R. *Rising Titans, Falling Giants: How Great Powers Exploit Power Shifts*. Ithaca, NY: Cornell University Press, 2018.

Jacques, Martin. *When China Rules the World: The End of the Western World and the Birth of a New Global Order*. 2nd edition. New York, NY: Penguin Books, 2012.

Jaggers, Keith, and Ted Robert Gurr. "Tracking Democracy's Third Wave with the Polity III Data." *Journal of Peace Research* 32, no. 4 (2016): 469–82.

Jain, Ash, and Matthew Kroenig, "Present at the Re-Creation: A Global Strategy for Revitalizing, Adpating, and Defending a Rules-Based International System," *Atlantic Council Strategy Paper* (Washington DC: Atlantic Council), October 2019.

"Just How Badly Is China's Economy Doing?" *South China Morning Post*, January 3, 2019.

Kagan, Donald. *The Peloponnesian War*. New York, NY: Penguin Books, 2004.

Kagan, Robert. *Dangerous Nation: America's Foreign Policy from Its Earliest Days to the Dawn of the Twentieth Century*. Reprint edition. New York, NY: Vintage, 2007.

Kagan, Robert. *The World America Made*. First Edition edition. New York: Knopf, 2012.

Kagan, Robert. *The Jungle Grows Back: America and Our Imperiled World*. First Edition New York: Knopf, 2018.

Kennan, George F. "The Sources of Soviet Conduct [Excerpt]." *Foreign Affairs* 25 no. 4 (July 1947): 566–82.

Kennedy, Paul. "The Greatest Superpower Ever." *New Perspectives Quarterly* 19, no. 2 (2002): 12.

Kennedy, Paul. *The Rise and Fall of the Great Powers*. New York, NY: Vintage, 1989.

Kim, Cynthia, and Adam Jourdan. "Ghost Stores, Lost Billions as Korea Inc's China Woes Grow." *Reuters*, September 21, 2017.

Kissinger, Henry. *Diplomacy*. Reprint edition. New York, NY: Simon & Schuster, 1995.

Kissinger, Henry. *On China*. New York, NY: Penguin Books, 2012.

Klein, James P., Gary Goertz, and Paul F. Diehl. "The New Rivalry Dataset: Procedures and Patterns." *Journal of Peace Research* 43, no. 3 (May 2006): 331–48.

Krauthammer, Charles. "The Unipolar Moment." *Foreign Affairs*, January/February 1990.

Kristensen, Hans M., and Robert S. Norris. "Nuclear Notebook: Chinese Nuclear Forces, 2018." *Bulletin of the Atomic Scientists* 74, no. 4 (2018): 289–95.

Kroenig, Matthew. "Why Democracies Dominate: America's Edge over China." *The National Interest*, July/August 2015.

Kroenig, Matthew. "Facing Reality: Getting NATO Ready for a New Cold War." *Survival* 57, no. 1 (2015): 49–70.

Kroenig, Matthew. *The Logic of American Nuclear Strategy: Why Strategic Superiority Matters*. New York, NY: Oxford University Press, 2018.

Kroenig, Matthew, and Jay Stowsky. "War Makes the State, but Not as It Pleases: Homeland Security and American Anti-Statism." *Security Studies* 15, no. 2 (2006): 225–70.

Kroenig, Matthew, and Tristan Volpe. "3-D Printing the Bomb? The Nuclear Nonproliferation Challenge." *Washington Quarterly* 38, no. 3 (2015): 7–19.

Kupchan, Charles. *No One's World: The West, the Rising Rest, and the Coming Global Turn*. New York: Oxford University Press, 2012.

Kupchan, Charles. *The End of the American Era: U.S. Foreign Policy and the Geopolitics of the Twenty-First Century*. New York: Knopf, 2002.

Lai, Brian, and Dan Reiter. "Democracy, Political Similarity, and International Alliances, 1816–1992." *Journal of Conflict Resolution* 44, no. 2 (2000): 203–27.

Lake, David A. "Powerful Pacifists: Democratic States and War." *American Political Science Review* 86, no. 1 (1992): 24–37.

Leeds, Brett Ashley. "Alliance Reliability in Times of War: Explaining State Decisions to Violate Treaties." *International Organization* 57, no. 4 (2003): 801–27.

Leeds, Brett Ashley. "Do Alliances Deter Aggression? The Influence of Military Alliances on the Initiation of Militarized Interstate Disputes." *American Journal of Political Science* 47, no. 3 (2003): 427–39.

Leeds, Brett Ashley, Michaela Mattes, and Jeremy S. Vogel. "Interests, Institutions, and the Reliability of International Commitments." *American Journal of Political Science* 53, no. 2 (2009): 461–76.

Lenin, Vladimir Ilyich. *Essential Works of Lenin: "What Is to Be Done?" And Other Writings*. 1st edition. New York, NY: Dover Publications, 1987.

Levine, Ross. "Stock Markets, Economic Development, and Capital Control Liberalization." *Investment Company Institute Perspective* 3, no. 5 (1997): 8.

Levine, Ross, and Sara Zervos. "Capital Control Liberalization and Stock Market Development." *World Development* 26, no. 7 (1998): 1169–83.

Levitsky, Steven, and Daniel Ziblatt. *How Democracies Die*. Reprint edition. New York, NY: Broadway Books, 2019.

Levy, Jack S., and William Mulligan. "Shifting Power, Preventive Logic, and the Response of the Target: Germany, Russia, and the First World War." *Journal of Strategic Studies* 40, no. 5 (July 29, 2017): 731–69.

Levy, Jack S., and William R. Thompson, "Balancing on Land and at Sea: Do States Ally against the Leading Global Power?" *International Security* 35, no. 1 (Summer 2010): 7–43.

Lieber, Keir A., and Daryl G. Press. "The End of MAD? The Nuclear Dimension of U.S. Primacy." *International Security* 30, no. 4 (2006): 7–44.

Lieber, Robert J. *Power and Willpower in the American Future: Why the United States Is Not Destined to Decline.* Cambridge: Cambridge University Press, 2012.

Lieber, Robert J. *Retreat and Its Consequences: American Foreign Policy and the Problem of World Order.* Cambridge: Cambridge University Press, 2016.

Livius, Titus. *The History of Rome: The Only Complete and Unabridged Edition in One Volume.* Edited by Jake E. Stief, translated by D. Spillan, Cyrus Edmonds, and William A. M'Devitte. Santa Fe, NM: Stief Books, 2018.

Long, Austin, and Brendan Rittenhouse Green. "Stalking the Secure Second Strike: Intelligence, Counterforce, and Nuclear Strategy." *Journal of Strategic Studies* 38, no. 1–2 (January 2, 2015): 38–73.

Lowe, Christian. "Georgia War Shows Russian Army Strong but Flawed." *Reuters*, August 21, 2008. https://www.reuters.com/article/us-georgia-ossetia-military/georgia-war-shows-russian-army-strong-but-flawed-idUSLK23804020080821.

Ma, Damien. "The Year the Training Wheels Came off China." *Foreign Policy*, December 31, 2014.

Ma, Damien, and William Adams. *In Line behind a Billion People: How Scarcity Will Define China's Ascent in the Next Decade.* 1st edition. Upper Saddle River, NJ: Pearson FT Press, 2013.

Machiavelli, Niccolò, and Albert Russell Ascoli. *The Essential Writings of Machiavelli.* Translated by Peter Constantine, Modern Library pbk. edition. New York, NY: Modern Library, 2007.

MacMillan, Margaret, and Richard Holbrooke, *Paris 1919: Six Months That Changed the World.* 1st edition. New York, NY: Random House, 2002.

Mahan, Alfred. *Influence of Sea Power upon History, 1660–1783.* Gretna: Pelican Publishing, 2003.

Maddison, Angus. *The World Economy.* Development Centre Studies. Paris, France: Development Centre of the Organisation for Economic Co-operation and Development, 2006.

Majumdar, Dave. "China's New J-20 Stealth Fighter Has Officially Entered Service." *The National Interest*, September 28, 2017.

Marshall, Monty G., Ted Robert Gurr, and Keith Jaggers. "Polity IV Project: Political Regime Characteristics and Transitions, 1800–2016." *Center for Systemic Peace*, 2017.

McDonald, Patrick J. *The Invisible Hand of Peace: Capitalism, the War Machine, and International Relations Theory.* 1st edition. New York: Cambridge University Press, 2009.

McFaul, Michael. *From Cold War to Hot Peace: An American Ambassador in Putin's Russia.* New York, NY: Houghton Mifflin Harcourt, 2018.

McGregor, Malcolm Francis. *The Athenians and Their Empire.* Vancouver: UBC Press, 1987.

McNeill, William H. *The Pursuit of Power: Technology, Armed Force, and Society since A.D. 1000.* New York, NY: ACLS Humanities E-Book Project, 2009.

McReynolds, Joe. "China's Evolving Perspectives on Network Warfare: Lessons from the Science of Military Strategy." *Jamestown Foundation* China Brief 15 no. 8, April 16, 2015. https://jamestown.org/program/chinas-evolving-perspectives-on-network-warfare-lessons-from-the-science-of-military-strategy/.

Mead, Walter Russel. *Power, Terror, Peace, and War: America's Grand Strategy in a World at Risk.* New York, NY: Vintage, 2005.

Mearsheimer, John J. "Back to the Future: Instability in Europe after the Cold War." *International Security* 15, no. 1 (Summer 1990), 5–56.

Mearsheimer, John J. *The Tragedy of Great Power Politics.* New York, NY: W. W. Norton, 2001.

Millward, James A. "Opinion: What It's Like to Live in a Surveillance State." *New York Times,* February 5, 2018. https://www.nytimes.com/2018/02/03/opinion/sunday/china-surveillance-state-uighurs.html.

Milner, Helen V., and Keiko Kubota. "Why the Move to Free Trade? Democracy and Trade Policy in the Developing Countries." *International Organization* 59, no. 1 (2005): 107–43.

Minzner, Carl. *End of an Era: How China's Authoritarian Revival Is Undermining Its Rise.* New York, NY: Oxford University Press, 2018.

Modelski, George. *Leading Sectors and World Powers: The Coevolution of Global Economics and Politics.* Edited by Charles W. Kegley Jr. and Donald J. Puchala. Columbia, S.C: University of South Carolina Press, 1996.

Monfasani, John. "Machiavelli, Polybius, and Janus Lascaris: The Hexter Thesis Revisited." *Italian Studies* 71, no. 1 (2016): 39–48.

Morrow, James D. "Alliances: Why Write Them Down?" *Annual Review of Political Science* 3, no. 1 (2000): 63–83.

Moukarzel, Pierre. "Venetian Merchants in Thirteenth-Century Alexandria and the Sultans of Egypt: An Analysis of Treaties, Privileges and Intercultural Relations." *Al-Masāq* 28, no. 2 (May 3, 2016): 187–205.

Nathan, Andrew, and Andrew Scobell. *China's Search for Security.* New York, NY: Columbia University Press, 2012.

Nau, Henry R. "Where Reaganomics Works." *Foreign Policy,* no. 57 (1984): 14–37.

Nau, Henry R. *The Myth of America's Decline: Leading the World Economy into the 1990s.* 1st edition. New York: Oxford University Press, 1990.

Nau, Henry R., and Richard C. Leone. *At Home Abroad: Identity and Power in American Foreign Policy.* 1st edition. Ithaca: Cornell University Press, 2002.

Nechepurenko, Ivan. "Kremlin Critic Says Russian Premier, Dmitri Medvedev, Built Property Empire on Graft." *New York Times,* December 22, 2017.

Nexon, Daniel H. *The Struggle for Power in Early Modern Europe: Religious Conflict, Dynastic Empires, and International Change.* Princeton, NJ: Princeton University Press, 2009.

Noack, Rick. "Even as Fear of Russia Is Rising, Its Military Spending Is Actually Decreasing." *Washington Post,* May 2, 2018.

Nordenman, Magnus. "China and Russia Joint Sea 2017 Baltic Naval Exercise Highlight New Normal in European Maritime." *USNI News* (blog), July 5, 2017.

North, Douglass C. *Institutions, Institutional Change, and Economic Performance.* Cambridge, UK: Cambridge University Press, 1990.

North, Douglass C., and Barry R. Weingast. "Constitutions and Commitment: The Evolution of Institutions Governing Public Choice in Seventeenth-Century England." *Journal of Economic History* 49, no. 4 (1989): 803–32.

Norwich, John Julius. *A History of Venice.* 1st Vintage Books edition. New York, NY: Vintage, 1989.

Nye, Joseph S., Jr. *Soft Power: The Means to Success in World Politics.* New York, NY: Public Affairs, 2005.

Nye, Joseph S., Jr. "How Sharp Power Threatens Soft Power." *Foreign Affairs,* January 24, 2018.

Olson, Mancur. "Dictatorship, Democracy, and Development." *The American Political Science Review* 87, no. 3 (1993): 567–76. https://doi.org/10.2307/2938736.

Osnos, Evan. *Age of Ambition: Chasing Fortune, Truth, and Faith in the New China.* New York, NY: Farrar, Straus and Giroux, 2014.

Organski, Abramo Fino Kenneth, and Jacek Kugler. "The War Ledger." *Bibliovault OAI Repository.* Chicago, IL: University of Chicago Press, 1981.

O'Sullivan, Meghan L. *Windfall: How the New Energy Abundance Upends Global Politics and Strengthens America's Power.* 1st edition. New York, NY: Simon & Schuster, 2017.

Owen IV, John M. *The Clash of Ideas in World Politics: Transnational Networks, States, and Regime Change, 1510–2010.* Princeton, N.J: Princeton University Press, 2010.

Paarlberg, Robert L. *Leadership Abroad Begins at Home: U.S. Foreign Economic Policy After the Cold War.* Brookings Institution Press, 1995.

Padgett, John F., and Paul D. McLean. "Economic Credit in Renaissance Florence." *Journal of Modern History* 83, no. 1 (2011): 1–47.

Parker, Geoffrey. "The 'Military Revolution,' 1560–1660—A Myth?" *Journal of Modern History* 48, no. 2 (1976): 196–214.

Parks, Miles. "Businessman Paints Terrifying and Complex Picture of Putin's Russia." *NPR.Org,* July 28, 2017. https://www.npr.org/2017/07/28/539802914/businessman-paints-a-terrifying-and-complex-picture-of-putins-russia.

Piketty, Thomas. *Capital in the Twenty-First Century.* Translated by Arthur Goldhammer. Reprint edition. Cambridge, MA: Belknap Press, an Imprint of Harvard University Press, 2017.

Pillsbury, Michael. *The Hundred-Year Marathon: China's Secret Strategy to Replace America as the Global Superpower.* New York, NY: Henry Holt 2015.

Plato, and Tom Butler-Bowdon. *The Republic: The Influential Classic.* Chichester, West Sussex, UK: Capstone, 2012.

Plutarch. *Lives of the Noble Grecians and Romans*. Edited by Arthur Hugh Clough. Oxford, UK: Benediction Classics, 2010.

Pollack, Kenneth M. *Armies of Sand: The Past, Present, and Future of Arab Military Effectiveness*. New York, NY, United States of America: Oxford University Press, 2019.

Polybius. *The Complete Histories of Polybius*. Translated by W. R. Paton. Digireads. com, 2009.

Przeworski, Adam, Michael E. Alvarez, Jose Antonio Cheibub, and Fernando Limongi. *Democracy and Development: Political Institutions and Well-Being in the World, 1950–1990*. New York, NY: Cambridge University Press, 2000.

"Putin Deplores Collapse of USSR." *BBC News,* April 25, 2005. http://news.bbc. co.uk/2/hi/4480745.stm.

Radia, Kirit. "Putin's Extravagant $700,000 Watch Collection." *ABC News*, June 8, 2012. https://abcnews.go.com/news/t/blogEntry?id=16523979.

Rasler, Karen A., and William R. Thompson. "Global Wars, Public Debts, and the Long Cycle." *World Politics* 35, no. 4 (1983):489–516.

Rasler, Karen A., and William R. Thompson. *War and State Making: The Shaping of the Global Powers*. Crows Nest, Australia: Unwin Hyman, 1989.

Reed, William. "Alliance Duration and Democracy: An Extension and Cross-Validation of 'Democratic States and Commitment in International Relations.'" *American Journal of Political Science* 41, no. 3 (1997): 1072–78.

Reiter, Dan, and Allan C. Stam. *Democracies at War*. Princeton, NJ: Princeton University Press, 2002.

Reiter, Dan, Allan C. Stam, and Alexander B. Downes. "Another Skirmish in the Battle over Democracies and War." *International Security* 34, no. 2 (2009): 194–204.

Riasanovsky, Nicholas V., and Mark Steinberg, *A History of Russia: Combined Volume*. 7th edition. New York, NY: Oxford University Press, 2004.

Rogers, Katie. "Trump Warns Russia to 'Get Out' of Venezuela." *New York Times*, March 28, 2019.

Rohac, Dalibor, Liz Kennedy, and Vikram Singh. "Drivers of Authoritarian Populism in the United States." *Center for American Progress*, May 10, 2018. https://www.americanprogress.org/issues/democracy/reports/2018/05/10/450552/drivers-authoritarian-populism-united-states/.

Rolland, Nadège. *China's Eurasian Century? Political and Strategic Implications of the Belt and Road Initiative*. Seattle: The National Bureau of Asian Research, 2017.

Ross, Michael L. "What Have We Learned about the Resource Curse?" *Annual Review of Political Science* 18 (May 2015): 239–59.

Rossabi, Morris. *History of China*. Hoboken, UK: John Wiley & Sons, 2013.

Rowlands, Guy. *The Financial Decline of a Great Power: War, Influence, and Money in Louis XIV's France*. 1st edition. Oxford: Oxford University Press, 2012.

Russett, Bruce, William Antholis, Carol R. Ember, Melvin Ember, and Zeev Maoz. *Grasping the Democratic Peace: Principles for a Post–Cold War World*. Princeton, NJ: Princeton University Press, 1993.

Sachs, Jeffrey. "Government, Geography, and Growth: The True Drivers of
  Economic Development." *Foreign Affairs* 91, no. 5 (August 2012), 142.

Sachs, Jeffrey, and A. M. Warner. "Economic Reform and the Process of Global
  Integration." *Brookings Papers on Economic Activity* (1995): 1–118.

Saiegh, Sebastian M. "Coalition Governments and Sovereign Debt Crises." *Economics
  and Politics* 21, no. 2 (2009): 232–54.

Sarotte, Mary Elise. "How an Accident Caused the Berlin Wall to Come Down."
  Washington Post, November 1, 2009.

Saunders, Elizabeth N. "War and the Inner Circle: Democratic Elites and the
  Politics of Using Force." *Security Studies* 24, no. 3 (July 3, 2015): 466–501.

Schake, Kori. *Safe Passage: The Transition from British to American Hegemony*. 1st
  edition. Cambridge, MA: Harvard University Press, 2017.

Schenkkan, Nate. *Nations in Transit 2017: The False Promise of Populism*. Freedom
  House, Washington DC, 2017.

Schmitt, Eric. "Russia's Military Mission Creep Advances to a New Front: Africa."
  The New York Times, April 1, 2019.

Schultz, Kenneth A., and Barry R. Weingast. "The Democratic
  Advantage: Institutional Foundations of Financial Power in International
  Competition." *International Organization* 57, no. 1 (2003): 3–42.

Schumpeter, Joseph A. *Capitalism, Socialism, and Democracy*. 3rd edition. New York,
  NY: Harper & Brothers, 1950.

Scissors, Derek M. "Is China's Economic Power a Paper Tiger?" *The National
  Interest*, November 27, 2017.

Secrieru, Stanislav. "The Real and Hidden Costs of Russia's Foreign Policy."
  European Union Institute for Security Studies, February 2018.

Shambaugh, David. *China's Communist Party: Atrophy and Adaptation*. 1st edition.
  Washington, D.C.: Berkeley: University of California Press, 2008.

Shambaugh, David. *China Goes Global: The Partial Power*. 1st edition. New York,
  NY: Oxford University Press, 2013.

Shea, Patrick E. "Financing Victory: Sovereign Credit, Democracy, and War."
  Journal of Conflict Resolution 58, no. 5 (August 1, 2014): 771–95.

Shirk, Susan L. *China: Fragile Superpower: How China's Internal Politics Could Derail
  Its Peaceful Rise*. Oxford; New York: Oxford University Press, 2007.

Shlapak, David, and Michael Johnson. *Reinforcing Deterrence on NATO's Eastern
  Flank: Wargaming the Defense of the Baltics*. Santa Monica: RAND Corporation, 2016.

Simmons, Beth. "Treaty Compliance and Violation." *Annual Review of Political
  Science* 13, no. 1 (2010): 273–96.

Simons, Robert A., Jing Wu, Jie Xu, and Yu Fei. "Chinese Investment in U.S. Real
  Estate Markets Using the EB-5 Program." *Economic Development Quarterly* 30, no.
  1 (2016): 75–87.

Singer, J. David, Stuart Bremer, and John Stuckey. "Capability Distribution,
  Uncertainty, and Major Power War, 1820–1965." *Peace, War and Numbers*
  (1972): 19–48.

Siverson, Randolph M., and Juliann Emmons. "Birds of a Feather: Democratic Political Systems and Alliance Choices in the Twentieth Century." *Journal of Conflict Resolution* 35, no. 2 (1991): 285–306.

Skocpol, Theda. *States and Social Revolutions: A Comparative Analysis of France, Russia, and China.* Cambridge; New York, NY: Cambridge University Press, 2015.

Snyder, Jack I. *Myths of Empire: Domestic Politcs and International Ambitions.* Ithaca, NY: Cornell University Press, 1991.

Socor, Vladimir. "Putin's Crimea Speech: A Manifesto of Greater-Russia Irredentism." *Eurasia Daily Monitor* 11, no. 56 (2018).

Stasavage, David. "Transparency, Democratic Accountability, and the Economic Consequences of Monetary Institutions." *American Journal of Political Science* 47, no. 3 (2003): 389–402.

Stasavage, David. "Cities, Constitutions, and Sovereign Borrowing in Europe, 1274–1785." *International Organization* 61, no. 3 (2007): 489–525.

Stasavage, David. "Polarization and Publicity: Rethinking the Benefits of Deliberative Democracy." *Journal of Politics* 69, no. 1 (2007): 59–72.

Steinfeld, Edward S. *Playing Our Game: Why China's Rise Doesn't Threaten the West.* New York, NY: Oxford University Press, 2010.

Stent, Angela. *Putin's World: Russia against the West and with the Rest.* New York, NY: Twelve, 2019.

Stent, Angela. *The Limits of Partnership: U.S.-Russian Relations in the Twenty-First Century.* Princeton, NJ: Princeton University Press, 2014.

Summerhill, William R. *Inglorious Revolution: Political Institutions, Sovereign Debt, and Financial Underdevelopment in Imperial Brazil.* New Haven, CT: Yale University Press, 2015.

Taagepera, Rein. "Expansion and Contraction Patterns of Large Polities: Context for Russia." *International Studies Quarterly* 41, no. 3 (1997): 475–504.

Talmadge, Caitlin. *The Dictator's Army: Battlefield Effectiveness in Authoritarian Regimes.* Ithaca, NY: Cornell University Press, 2015.

Tammen, Ronald, Jacek Kugler, Douglas Lemke, Alan C. Stam III, Mark Abdollahian, Carole Alsharabati, Brian Efird, and A. F. K. Organski. *Power Transitions: Strategies for the 21st Century.* New York, NY: Seven Bridges Press, LLC/Chatham House, 2000.

Taylor, Adam. "Ahead of Russian Elections, Putin Releases Official Details of Wealth and Income." *Washington Post*, February 7, 2018.

The Economist. "Cops for Hire." March 18, 2010. https://www.economist.com/europe/2010/03/18/cops-for-hire.

The Economist. "Milk without the Cow." October 22, 2016. https://www.economist.com/special-report/2016/10/22/milk-without-the-cow.

The Economist. "Will China's Belt and Road Initiative Outdo the Marshall Plan?" March 8, 2018. https://www.economist.com/finance-and-economics/2018/03/08/will-chinas-belt-and-road-initiative-outdo-the-marshall-plan.

The Economist, "How China's 'Sharp Power' Is Muting Criticism Abroad." The
    Economist, December 14, 2017. https://www.economist.com/briefing/2017/12/
    14/how-chinas-sharp-power-is-muting-criticism-abroad.
"The Imperial Presidency." *The Nation*, August 29, 2002.
Thucydides. *The Peloponnesian War*. New York, NY: E. P. Dutton,1910.
Thompson, William R. "Uneven Economic Growth, Systemic Challenges,
    and Global Wars." *International Studies Quarterly* 27, no. 3 (September 1,
    1983): 341–55.
Tuchman, Barbara W. *The Guns of August*. Reprint edition. New York,
    NY: Random House Trade Paperbacks, 1994.
Tocqueville, Alexis de. *Democracy in America*. Translated by Harvey C. Mansfield
    and Delba Winthrop. Chicago, IL: University of Chicago Press, 2002.
Tzu, Sun. *The Art of War*. First Thus edition. Las Vegas, NV: Filiquarian, 2007.
United States. *National Security Strategy of the United States of America*. The White
    House, 2017.
Van Evera, Stephen. *Causes of War: Power and the Roots of Conflict*. 1st edition. Ithaca,
    NY: Cornell University Press, 2001.
Van Creveld, Martin L. *Technology and War: From 2000 B.C. to the Present*.
    New York, NY; London, UK: Free Press, 1989.
Volz, Dustin, and Warren P. Strobel. "China and Russia, Aligned More Closely,
    Seen as Chief Security Threat to U.S." *Wall Street Journal*, January 29, 2019.
Vries, Jan de, and Ad van der Woude. *The First Modern Economy: Success, Failure,
    and Perseverance of the Dutch Economy, 1500–1815*. Cambridge; New York,
    NY: Cambridge University Press, 1997.
Walt, Stephen M. *The Origins of Alliances*. Cornell Studies in Security Affairs.
    Ithaca, NY: Cornell University Press, 1987.
Waltz, Kenneth Neal. *Theory of International Politics*. New York,
    NY: McGraw-Hill, 1979.
Weber, Max. *The Protestant Ethic and the Spirit of Capitalism and Other Writings*.
    Trans. Peter Baehr and Gordon C. Wells. New York, NY: Penguin
    Books, 2002.
Weeks, Jessica L. P. *Dictators at War and Peace*. 1st edition. Ithaca, NY; London,
    UK: Cornell University Press, 2014.
Weinberg, Gerhard L. *A World at Arms: A Global History of World War II*.
    Cambridge; New York, NY: Cambridge University Press, 1993.
Weiss, Jessica Chen. *Powerful Patriots: Nationalist Protest in China's Foreign Relations*.
    1st edition. New York, NY: Oxford University Press, 2014.
Wielenga, Friso. *A History of the Netherlands: From the Sixteenth Century to the
    Present Day*. Translated by Lynne Richards. London, UK: Bloomsbury
    Academic, 2015.
Wohlstetter, Roberta. *Pearl Harbor: Warning and Decision*. 1st edition. Stanford,
    CA: Stanford University Press, 1962.

"World's Top Oil Producers." *CNNMoney*. July 22, 2016. https://money.cnn.com/ interactive/news/economy/worlds-biggest-oil-producers/index.html.

Zakaria, Fareed. *From Wealth to Power*. Princeton, NJ: Princeton University Press, 1998).

Zakaria, Fareed. *The Post-American World: Release 2.0*. New York, NY: W. W. Norton, 2011.

INDEX

For the benefit of digital users, indexed terms that span two pages (e.g., 52–53) may, on occasion, appear on only one of those pages.

alliance building (*Cont.*)
and Athens, 61, 63, 68–69
and the Britain, 124
and British-German rivalry, 136
and China's autocratic
diplomacy, 187–88
and China's third revolution, 178
and the Greco-Persian Wars, 65–66
and lessons of democratic advantage
theory, xi, 215, 217, 218, 219–24
and modern theory of democratic
dominance, 16–17
and responses to German
militarism, 135–36
and the Roman Republic, 73–74,
80, 84–85
and Russian autocratic
diplomacy, 163–65
and the Venetian Republic, 95, 96
and World War I, 128–29
and World War II, 126, 133, 135
Allison, Graham, 7
Amalfi, 93
American Chamber of
Commerce, 188–89
American Civil War, 36, 56–58
American colonies, 118
American Enterprise Institute, 200
American War of Independence, 119, 120
Amsterdam, 103, 107, 110, 115
Anabaptism, 101
Anatolia, 82–83, 87
Andriscus, 83
Anglo-Dutch Wars, 112
Anglo-Saxon kings, 113–14
Anti-Access Area Denial (A2AD)
strategy, 178, 207
Antiochus II, 82
Antwerp, 103
aqueducts, 75, 84
aristocracy, 36, 37, 62, 140
Aristotle, 6, 68, 77
armored tanks, 129

arms control agreements, 146, 221
arms limitation treaties, 144
arms races, 135–36, 143–44, 196–97,
222–23
Arsenal, The, 90, 94
artificial intelligence (AI), 40, 167,
175, 179, 184, 85, 194, 201
arts and sciences
and Athens, 68
and the British Empire, 122
and Cold War migrations, 145
and the Dutch Golden Age, 107
and the Roman Republic, 75
and Tocqueville's assessment of
America, 36
and the Venetian Republic, 91
Asia, 203. *See also specific countries*
Asian trade and the Thirty Years'
War, 108–9
and China's third revolution, 176–77
and "competitive strategies"
framework, 222
and *Pax Britannica,* 123
standard of living, 21
Asia Society, 183
asiento, 117–18
Assad, Bashar Al, 40, 157
assassinations, 128–29, 157, 199
Athens
American diplomatic strength
compared to, 204
Assembly of, 69
and case selection for study, 58–59
and direct democracy, 72
extent of empire, 67*f*
as first democracy, 61
and Greco-Persian Wars, 61–66
and historical success of
democracies, 53
and lessons of democratic advantage
theory, 213–14
and overview of democratic
advantage theory, 4, 14–15

and the Punic Wars, 77
and support for democratic advantage
  theory, 66–70
U.S. diplomatic strength compared
  to, 203
Atlantic Council, xii
Atlantic Ocean, 117–18
"audience costs," 26
Augustus Caesar, 86
Australia
  and British global empire, 122–23
  and China's autocratic diplomacy,
    189, 191
  and China's autocratic military, 191
  and China's credibility
    problems, 45–46
  and Russia's autocratic
    economics, 161–63
  standard of living, 21
Austria, 122, 126–27, 132
Austrian Hapsburgs, 117
Austro-Hungarian Empire, 55, 128–29
autocracy and autocrats
  autocratic advantage theory, 8, 35,
    38–47, 193–94
  and British-German rivalry as
    support of democratic advantage,
    135, 136
  and case selection for study, 58–59
  and "China for a day" thesis, 43–44
  described, 38–42
  difficulties accumulating power, 104
  and domestic political
    institutions, 47–49
  and domestic threats, 31
  and economic advantage of
    democracies, 21
  and foreign policy advantage, 4–5
  and lessons of democratic advantage
    theory, 213–14
  and Middle Ages, 86
  and military disadvantages, 191
  and origins of World Wars, 126

and overview of democratic
  advantage theory, 18
and political theorists' critiques of
  democracy, 36–38
questioning autocratic advantage,
  17, 42–47
and the rise of Venice, 88
and Russia's autocratic
  economics, 160
and Spanish persecution, 100–1
and the Venetian Republic, 97
automation, 203
Aztecs, 100

"balance of threat," 25–26
Balkan Peninsula, 64, 81, 83
Baltic states, 132, 164–65
Bangladesh, 177
Bank of Amsterdam, 107
Bank of England, 115
banking, 105, 107. *See also* financial
  power and innovation
Barca, Hamilcar, 78, 79, 85
Barca, Hannibal, 79–80, 81–83, 85
"bastion strategy," 167
Battle of Asculum, 76
Battle of Beneventum, 76
Battle of Britain, 133
Battle of Cannae, 79
Battle of Chiogga, 94, 97
Battle of Claudine Forks, 74
Battle of Cynoscephalae, 82, 85
Battle of Fornovo, 95
Battle of Guadalcanal, 135
Battle of Heiligerlee, 101
Battle of Heraclea, 76
Battle of Lake Tasimene, 79
Battle of Lake Vadimo, 76
Battle of Lepanto, 98, 107–8
Battle of Maclodio, 94–95
Battle of Marathon, 62–63
Battle of Midway, 135
Battle of Mycale, 65

democratic advantage theory. *See also*
democracy and democratization
Athens as support for, 66–70
China as support for, 195
defining democracy, 17
and diplomatic strength, 25
Dutch Republic as support
for, 110–12
and economic power, 19, 23
and erosion of democratic
institutions in U.S., 8
Germany as support for, 135–37
Great Britain as support for, 123–25
and great power competition, 31–35
historical scholarship
supporting, 11–15
implications for American
leadership, 213–24
key elements of, 3–4
lessons of, 213–24
and military strength, 29
model of, 34*f*
modern theory of, 15–31
overview of cases, 58–60
and overview of democratic
advantage theory, 15–31
Roman Republic as support
for, 84–86
United Kingdom as support
for, 135–37
United States as support for, 148–51,
168–69, 208–9
Venetian Republic as support
for, 96–98
demographic trends, 165–66
Deng Xiaoping, 42, 174–75, 176,
193–94, 195
Destined for War (Allison), 7
détente, 144, 146–47
deterrence, 1, 43, 149
Detroit, Michigan, 118
dictators, 4–5, 21, 86. *See also* autocracy
and autocrats

diplomacy and diplomatic relations.
See also alliance building; *specific
countries*
and advantages of
democracies, 32–33
democracies vs. autocracies, 32
and democratic advantage theory
described, 25
and Greco-Persian Wars, 69
and lessons of democratic advantage
theory, 213, 223–24
and model of study, 34*f*
and modern theory of democratic
dominance, 16, 17
and pessimism about America's
future, 197
and threat of Russian autocracy, 168
directed-energy weapons, 206, 221
Discourses on Livy (Machiavelli), 5, 6,
12–13, 47
disinformation campaigns, 158
Djibouti, 179
domestic threats and security
and American democratic
institutions, 199
and American military
strength, 206–7
and China, 172, 194
and the French Revolution, 121
and lessons of democratic advantage
theory, 217, 218–19, 222–23
and the Macedonian Wars, 82
and military advantage of
democracies, 31
and model of study, 34*f*
and the Punic Wars, 78
and Russia, 167, 168
and the Spanish Empire, 112
and Sparta, 68–69
and the Thirty Years' War, 109
and the Venetian Republic, 89, 97
Doria, Pietro, 94
Drake, Francis, 104, 114

Great Britain. *See also* Britain and
    British Empire; England; United
    Kingdom (UK)
    and American economic
        strength, 200
    and the French Revolution, 120
    and lessons of democratic advantage
        theory, 213–14
    and long-cycle view great power
        competition, 53–54
    and the Opium Wars, 171
    origin of, 118
    and Wars of Louis XIV, 118
    and World War II, 133
Great Chinese Famine, 173
Great Council (Venice), 89, 98
Great Italian Wars, 11–12, 94–95,
    96, 102
Great Lakes, 118
Great Leap Forward, 42, 173
Great Recession, 161
Greater East Asia Co-Prosperity
    Sphere, 134
Greatness of the Romans and Their Decline,
    The (Montesquieu), 14
Greece and Greek city-states. *See also*
    Athens; *specific polities*
    and the Fourth Crusade, 91–92
    and Greco-Persian Wars, 14, 61–66
    and the Macedonian Wars, 81–84
    and overview of democratic
        advantage theory, 13–15
    and the Roman Republic, 76
    and the Venetian Republic, 87
gross domestic product (GDP), 200
Grotius, Hugo, 108
ground warfare tactics, 130, 136
guest workers, 190
Gulf States, 203
Gulf Wars, 30, 79–80

Haiti, 21
Hapsburg Empire, 100

hard power, 4, 28, 33. *See also* military
    power and innovation
hastati, 75
helots, 63, 65, 68–69
Henry VII, 114
Henry VIII, 114
Herodotus, 3, 14
Hiero II, 77
Hippocrates, 15
Hiroshima, Japan, 135
Histories, The (Herodotus), 14
History of Rome (Livy), 13
Hitler, Adolf
    and autocratic advantage theory, 44
    and Britain's rise to power, 113
    and critiques of democracy, 37–38
    and diplomatic advantage of
        democracies, 25
    and the Holocaust, 136
    and the interwar years, 130–32
    and lessons of democratic advantage
        theory, 213–14
    and overview of democratic
        advantage theory, 4, 5, 16
    and support for democratic advantage
        theory, 135, 136–37
    and World War II, 132–33, 134, 135
HIV/AIDS, 165–66
Holland, 100, 102, 104. *See also*
    Netherlands
Holocaust, 136
Holy Land, 91–92
Holy Roman Empire, 11–12, 88, 89,
    100–1, 116–17, 126–27
Hong Kong, 123, 171
Hong Xiuquan, 172
hoplite warriors, 64, 82
hostage crises, Iran, 144
Hu Jintao, 174–75
Huawei, 45–46
human rights, 4, 5–6, 27, 40, 43,
    215, 220
Hundred Flowers Campaign, 173

Middle East, 2, 157, 164, 201, 203
middle income trap, 182–83
Milan, Italy, 95
military power and innovation
    and American democratic
        advantage, 208
    and Athens, 63
    autocratic military of China, 191
    and British-German rivalry, 136
    and China's autocratic military, 192
    and China's rising power, 170
    and China's third revolution, 177,
        178, 179
    and Chinese emergence as global
        power, 2
    and the Cold War, 145–46
    and democratic advantage theory
        described, 29, 32–33, 34f
    and the Dutch Golden Age, 107
    and the Dutch Republic, 110
    and the Dutch Revolt, 104–5
    erosion by autocratic Russian
        system, 168
    freerider problem, 219
    and the Greco-Persian Wars, 65
    and lessons of democratic advantage
        theory, 213, 218, 219–20, 221–23
    and the Macedonian Wars, 82
    and model of study, 34f
    and modern theory of democratic
        dominance, 15–17
    and "next generation" warfare, 158
    and problems of autocracies, 112
    and the Punic Wars, 78, 79–80
    and rise of Germany, 128
    and rise of U.S. power, 140, 149
    and the Roman Republic, 73,
        74–75, 85
    and Russian autocracy, 168
    and Russian autocratic
        military, 165, 166, 167
    and Russian resurgence under
        Putin, 158

strategic arms and warfare, 90,
    134, 135, 146–47, 149, 168,
    206, 221–23
and submarine warfare, 129–30,
    135–36, 146, 193
supremacy of U.S., 1
and the Venetian Republic, 97
and the Venetian-Genoese Wars, 94
weaponry innovations, 75
weapons proliferation, 148
and World War I, 129
and World War II 136
missile defense systems, 146–47,
    206, 222
Mississippi River, 118
mob rule, 17–18
modernization, 172
Molotov, Vyacheslav, 25
Molotov-Ribbentrop Pact, 25,
    26–27, 132
monarchies, 18, 86, 100, 127
Mongol Empire, 59, 90, 93
Monongahela River, 118
Monroe, James, 139
Monroe Doctrine, 139
Monte Vecchio system, 90–91, 96
Montenegro, 25, 147, 158
Montesquieu, Charles de Secondat,
    baron de, 3, 14, 71, 138–39
Montreal, Canada, 118
multipolar balance of power, 197–98,
    205–6, 215
Munich Peace Conference, 132
Muslim minorities in China, 5–6,
    179, 199
Mussolini, Benito, 133, 134
mutual-defense agreements, 73, 187.
    See also alliance building
Myanmar, 177

Naarden, Netherlands, 102
Nagasaki, Japan, 135
Namur, Belgium, 116–17

extent of, 84*f*
and historical success of
democracies, 53
and lessons of democratic advantage
theory, 213–14, 218–19
and the Macedonian Wars, 81–84
origins and rise of, 71–73
and origins of English power, 113–14
and overview of democratic
advantage theory, 4, 13–15, 17
and Punic Wars, 76–81
and the rise of Venice, 87
and support for democratic advantage
theory, 84–86
Roman Senate, 72, 84–85
Romania, 27, 147
Rome, Italy, 15. *See also* Roman
Republic
Romulus and Remus, 71–72
"root causes" view of international
success, 48–49
Royal Exchange, 115
rule-of-law, 3–4, 32
rules-based international order, 175
Russia and the Russian Federation. *See*
also Soviet Union
American democracy contrasted
with, 199
and American diplomatic
strength, 205
and American military
strength, 205–8
and American-led economic
sanctions, 202–3
and autocratic advantage theory, 38,
41, 42–43, 44
autocratic economics under
Putin, 160
and China's autocratic
diplomacy, 188
and China's autocratic military, 193
and China's third revolution, 176,
177, 178

and Chinese political
background, 171–72
and the Concert of Europe, 122
and effects of democratization, 56
and financial advantages of
democracies, 24
and German militarization, 128
and international distribution of
power, 56–58
and lessons of democratic advantage
theory, 214–15, 217–18, 221,
222–23, 224
and "major power" definitions, 55
and military advantage of
democracies, 29
and military modernization, 2
and the Napoleonic Wars, 121, 125
and overview of democratic
advantage theory, 5–6
and pessimism about America's
future, 197
political background of
autocracy, 159
and the post-Cold War order, 148
resurgence since Cold War, 155–59
and support for democratic advantage
theory, 168–69
and tyranny of Putin, 159–60
and World War I, 128–29
and World War II, 133, 136
Russia Today, 158
ruthlessness, 4–5, 35, 38, 40, 45–46,
85, 151, 176, 185
Ruyte, Michiel de, 107–8, 112

Sabine tribe, 71–72
Saguntum, 79
SALT I Treaty, 144
Samnites, 74, 75, 76, 84–85
sanctions, 134, 162, 164, 202–3,
204, 222
Santa Anna, Antonio López, 139
Sardinia, 78–79

Triple Alliance, 128
Triple Entente, 128
trireme warships, 63
Trump, Donald, 26, 41, 204–5
Tsingtao, 171–72
Tudors, 114
Tulip mania, 106–7
Turkey, 204
Twelve Years' Truce, 105, 108
tyranny of the majority, 17–18, 36
Tyre, 91–92

Uighur minority in China, 5–6, 179, 194
Ukraine
  and NATO membership, 147
  and Russian autocratic
    diplomacy, 164–65
  and Russian autocratic
    military, 166–67
  Russian invasion of, 2, 45, 157, 158,
    164–65, 166–67, 176
Umbrians, 74, 76
Union of the Crowns, 118
Union of Utrecht, 103
United Front (China), 178
United Kingdom (UK). *See also*
    Britain and British Empire;
    England; Great Britain
  and case selection for study, 58–59
  and the French Revolution, 120
  and lessons of democratic advantage
    theory, 213–14
  and "major power"
    definitions, 55–56
  and Polity scores, 55
  standard of living, 21
United Nations, 143
United Provinces, 103
United Russia Party, 160
United States
  alliance system, 147, 156–57, 163,
    191 (*see also* North Atlantic Treaty
    Organization)

  and case selection for study, 58–59
  and China's autocratic diplomacy,
    187–90, 191
  and China's autocratic
    economics, 185
  and China's autocratic military, 191,
    192–93, 194
  and China's credibility
    problems, 45–46
  and China's trade practices, 182
  and Chinese political
    background, 171
  and the Cold War, 141–47
  democratic advantage over
    China, 195
  democratic institutions of, 198–99
  diplomatic power of, 203–5
  and domestic security
    expenditures, 167
  economic power of, 199–203
  and effects of authoritarianism, 56
  erosion of democratic institutions, 8
  and the French Revolution, 120
  and international distribution of
    power, 56–58, 57f
  and lessons of democratic advantage
    theory, 213–14
  and long-cycle view great power
    competition, 53–54
  and "major power"
    definitions, 55–56
  military power of, 205–8
  and modern theory of democratic
    dominance, 17
  oil and gas resources, 161
  pessimism about future of, 196–98
  and post-Cold War world, 147–48
  rise of, 138–40
  Roman Republic's influence, 72
  and Russian autocratic
    diplomacy, 164–65
  and Russian election interference, 2,
    41, 45, 158, 159–60, 167